Reading at the Piano

A progressive course for all beginners

by

Nina Dalby

Revised and Edited
by
Ronald Lees

Acknowledgements

I am grateful to Simon Dalby for the gift of the author's copyright of this book. Ann Maycock and Ann Healy-Mayes encouraged me to publish it. Maria Mulcachy showed great patience in typesetting it. William Lees's assiduous refinement of the raw text and Fedelmia O'Herlihy's forensic proof reading and editorial suggestions were invaluable. Phillipa Lees supported the project at home, and John Loesberg generously shared his publishing expertise. The dynamic cover design is by Deirdre Frost.

Ronald Lees

Preamble: how to use this book

Difficulty in reading music is the most common reason given for 'giving up' piano playing. In examinations, piano candidates are notoriously worse at sight-reading than players of orchestral instruments. There are three main reasons for this: firstly, looking at the hands instead of positioning them by feel; secondly, the lack of ensemble playing (helpful for continuity); and thirdly, insufficient daily reading practice.

Nina's book provides the ideal opportunity to develop fluent reading from the earliest stages. It is not a book to flourish before a pupil a few weeks before an exam to 'prepare' for the sight-reading test, but a purposeful course for daily use at home by the pupil. Her impeccable analysis ensures a seamless progression through the two hundred and sixty-nine pieces up to about Grade Three level. The deliberately uncluttered text is free of gimmicks and is suitable for beginners of all ages. It includes sufficient instruction to guide anyone wishing to 'go it alone' and can be used alongside any traditional tutor.

Here are four practical ways of establishing good reading habits:

Insist that once the hands are in position, the notes are located by feel and the eyes stay resolutely on the music. The numerous examples in one-hand position are designed to build this skill. Later, all notes within reach of this position (extensions) are to be played in this way. Block the view of the hands with a book to ensure that this happens.

Stimulate the eyes to take in as much as possible in one glance. 'Snap-shot' a whole bar – show it for a brief moment, then ask the pupil to play it. Extend this to two bars, and so on. Ensure that the eyes are already scanning ahead before playing begins.

Inculcate orderly habits: decide on a slow enough tempo to ensure that the time will not falter. Clapping the rhythm first (even in the early examples) sets up the process. Mistakes should not be corrected – recovery and continuity are paramount.

Improvise a simple metronome-style accompaniment to provide ensemble experience from the start. This also internalises counting and expands the pupil's awareness by being a listener at the same time as a performer.

Above all, ensure that the pupil understands the difference between learning a piece on the edge of their ability and *reading within their capacity to maintain a musical flow*. The full value of this reading programme will only be gained if it becomes a routine part of daily home practice. Earlier pieces may be re-read at an increased tempo as progress is made through the book. No-one talks of 'sight-reading' the written word, it is simply read. Reading and playing music needs to be thought of in the same light.

These very simple measures produce results.

Ronald Lees

Nina Dalby

During her many years as a piano teacher at the Cork School of Music, Ireland, Nina Dalby's name became synonymous with excellence in sight-reading. She was an ardent advocate of the benefits of sight-reading and painstakingly worked out a simple and practical series of helpful hints, crystallized in this book, to aid beginners. Originally entitled *Play It Yourself*, this was only circulated in manuscript. Her two books for beginners, now out of print, *Opus One* and *Opus Two*, which I helped to edit, were published by Ossian Publications in 1983. Following her death in 1996, Simon, her son, donated the author's copyright of her works to me as I had long wanted to make them available to a wider audience. They were used with great success as core texts for the BMus Piano Pedagogy Course and the Group Piano Project for Beginners in the School, and continue to be used by piano teachers who are reluctant to let go of their tattered copies.

Nina was born in Cork during the First World War and studied under Eric Grant at the Royal Academy of Music, London, during the 1930s, graduating with the LRAM Diploma in Piano. Her career as a teacher of piano was interrupted by her service as a meteorological officer in the British Woman's Auxiliary Air Force for part of the Second World War. She married Leslie Dalby in 1955, and was appointed to the Cork School of Music in the 1960s.

Nina possessed a wonderful mixture of artful persuasion, discipline and humour, which endeared her to her pupils who would work for *her* as much as they would work for themselves. She understood fully that difficulty in reading is the most common reason given for abandoning the piano, and indeed it was her mission to banish this impediment.

RL

Contents

Introduction

The ability to play at sight is the basis of musical literacy. Sadly, it is rarely rated as importantly as it should be by teachers, pupils and examining bodies. Most young pianists class themselves as poor readers. This need not be so. The difficulty usually lies in their lack of knowledge of the best way to tackle the problem. Also they frequently attempt to read music that is too difficult. This book sets out to help in these areas.

Time

Most important of all, time is built up from crotchets ♩ in **2/4** in Section One to give pupils ample practice of a steady beat before attempting subdivisions later on. Above all else, the beat must be kept steady and on-going, regardless of any slips in notes. This must be inculcated from the beginning and adhered to always. Regardless of time signatures, avoid counting subdivisions instead of the beat *as a unit*, hence the use of mnemonics to encourage this. Plodding, non-musical playing results from an unrhythmical feel of the beat. Music that 'swings' feels satisfactory to the pupil, so from the earliest pieces we must help them to be aware of the importance of feeling the stress on the first beat of the bar. Otherwise, why have a time signature?

I have deliberately avoided beat subdivisions smaller than ♪ – once a good feeling of pulse is established, more difficult divisions of the beat will present few problems. **6/8** in Section Four, is the only possible exception.

Notes

I have built up pieces starting from as few as two notes in each hand, played separately, so that examples will always be within the pupil's scope, even for a complete beginner. Pieces are mostly hands separately, except for simple, single-note harmonization of cadences in Sections Three and Four. My aim is to keep examples easy enough to enable pupils to see where they are going, and not just read notes in isolation as so many do. After all, much of the music we play moves by steps and small intervals. I have avoided all but familiar dissonances so that pupils do not think they are playing wrong notes, the most common cause of going back to correct – which must be avoided at all costs. Pieces are deliberately short so that pupils can 'analyse' what they are going to play before they begin. Few pupils in the early stages have a sense of key. Key signatures are therefore restricted to C major/A minor, G major/E minor and F major/D minor until the pupil becomes secure in the feel of interval shapes. Progressing to other keys then becomes easier.

4

Fingering

This is built on five-finger groups throughout Sections One, Two and Three. Consequently little fingering help is given other than for the first note in each hand. Pupils should be encouraged to feel for the correct finger within the group – no needless looking down at hands.

I have made all examples as uncluttered looking as possible so that there is no distraction from the essential basics of time and notes. This explains the absence of tempo indications, dynamics and such things as staccato, ties... even chords. All these will add on easily with the ability to read notes and time correctly. Each section has numerous examples. Pupils need much practice at each stage before going on to the next section. Too often they struggle to read music that is beyond their capacity – a recipe for discouragement. Each section is prefaced by suggestions as to the easiest ways to tackle the pieces. I am assuming that pupils using this book already understand the elementary basics of notes and time, so these are not explained. No section of this book is specifically geared to any special examination requirement.

Nina Dalby

Action Plan - reading, re-reading, browsing

The essence of this programme lies in establishing regular reading, re-reading and browsing, as distinct from the common perception of playing at sight. There is nothing wrong with familiarity. Fill the gap between 'sight-reading' as an examination requirement and 'learning' a piece by making new and old material part of **daily reading practice**. Frequency and quantity are vital.

In Section One, a good weekly target would be to begin with ten pieces. Suggest playing two on the first day, then those two plus two new ones on the next day, and so on, playing them all on day six. At the end of the section, spend a week or two going through them all again at a quicker tempo, or adding detail such as dynamics or articulation. Make reading as regular as practising scales and arpeggios. Only a few minutes are needed daily. Moving on to Section Two, ten pieces a week would also be appropriate, reducing to five a week in Sections Three and Four. During lessons, occasionally go back to one or two pieces from earlier sections and set a brisk tempo for the pupil. Pacing the rate of progress is crucial – the pieces are so numerous and carefully graded that an appropriate rate can be established easily. Nothing succeeds like success!

RL

Section One

Suggestions to help
Before playing, notice these things:

Pieces 1 – 4
One hand only plays each piece

Time $\frac{2}{4}$ uses only *one-count* ♩ and *two-count* ♩ notes

Clap the time pattern of the whole piece, counting rhythmically – the first beat of the bar a little stronger than the second

Notes – Only two notes, next door to each other from Middle C

Fingering – Place the finger indicated on the first note and then place the others silently over the remainder of the five-finger group of notes lying under each hand

Play the pieces at a slow enough speed to keep going

Count rhythmically. <u>NO STOPS</u> – the beat must keep going even if you play a wrong note. Do not stop to correct

Feel with your fingers from one note to the next – there is no need to look down at your hands

Pieces 5 – 9
Now we extend to the three next-door notes in either hand from Middle C. Look at their movement pattern before you begin, e.g. in Nos. 5 and 6 all notes move by step, except for the skip in bars 2 and 3. In these two pieces, more than two notes going by step in the same direction are marked ⌐‾‾‾⌐ to show you how to look out for these *strings* of notes moving by step. Train yourself to watch for *strings* in all music that you play. In No. 7, notice that twice in this piece you repeat a note – find them – it is easy to play a wrong note in these places.

Next door notes – next door fingers
Skip a note – skip a finger

Pieces 10 – 48
Still three-note tunes from Nos. 10 – 23, but now they are divided between the hands. These are followed by four-note and five-note tunes. Before you play, place both hands over the finger groups in each hand, so that there will be no break in counting when hands change over. Notice how much of the music moves by step.

Piece 19

$\frac{3}{4}$ appears for the first time

Remember the things to look for before you begin to play

Section One

Two-note pieces

Three-note pieces

♩ = 120 first time
140 170 200 208

6

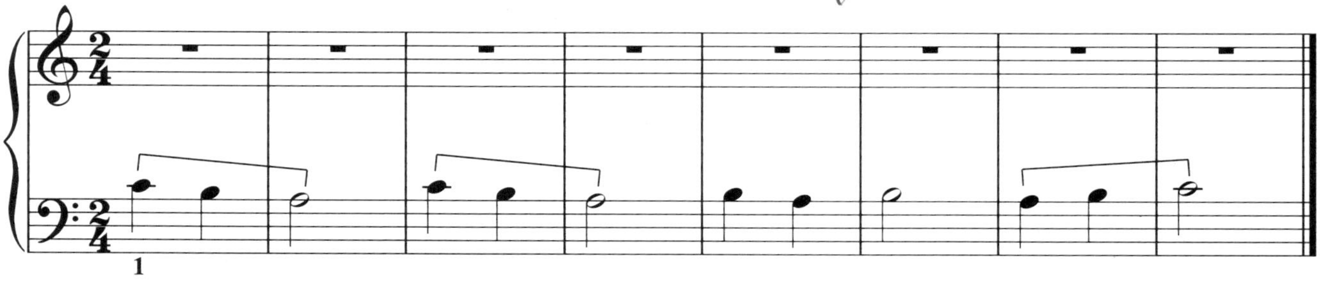

7

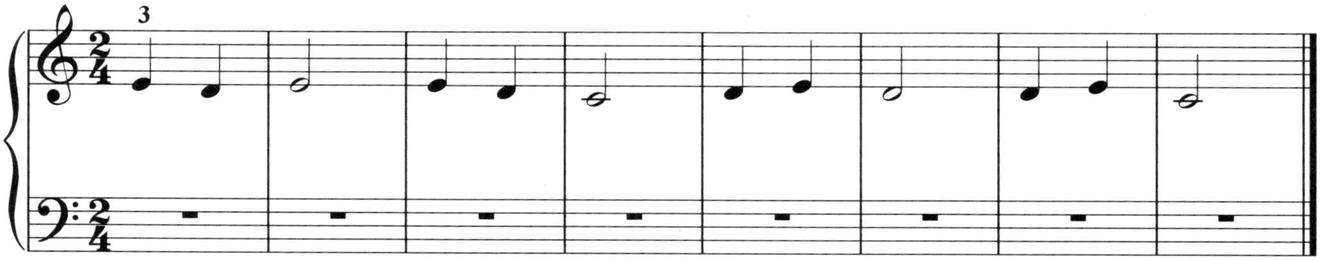

8

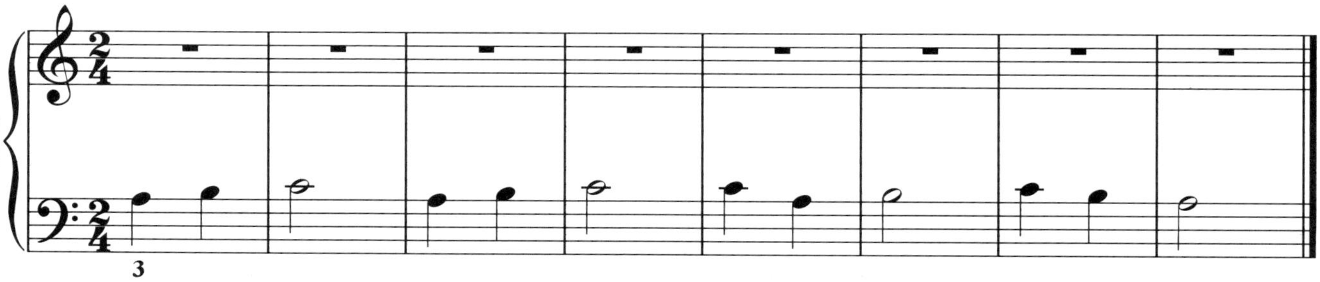

9

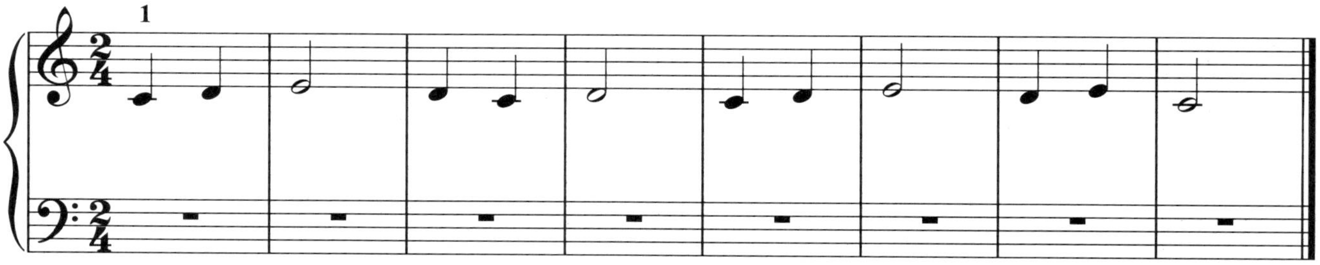

10

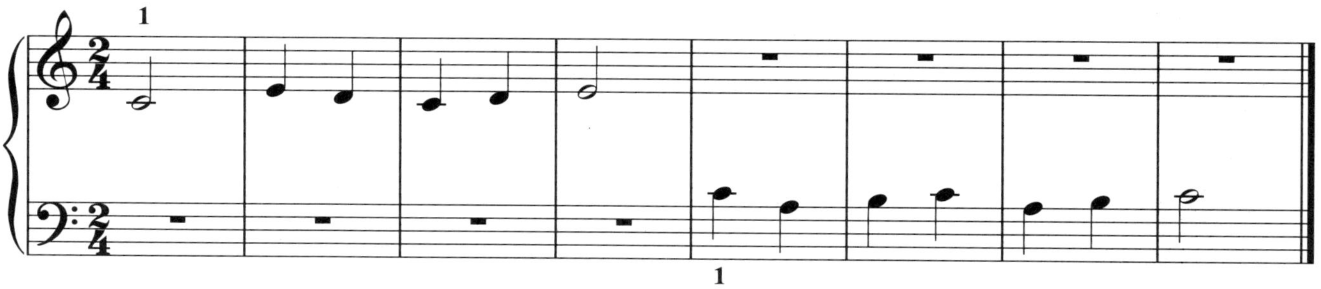

11

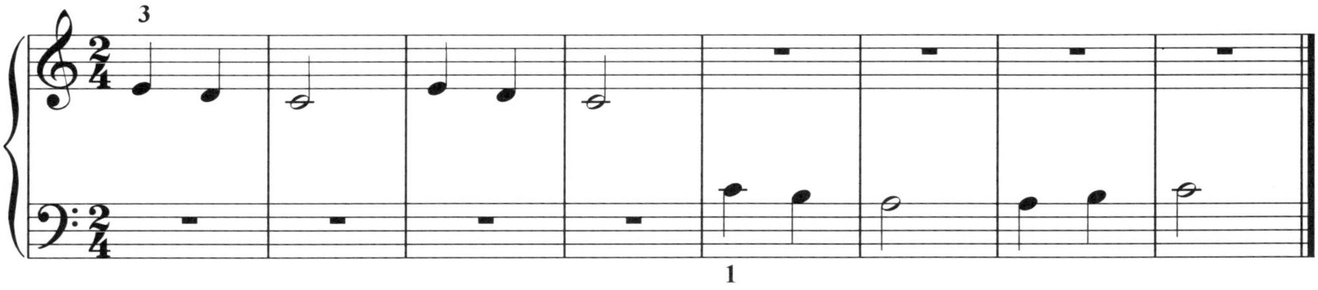

12

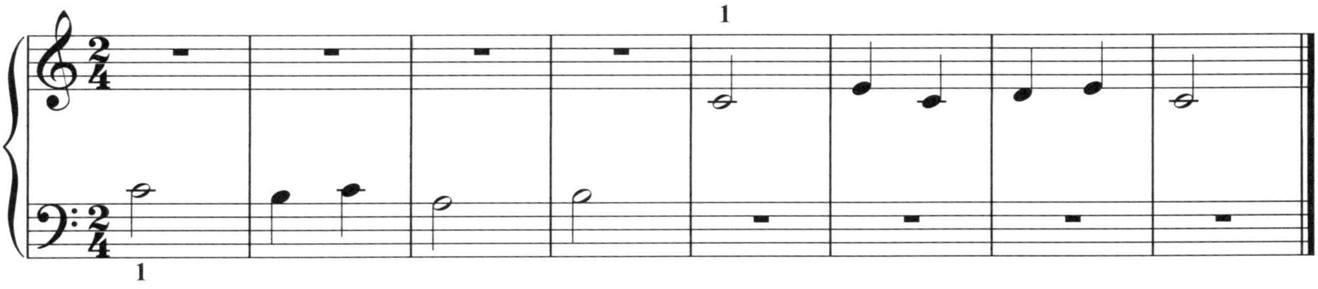

13

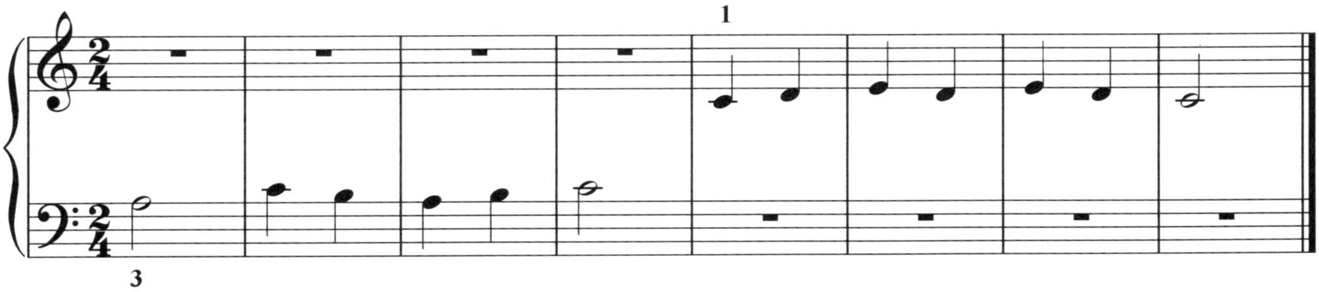

14

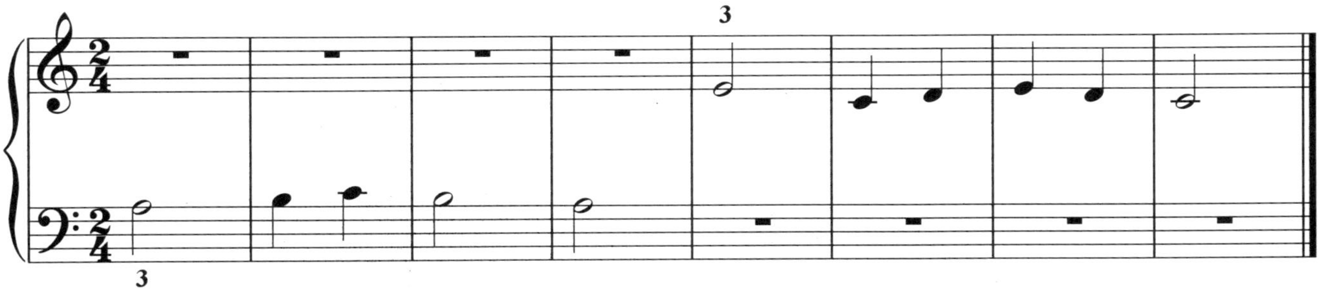

15

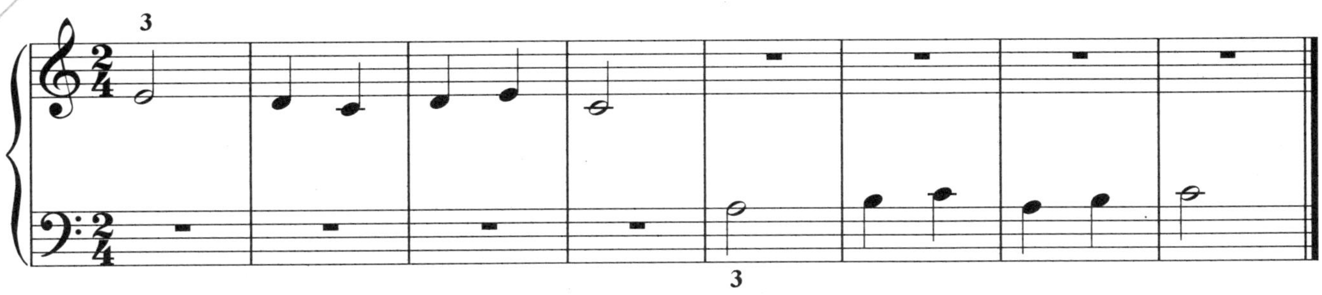

Three-note pieces in **3/4**

Four-note pieces

26

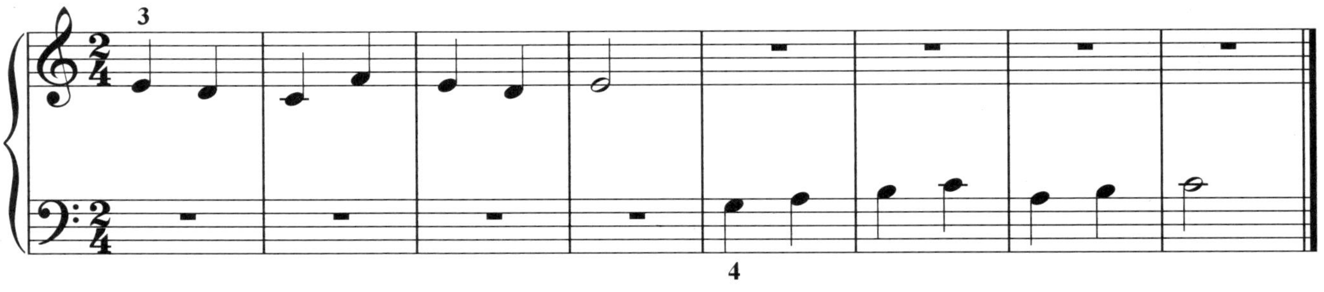

27

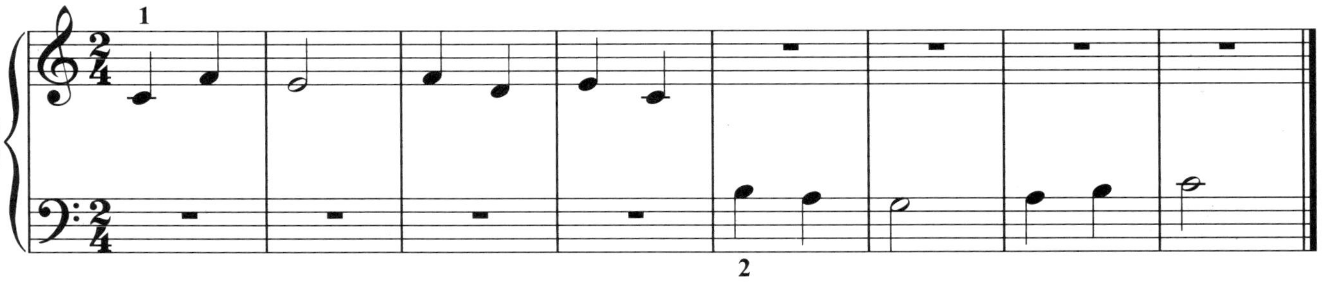

28

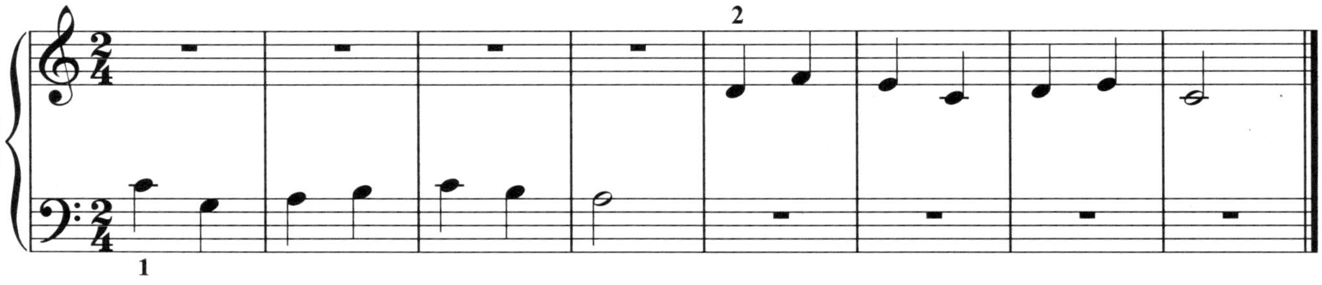

29

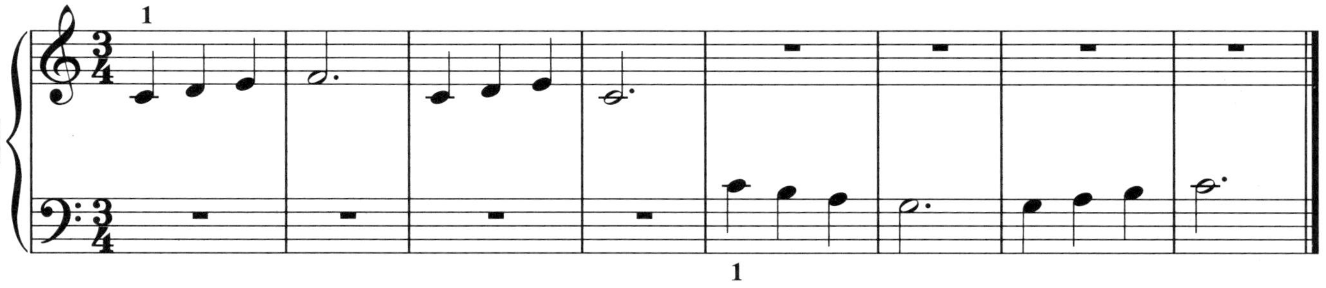

30

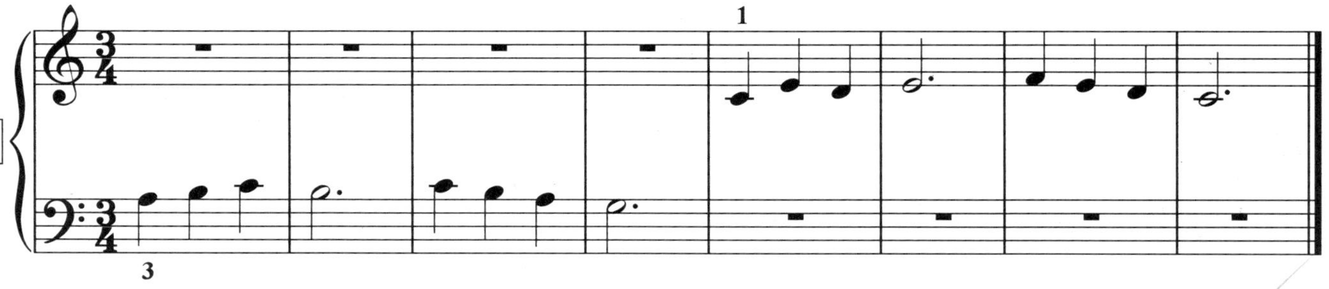

Five-note pieces

14

41

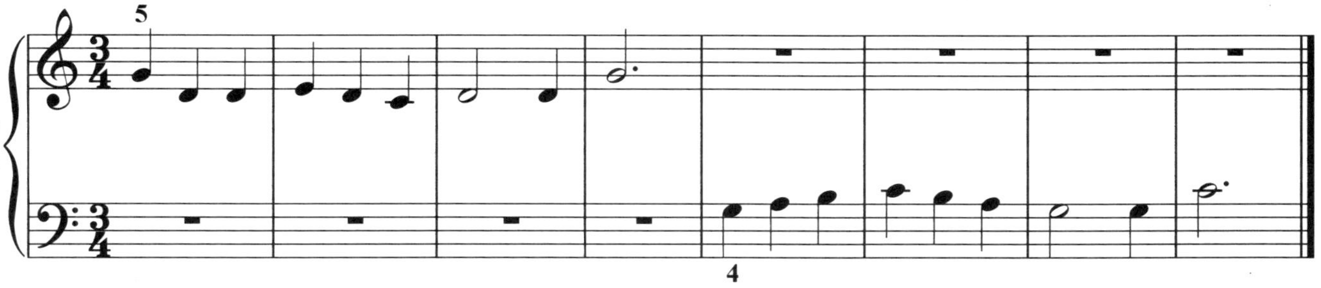

42

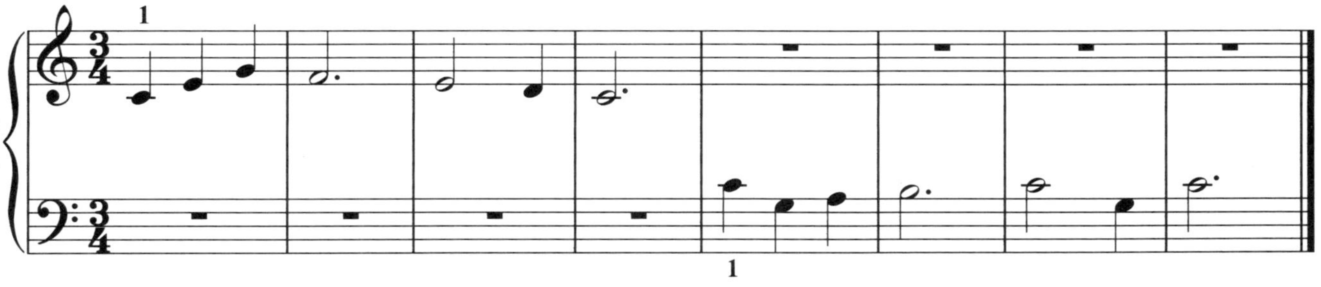

43

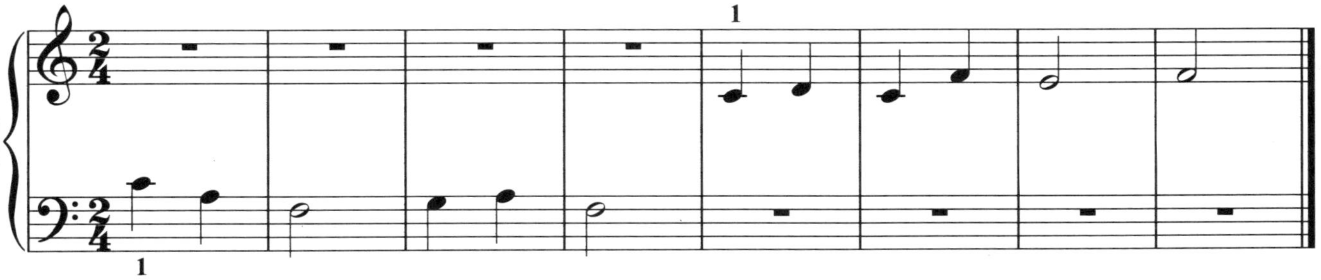

44

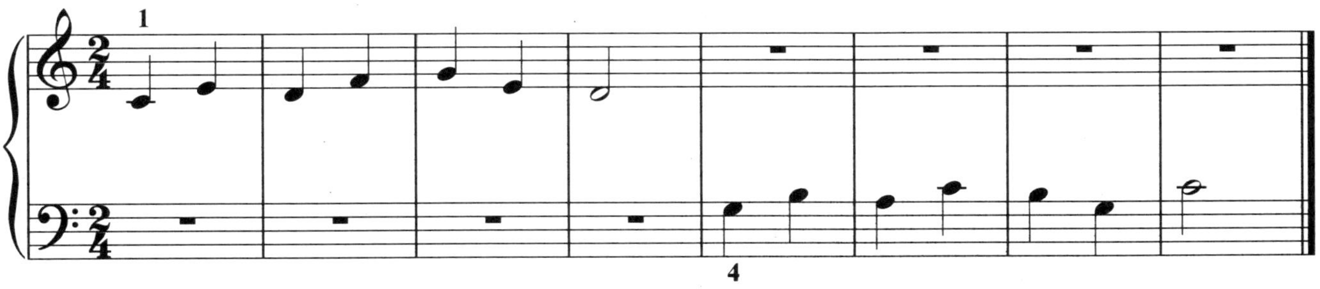

45

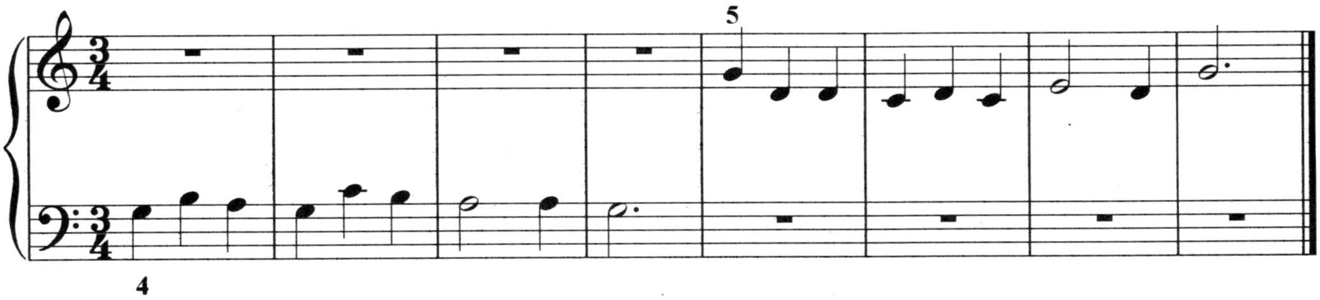

46

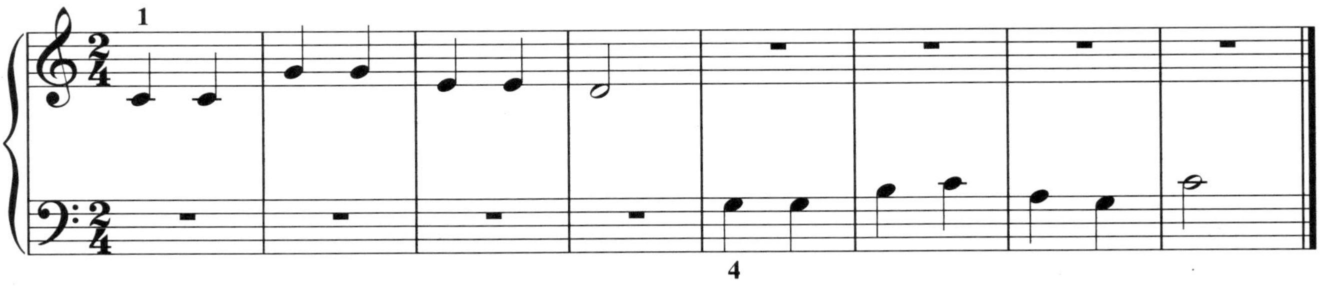

47

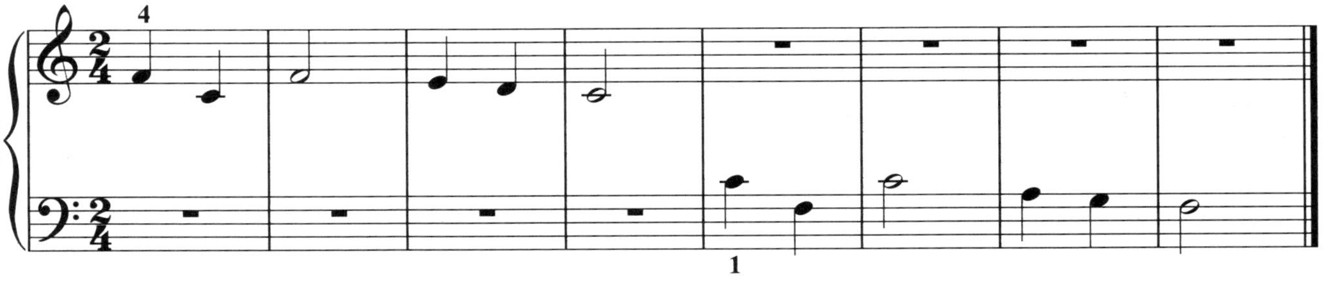

48

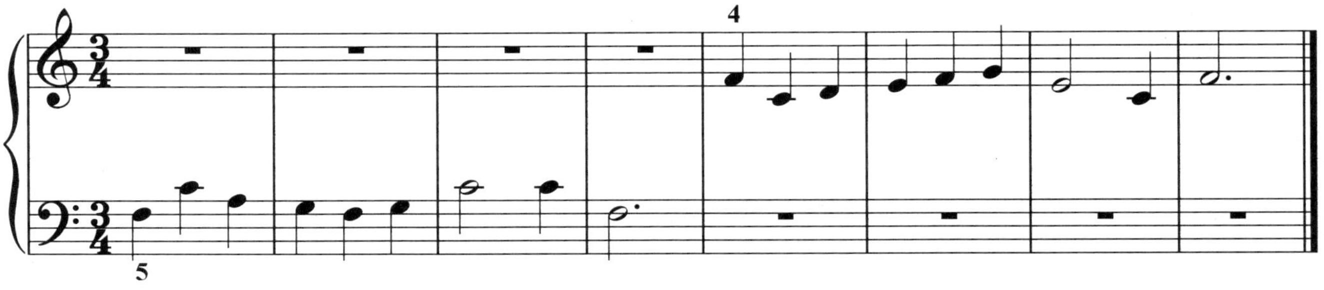

Section Two

We now move on to five-finger groups other than from Middle C.
Look for the following 'Landmark' notes in each hand to help you find and work out notes quickly.

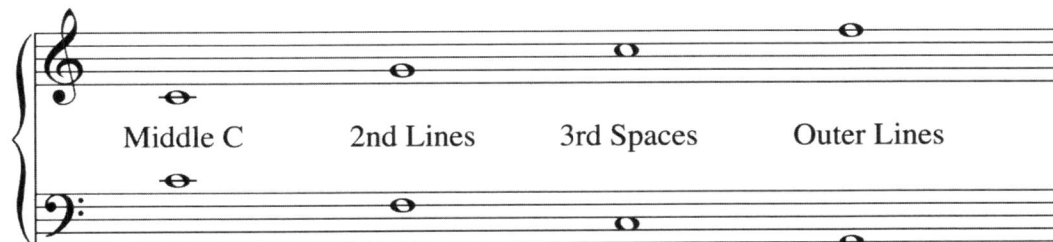

Middle C	2nd Lines	3rd Spaces	Outer Lines

RH   2nd line up is G for Granny
LH   2nd line down is F for Father

RH   3rd space up is C above middle C
LH   3rd space down is C below middle C

RH   Top line is F for Far up
LH   Bottom line is G for Ground at the bottom

The outer lines in either hand will be used only occasionally in this book, but they will help later when you extend the scope of your reading.
If you have a problem finding a note, work it out from the nearest 'Landmark'.

Piece 7 onwards

Key signatures containing F♯ and B♭ are introduced.
One ♯ in the key signature is always F♯ (keys G major/E minor)
One ♭ in the key signature is always B♭ (keys F major/D minor)

Make sure you remember a ♯ or ♭ in the key signature – leaving them out is a fault that occurs too often in sight-reading. When you have either a ♯ or ♭, it is a help to put the correct finger over them before you begin to play. From now on make it a rule to notice the key signature at the beginning of all pieces.

Piece 19 onwards

Now we add on ♫ ; ♩ = ♫

When there are ♫ in a piece, here is an easy way to count – instead of counting numbers in a bar, try counting this way:

For ♩ say WALK

For ♫ say RUN-NING

For 𝅗𝅥 say WALK-WAIT

For 𝅗𝅥. say WALK-WAIT-WAIT

Clap the time of pieces saying these words for the time values. It will also help you to get the swing of the beat – RHYTHM!

Section Two

Any five-finger group

Introducing new key signatures

11

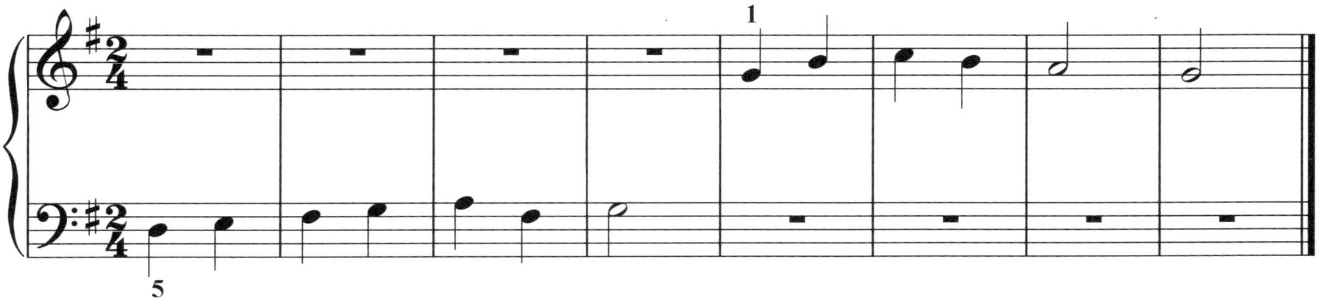

12

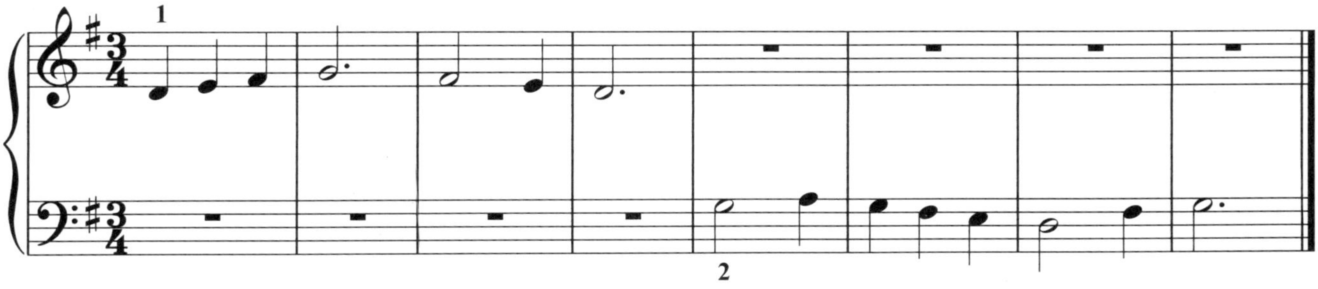

13

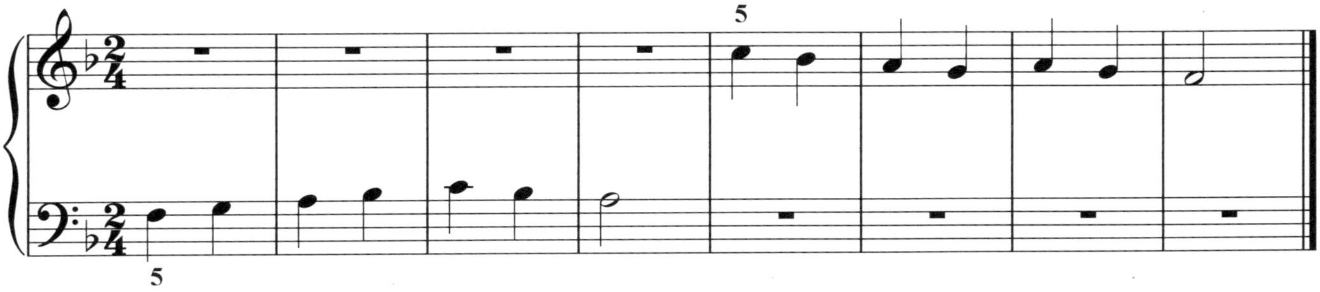

14

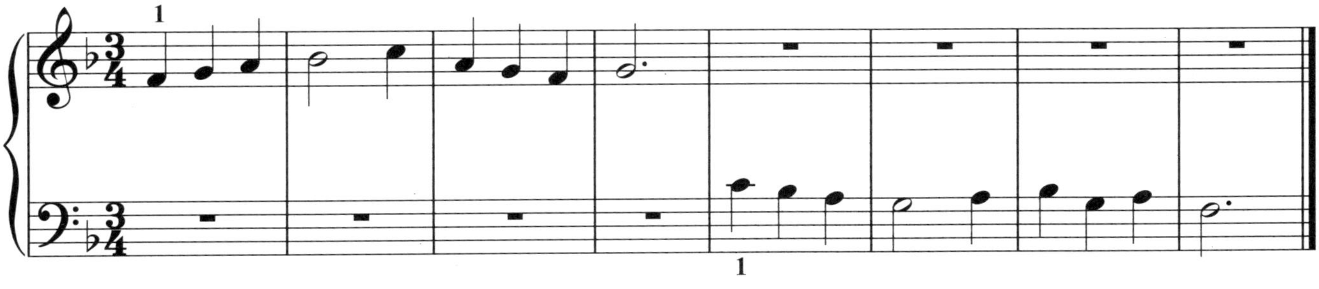

15

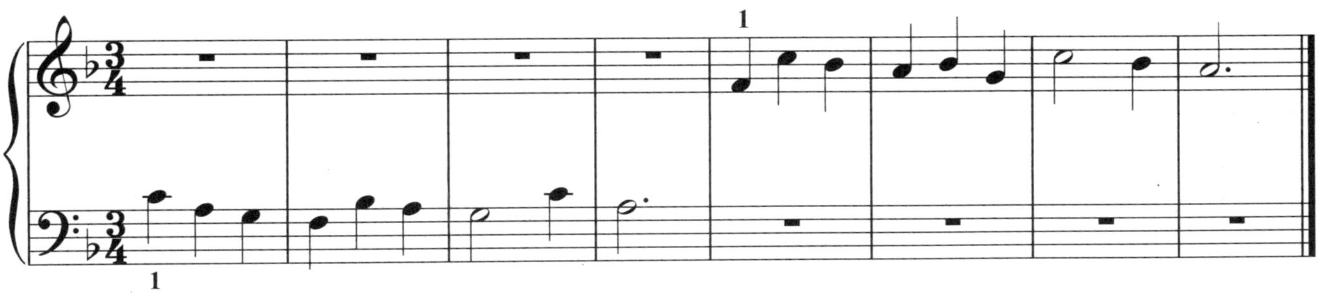

16

17

18

Introducing ♫

19

22

20

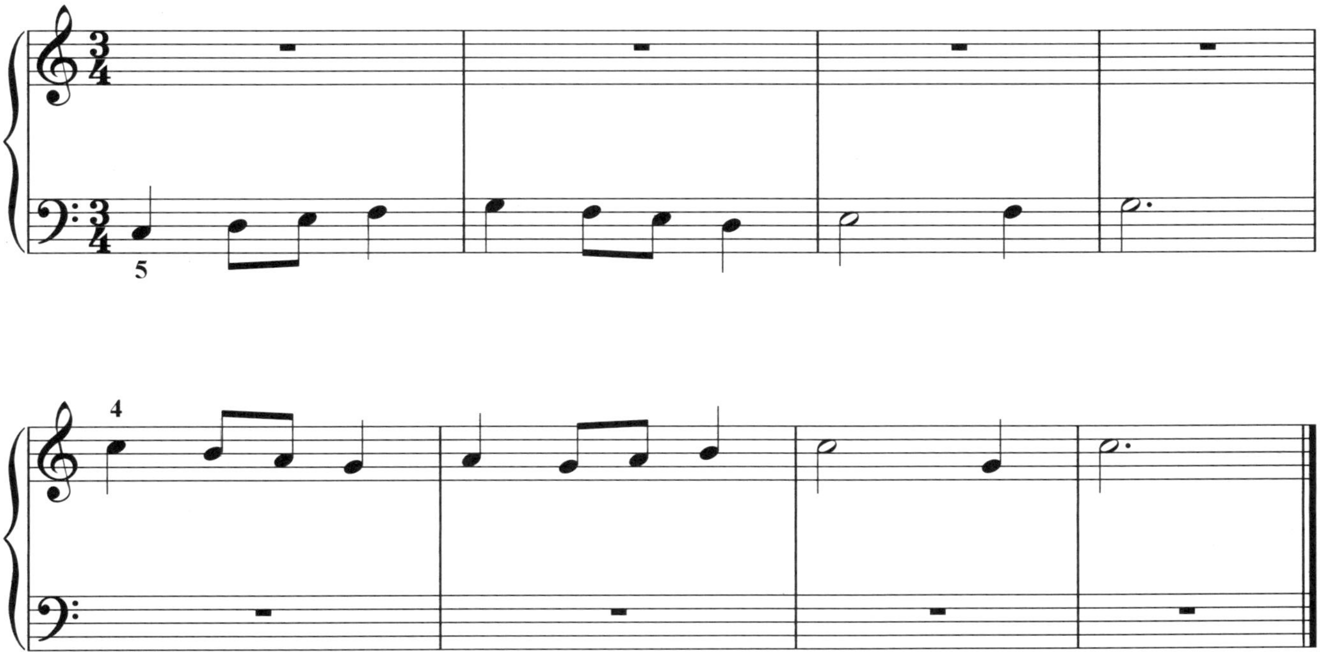

21

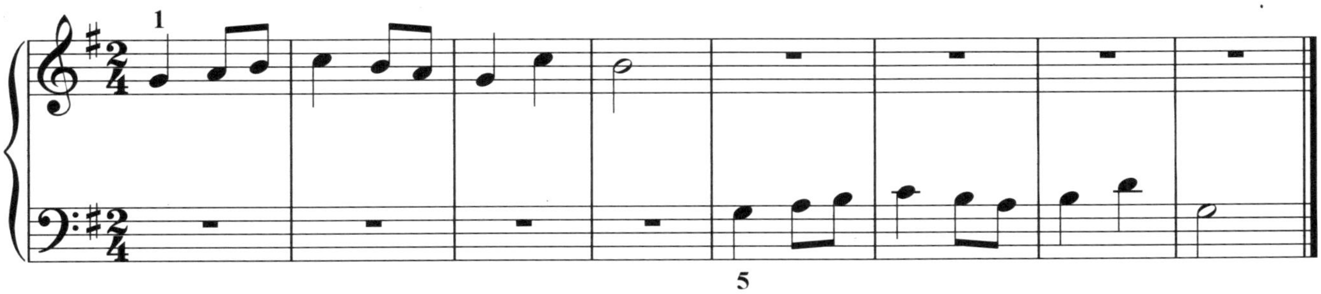

22

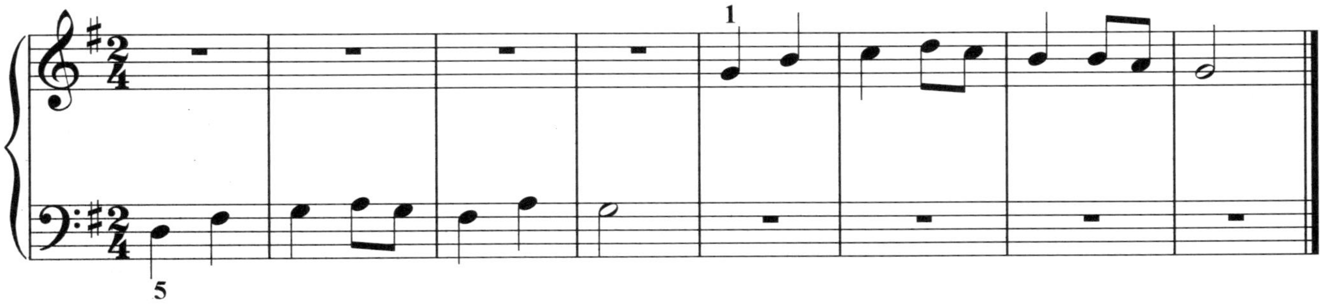

23

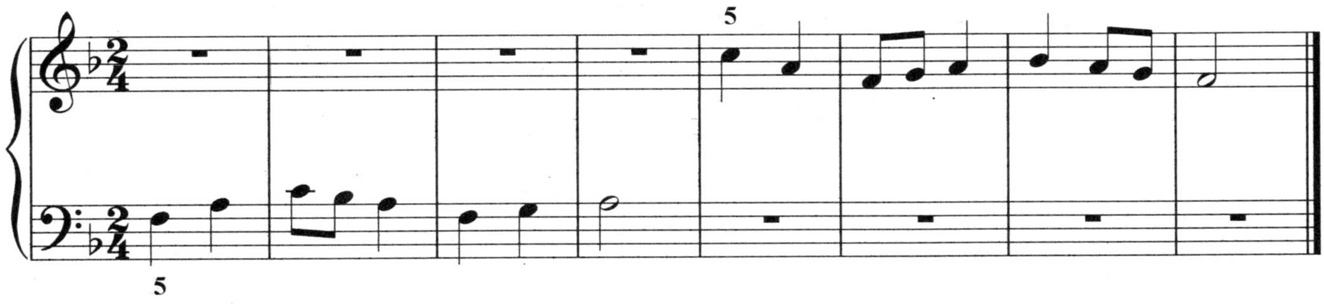

24

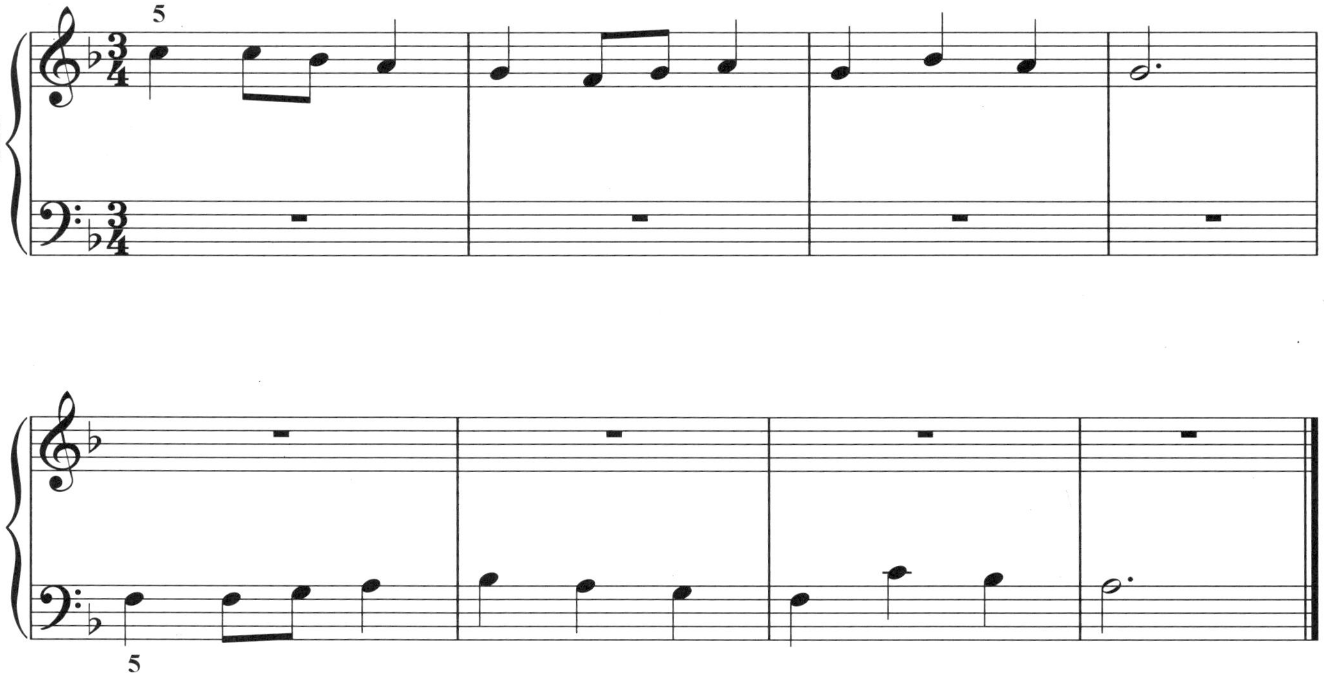

25

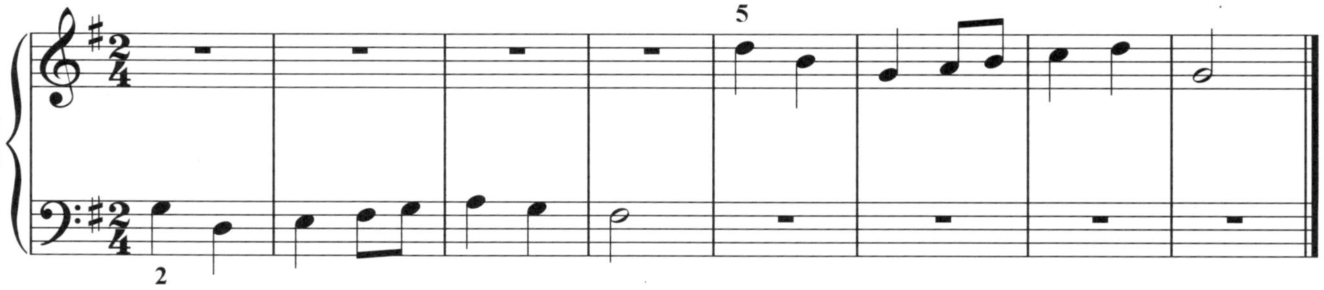

26

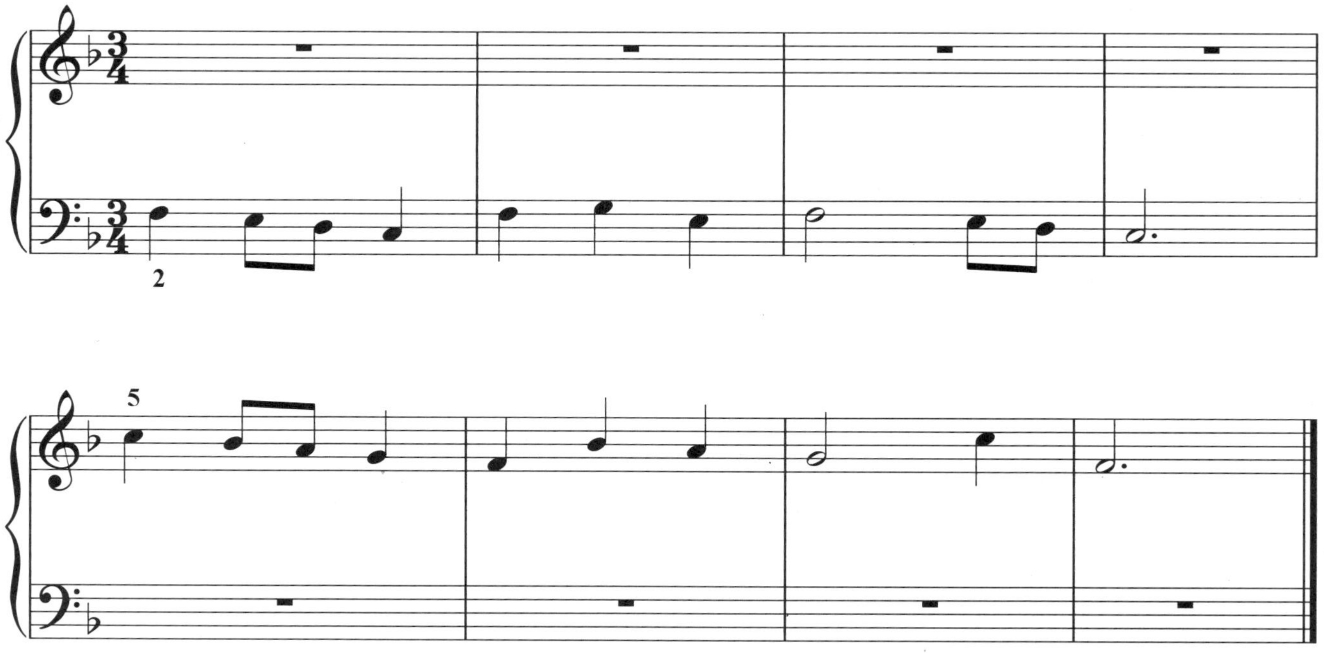

27

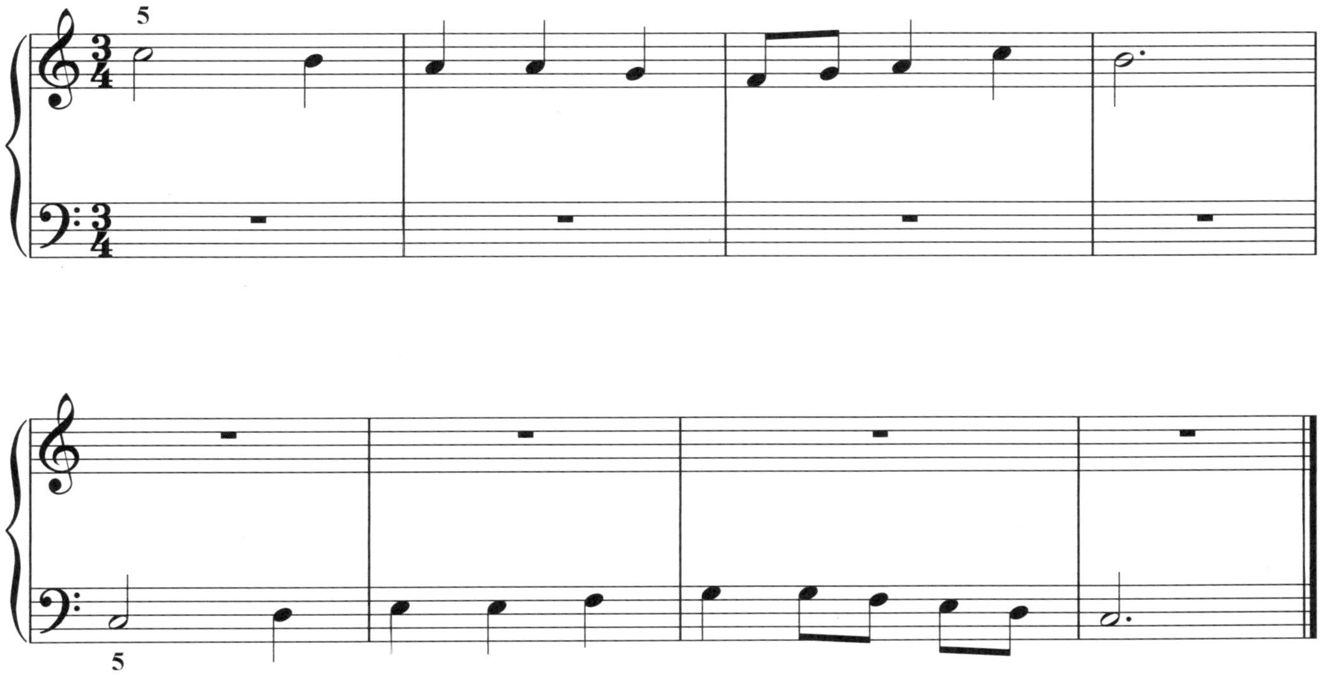

28

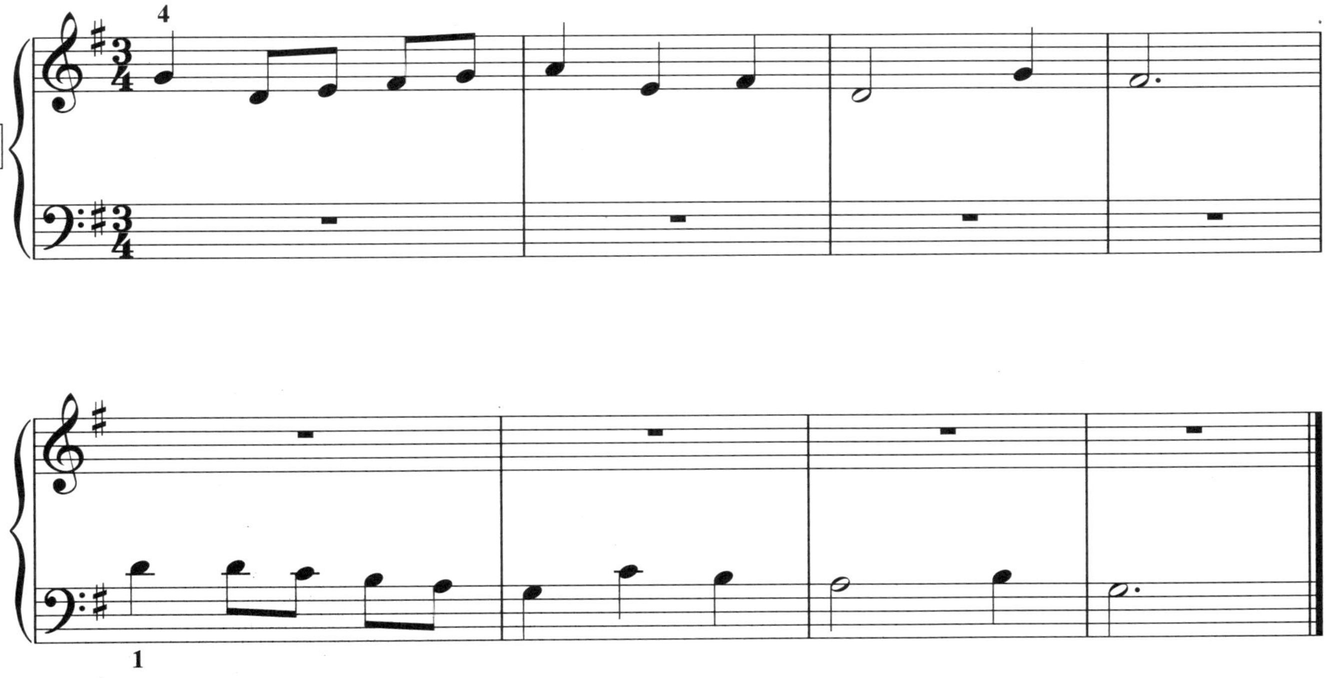

29

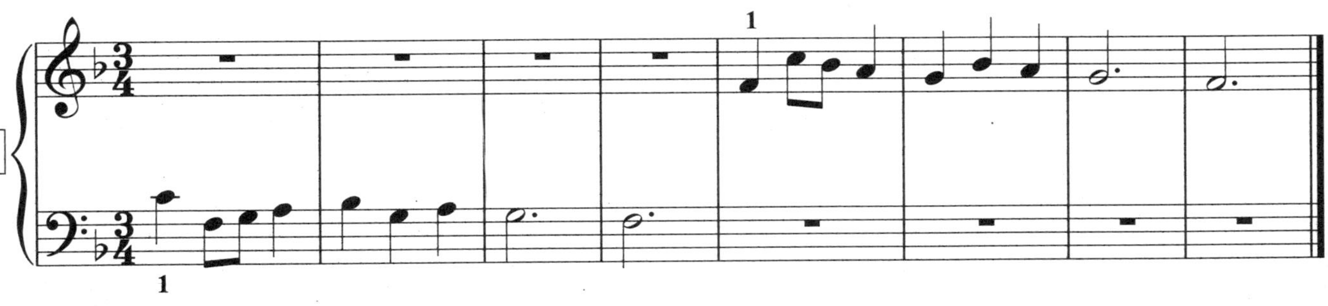

30

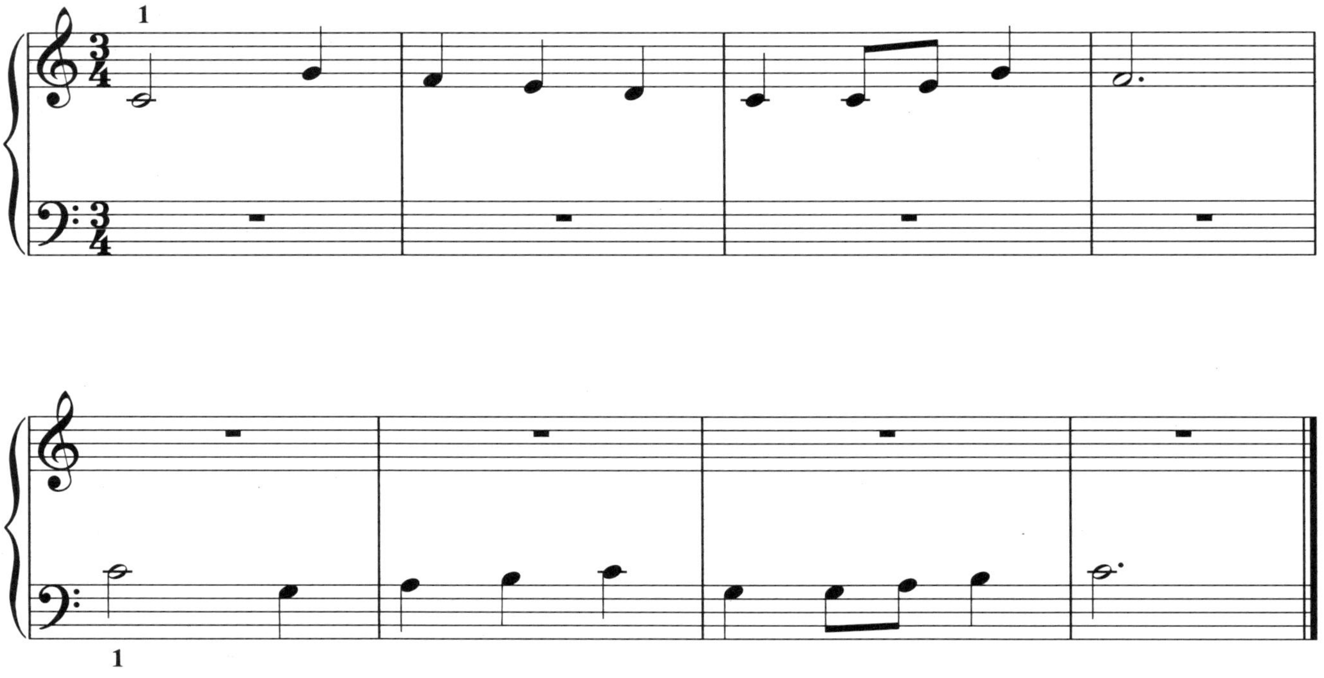

31

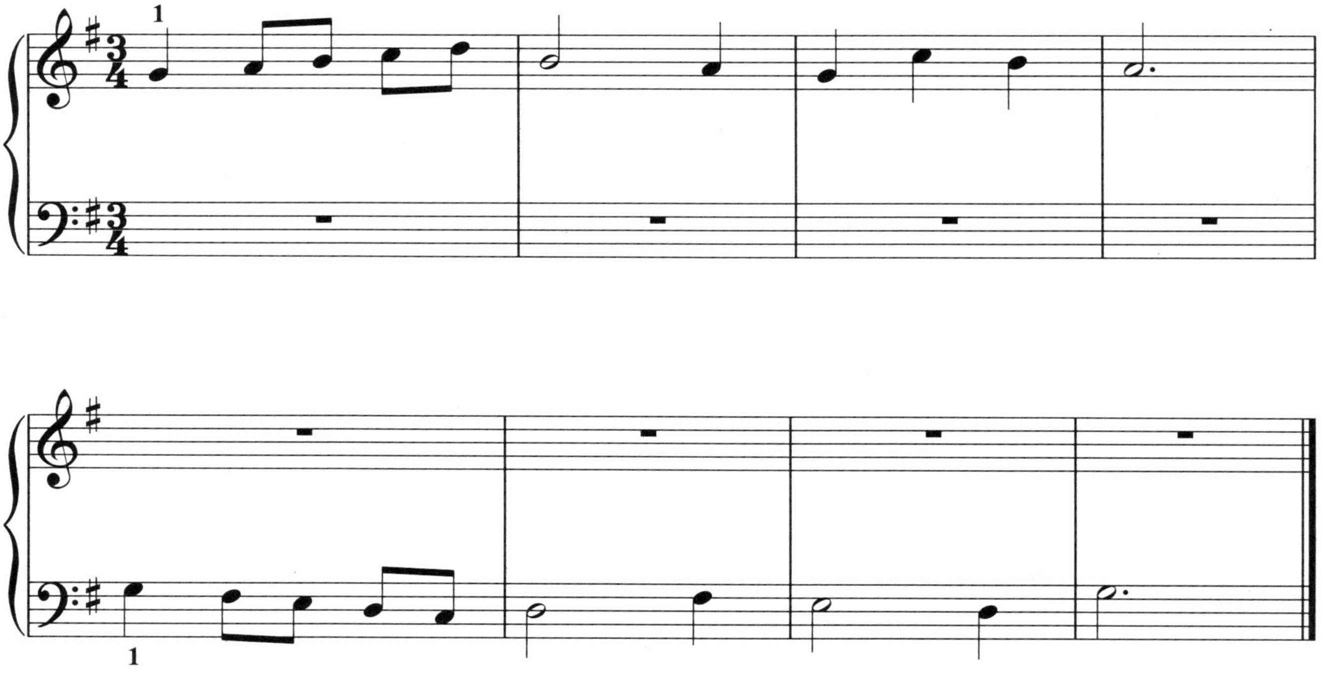

32

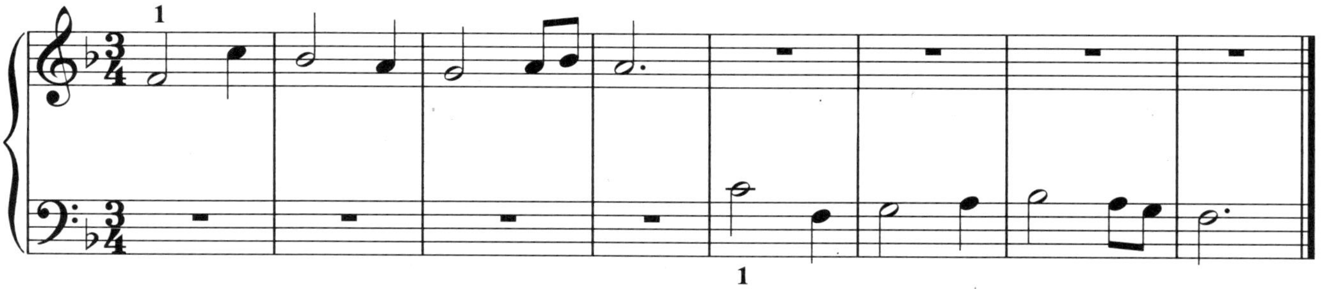

33

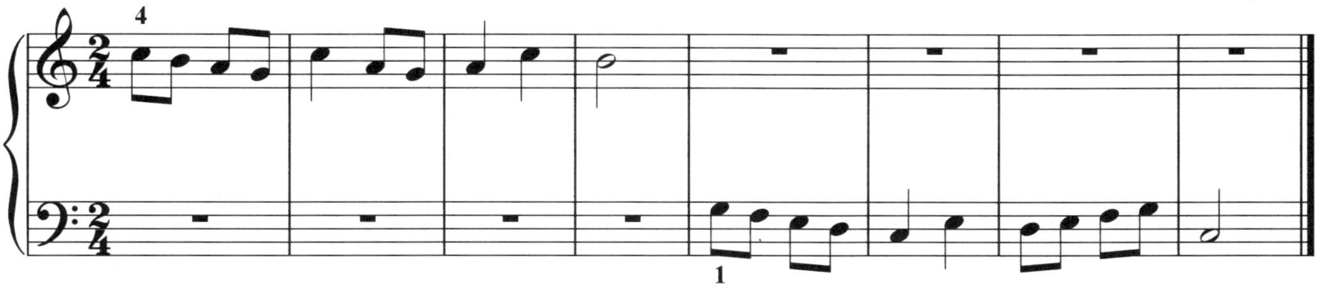

34

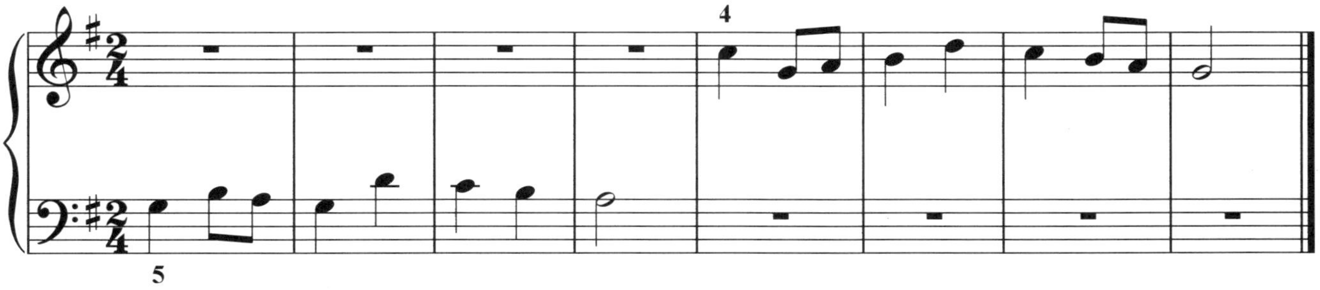

35

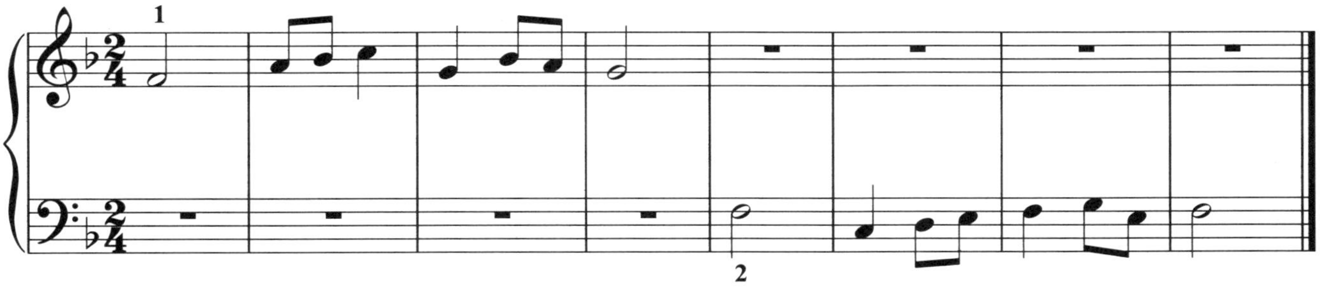

36

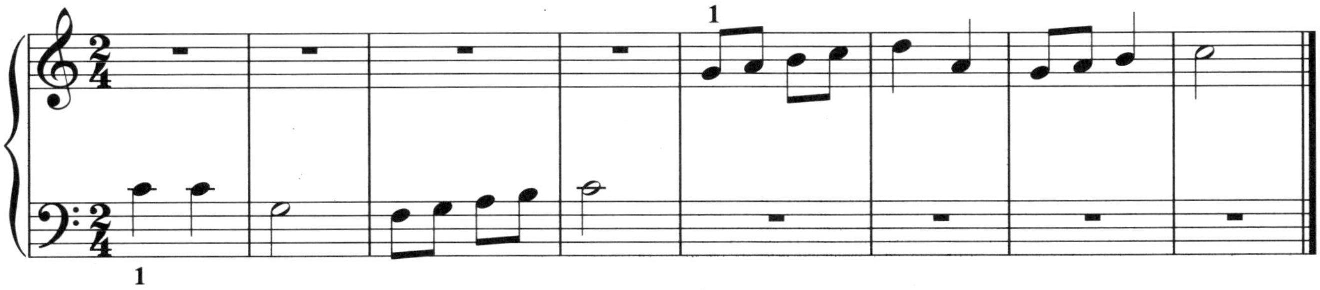

37

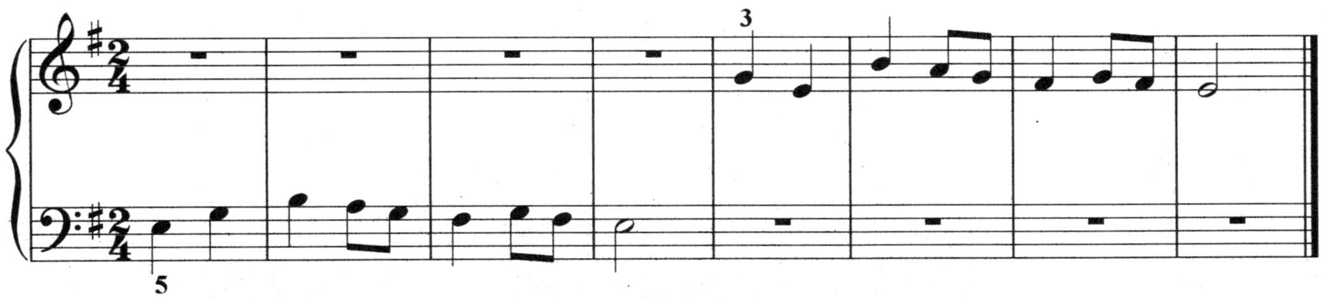

38

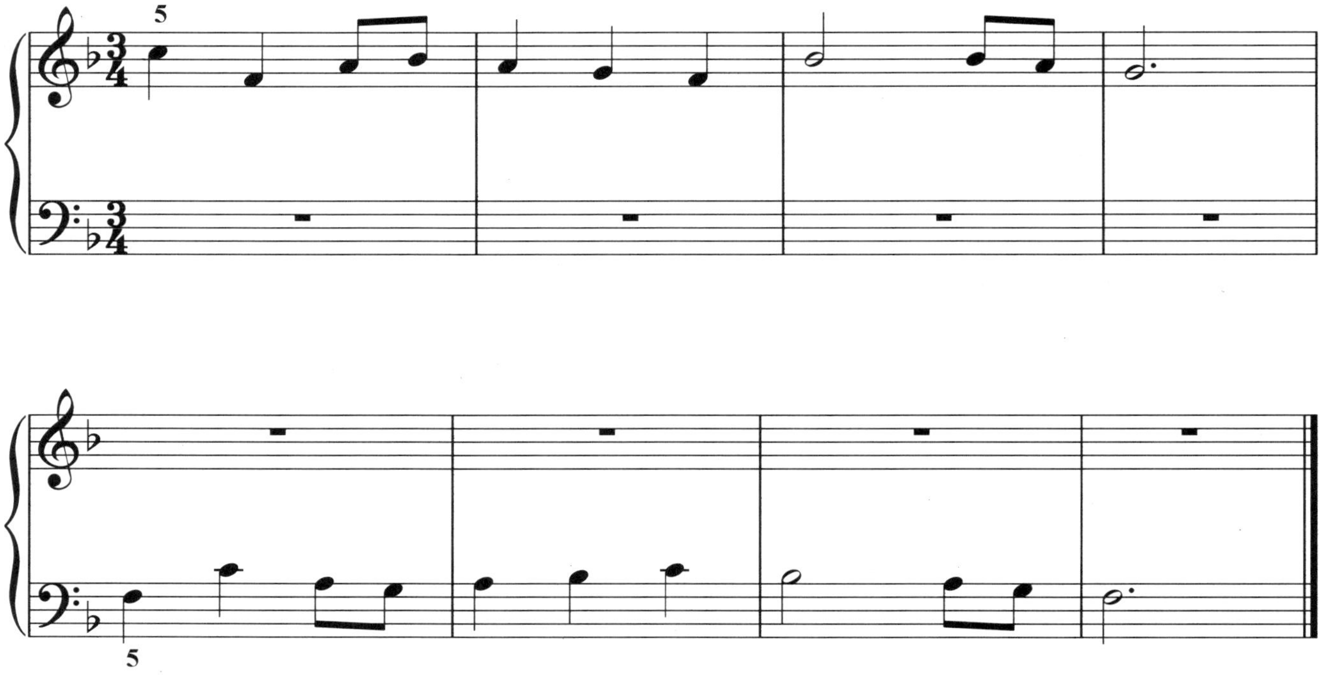

39

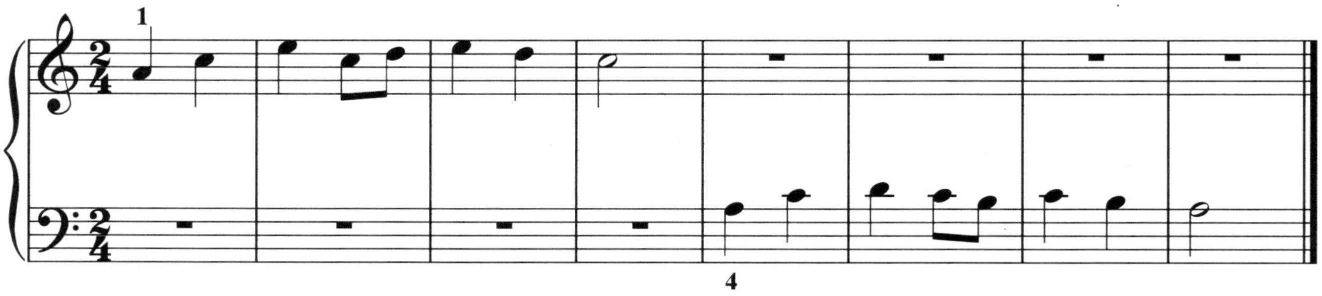

40

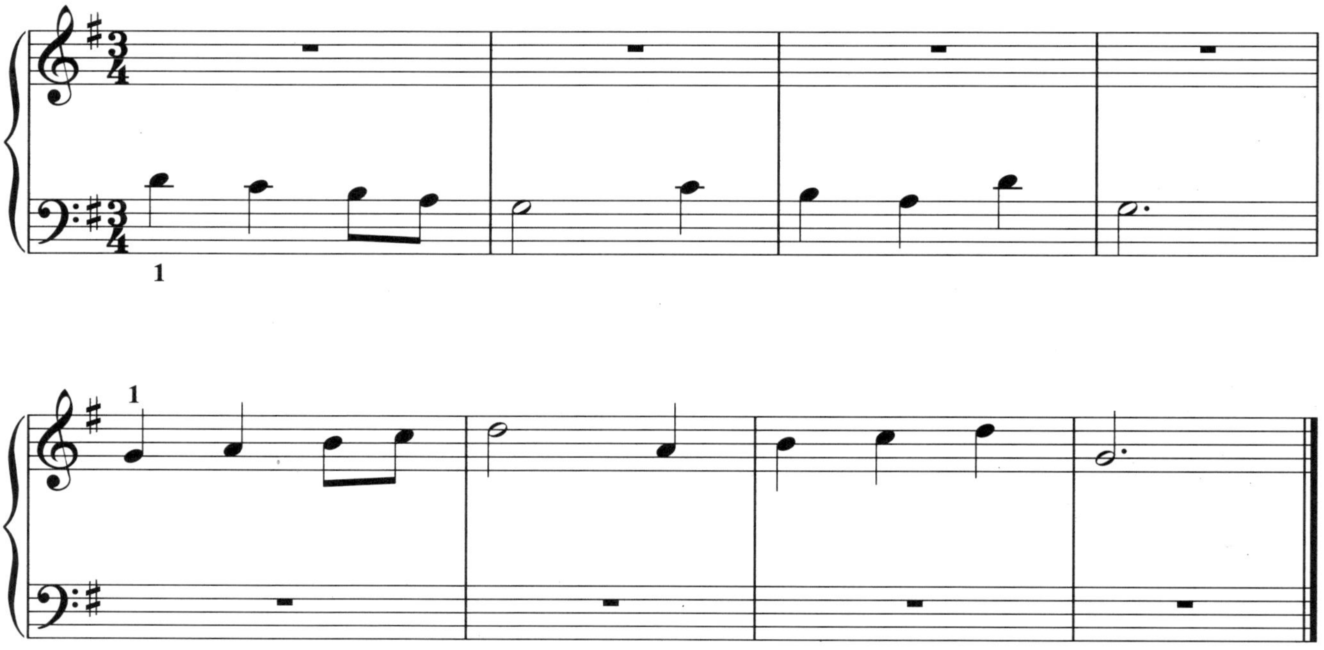

41

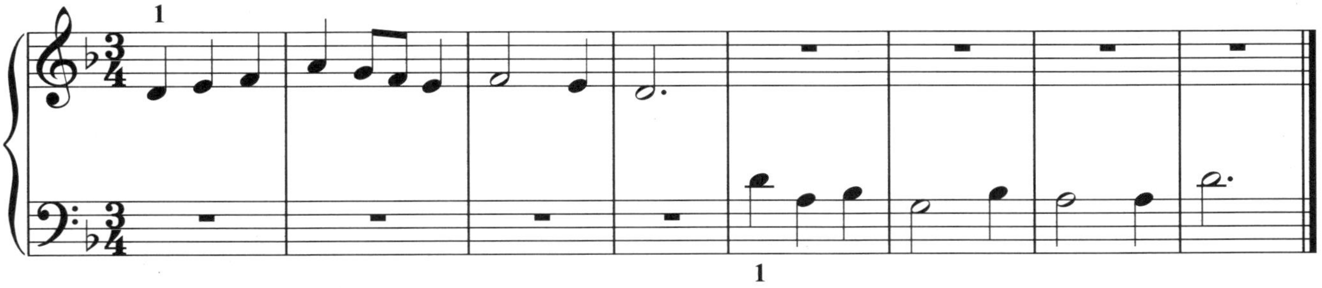

42

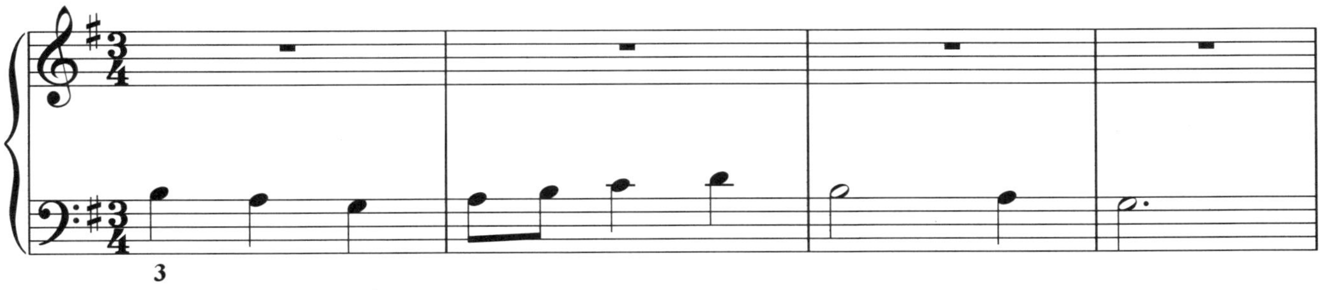

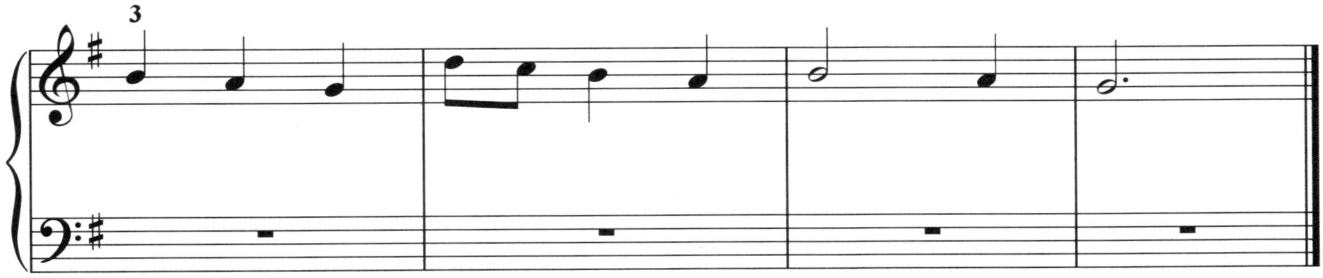

43

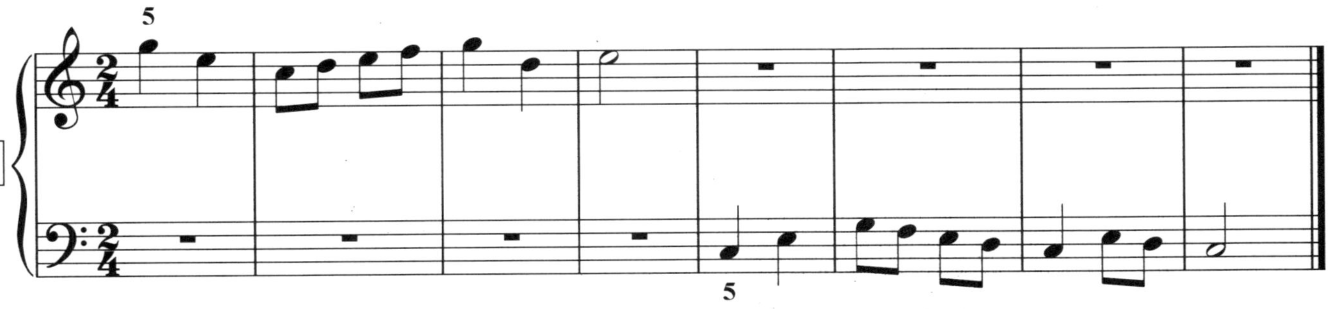

44

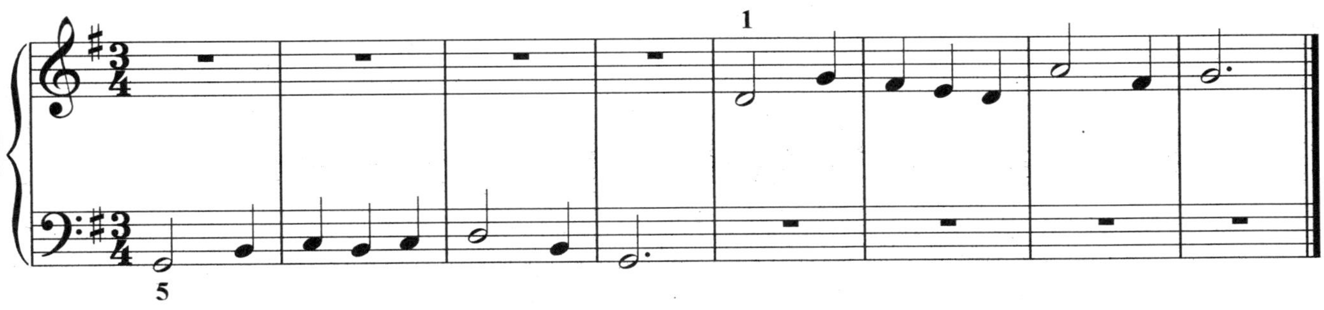

45

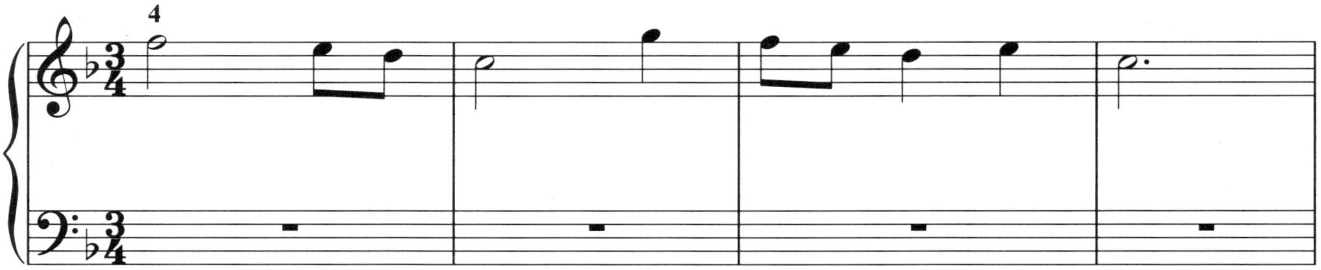

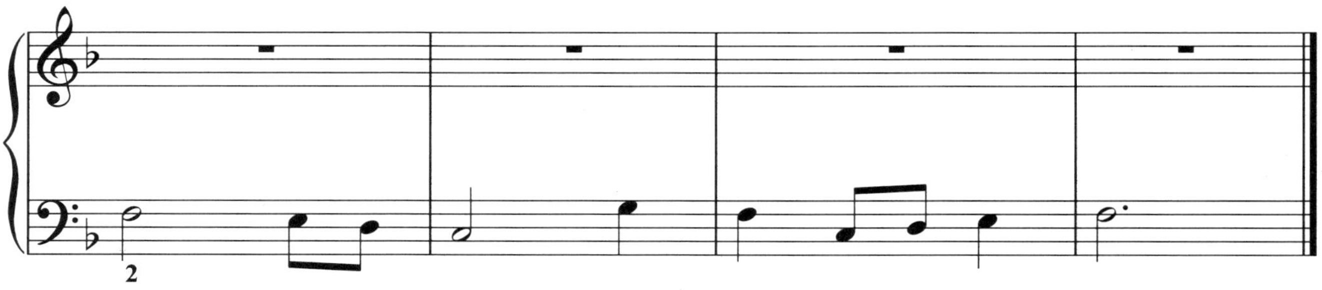

46

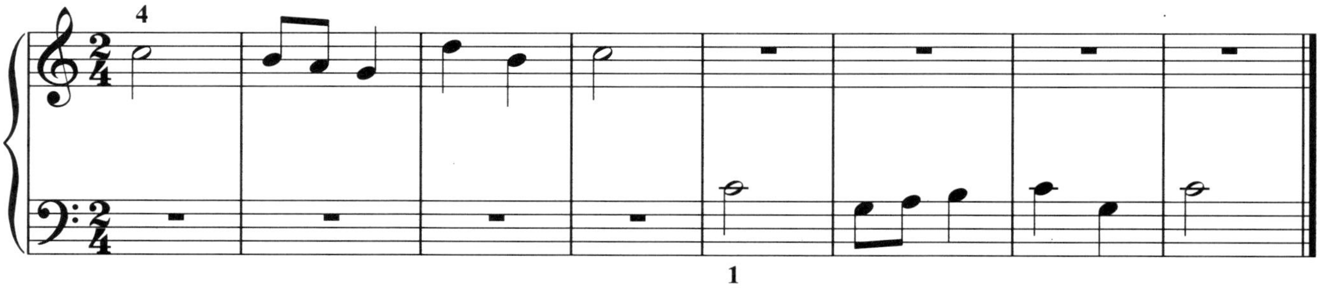

47

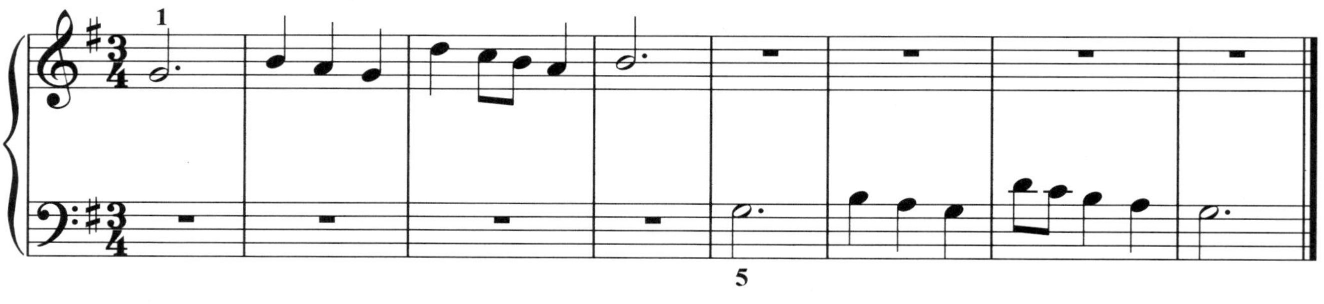

48

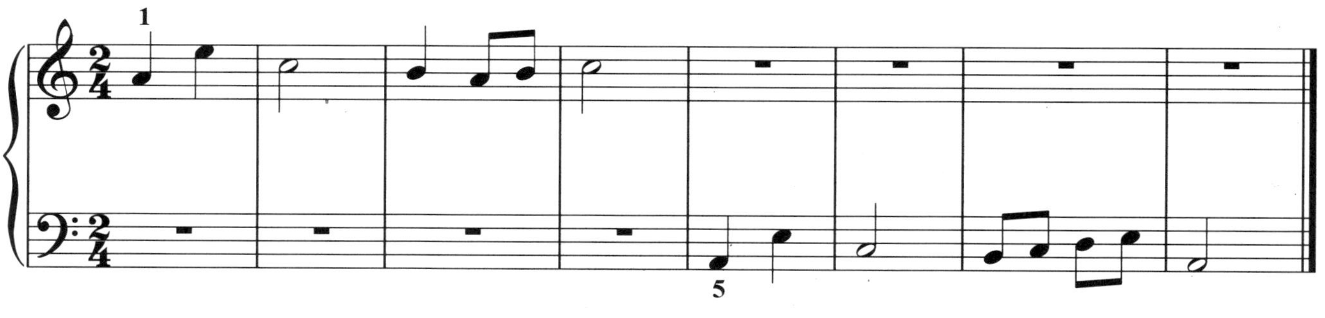

49

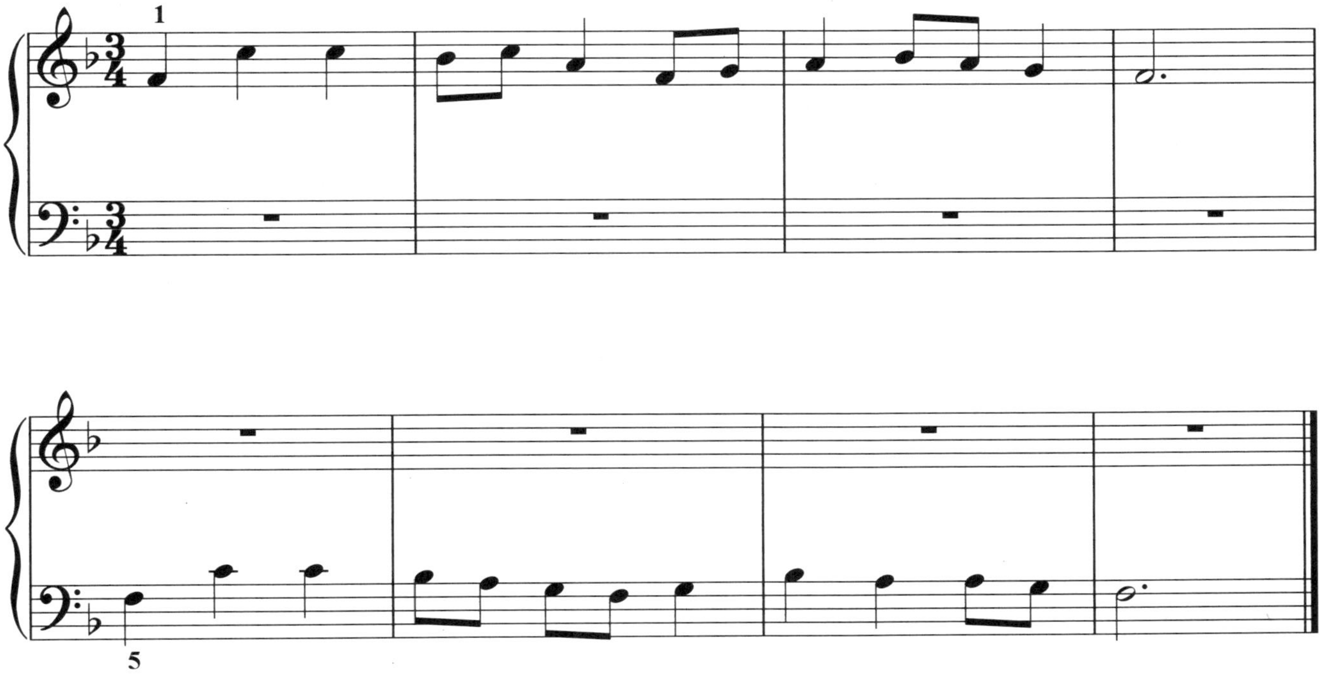

50

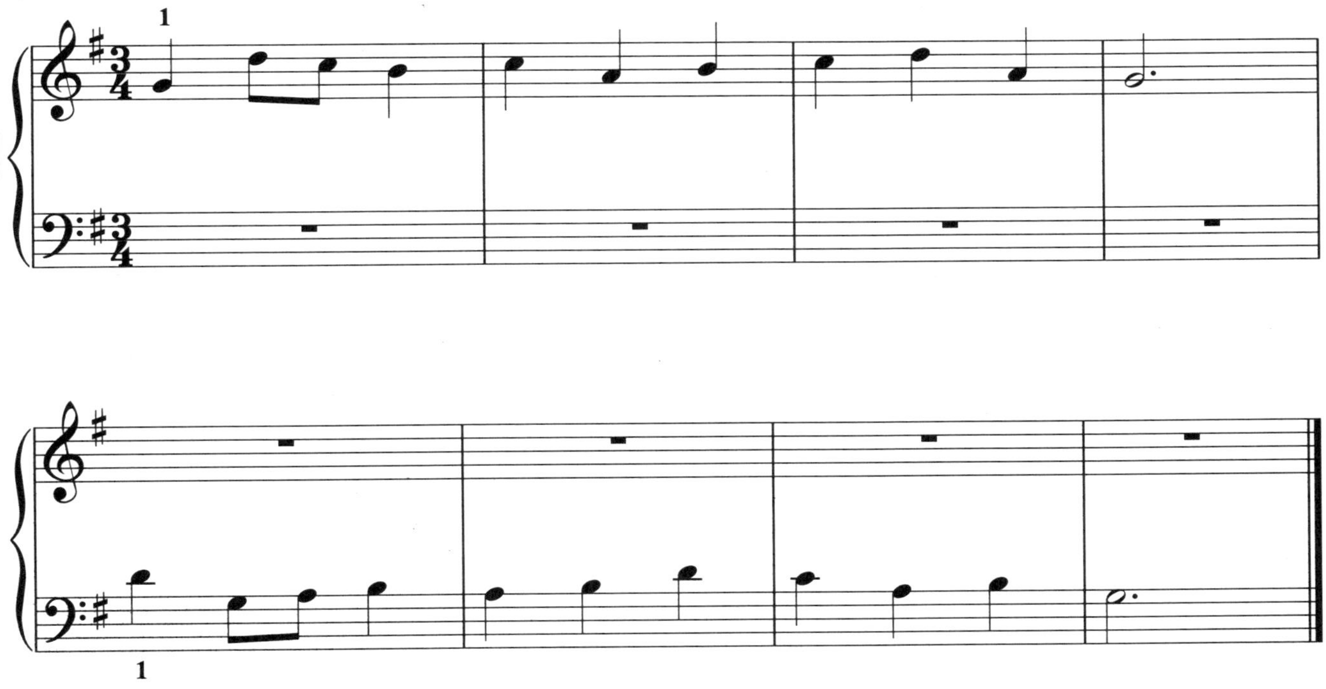

51

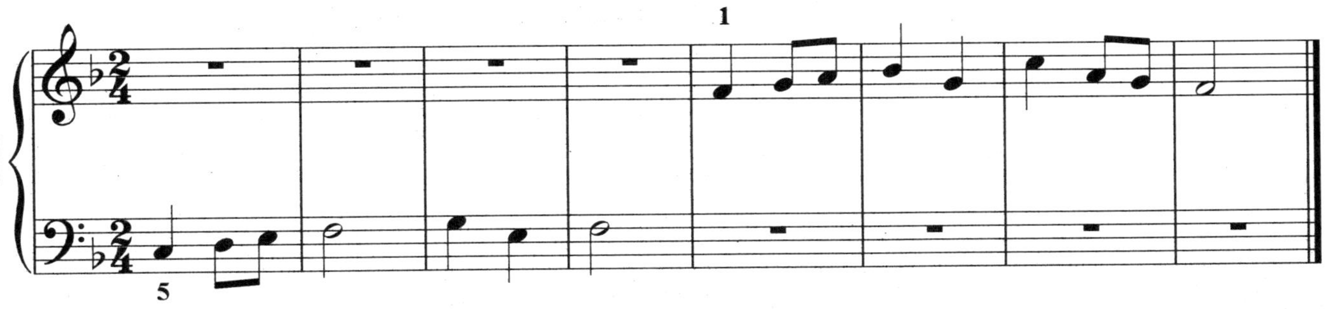

52

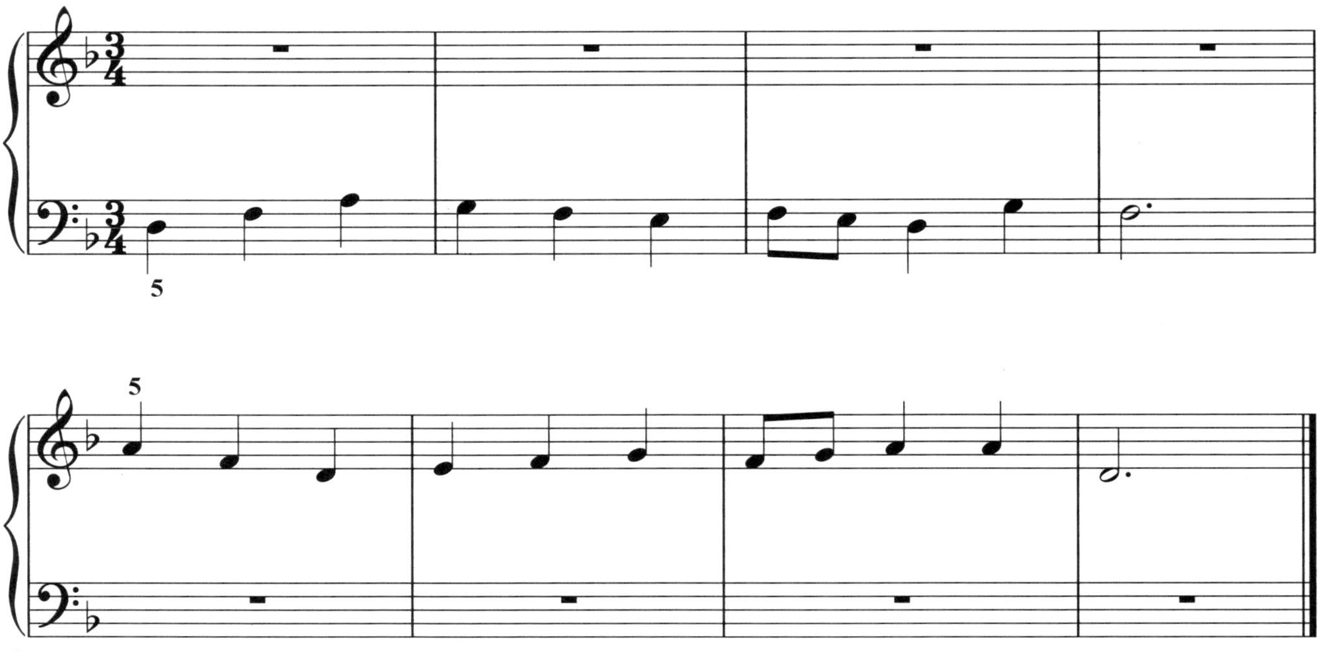

53

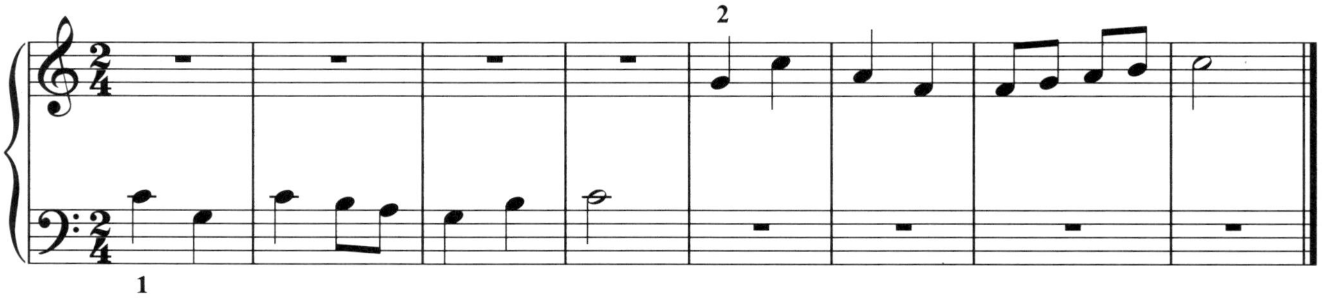

54

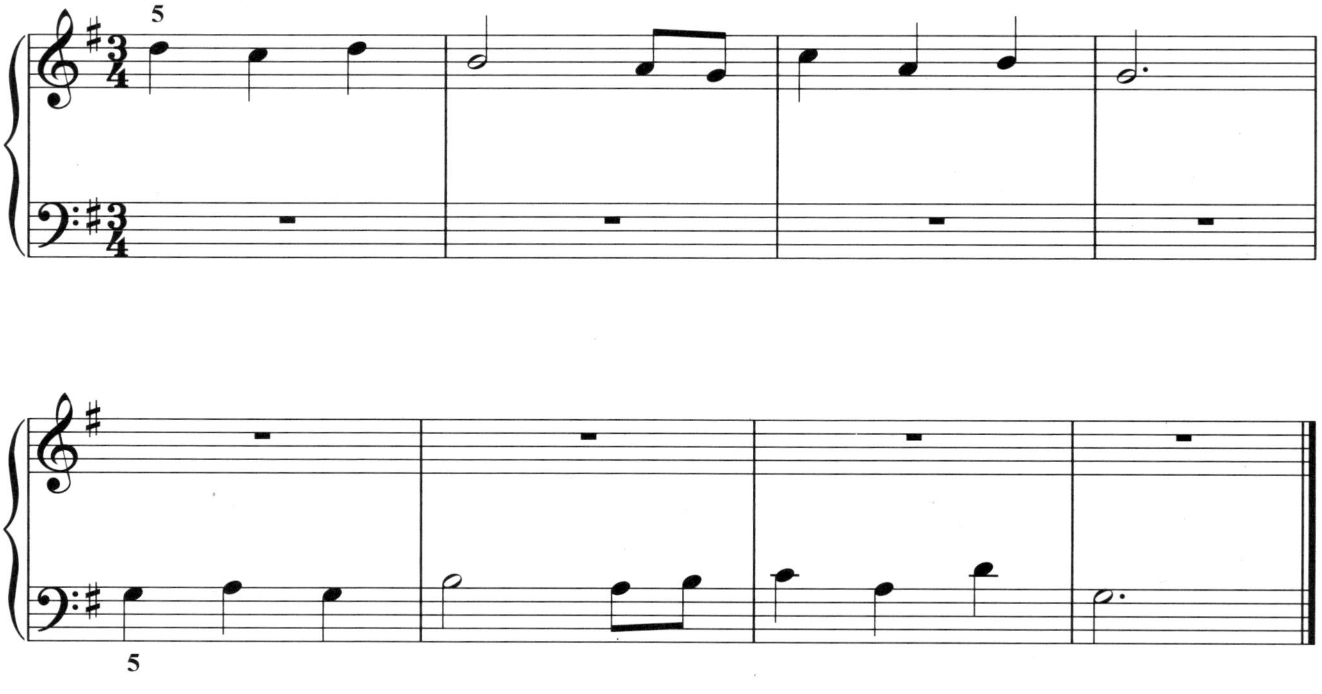

blank

Section Three

In this section, all pieces have a few bars where the hands play together. This is not difficult if you first look carefully at these bars before you play the piece.

Let us notice in No. 1 where the hands play together:

The LH repeats the same two notes, a step apart each time.
The RH steps in the opposite direction to the LH in the middle of the piece.
The RH steps in the same direction as the LH at the end of the piece.

Arrows show you the directions in this piece.

Pieces 1 – 18
Hands have one-step moves when they play together. From No. 11 onwards, there are bigger intervals in some pieces where hands are playing together, but usually one of the hands has only a step move. Always sort these points out before you begin, then there should not be difficulties when you play.

Piece 19 onwards

Introducing ♩. ♪ This is the same as ♩ ♫ the dot replacing the tied first half of the beat.
The easiest way to count this is to say "WALK- DOT - ON"

♩   .   ♪

WALK – DOT – ON

Remember to clap the tune through before you play.

Section 3

Hands together

5

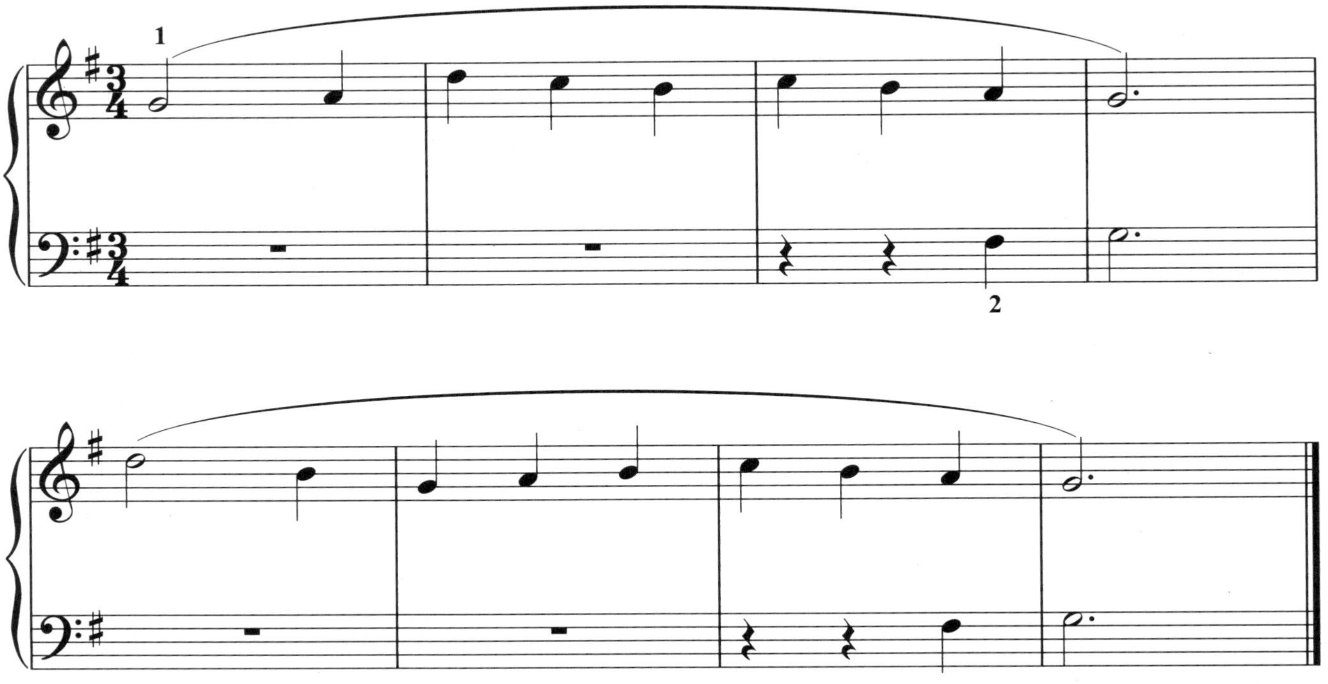

6

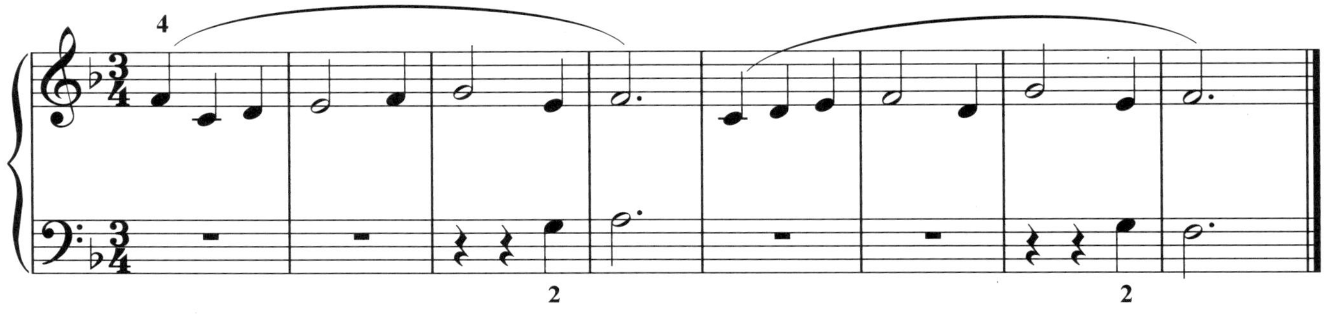

7

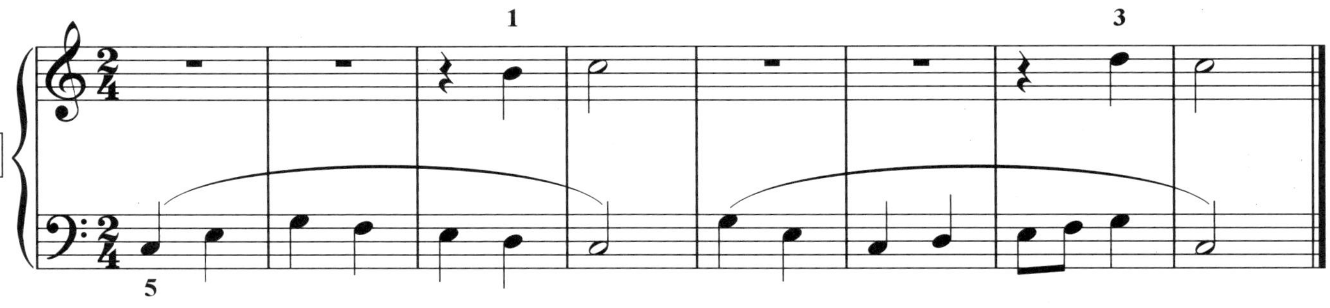

8

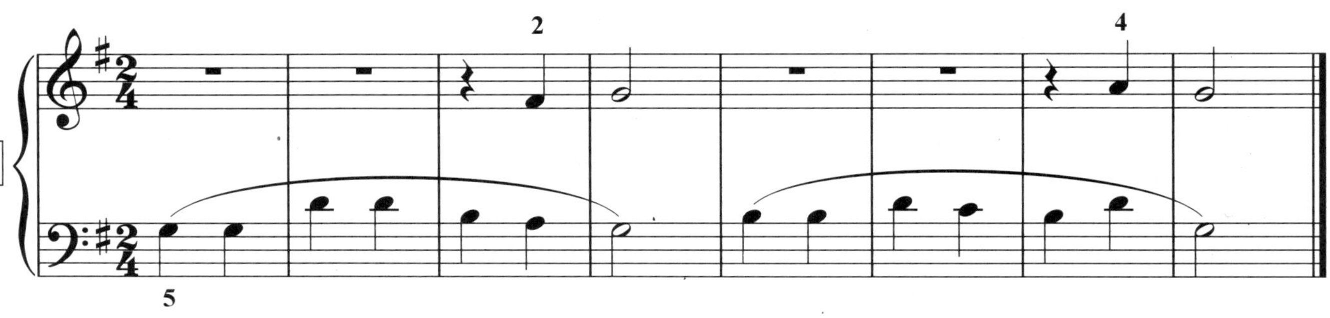

9

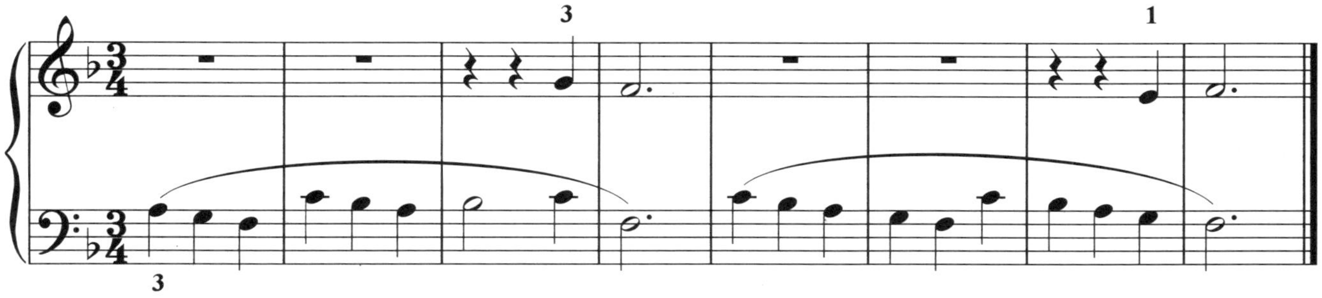

10

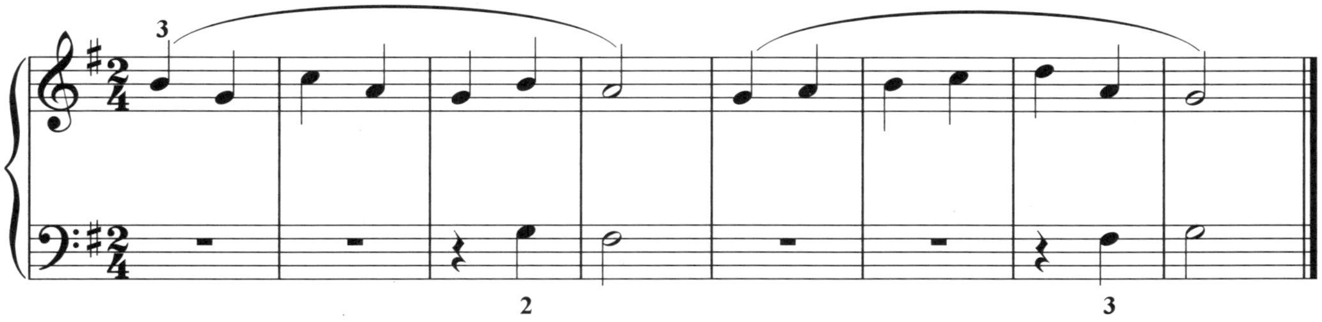

11

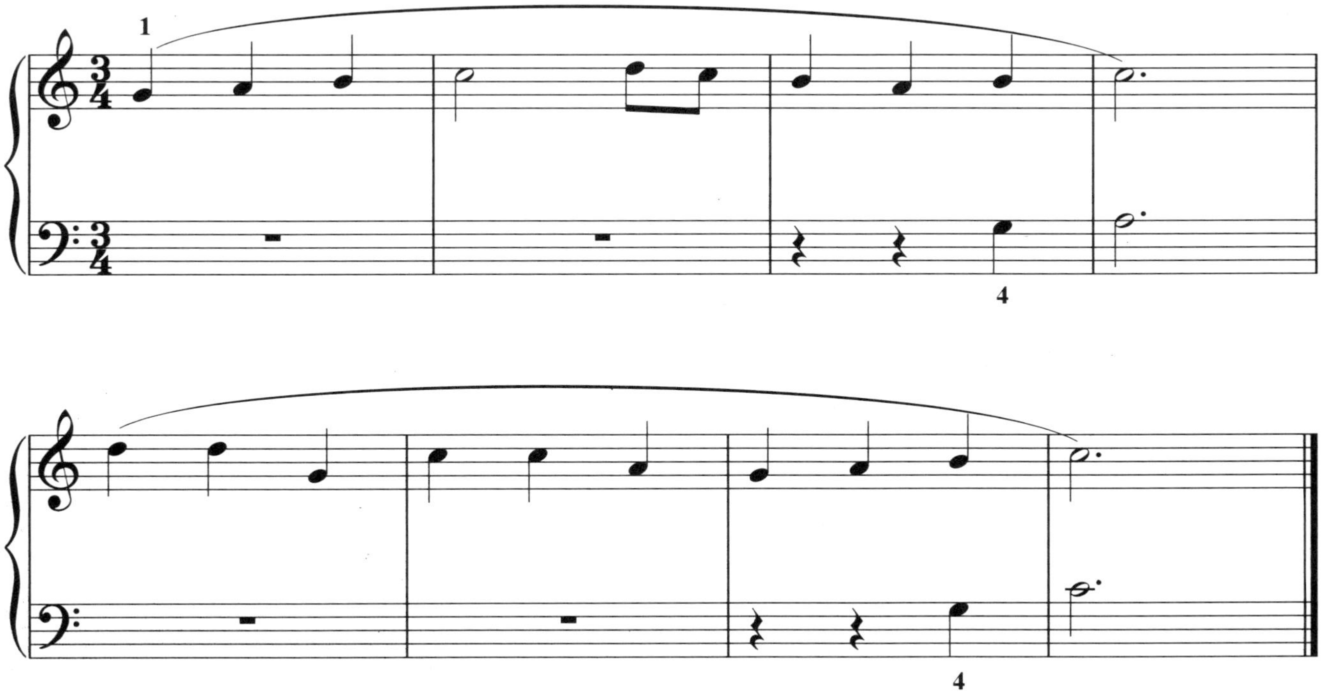

12

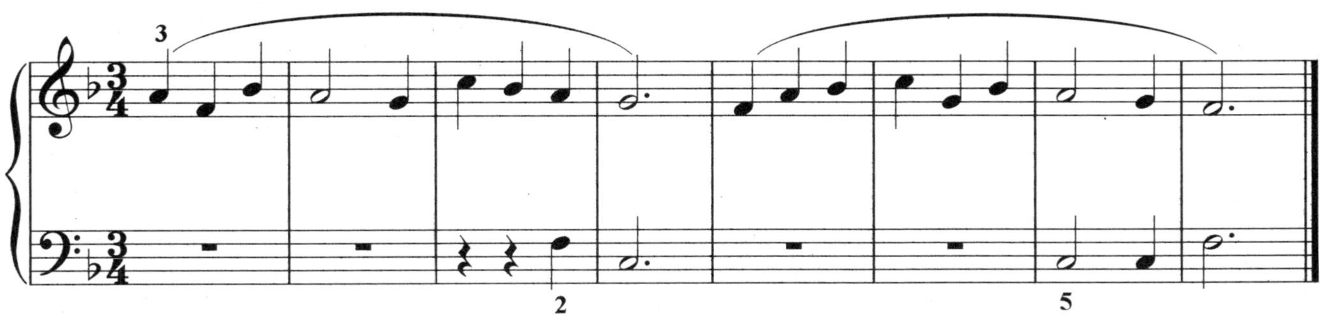

38

17

18

Introducing ♩. ♪

19

20

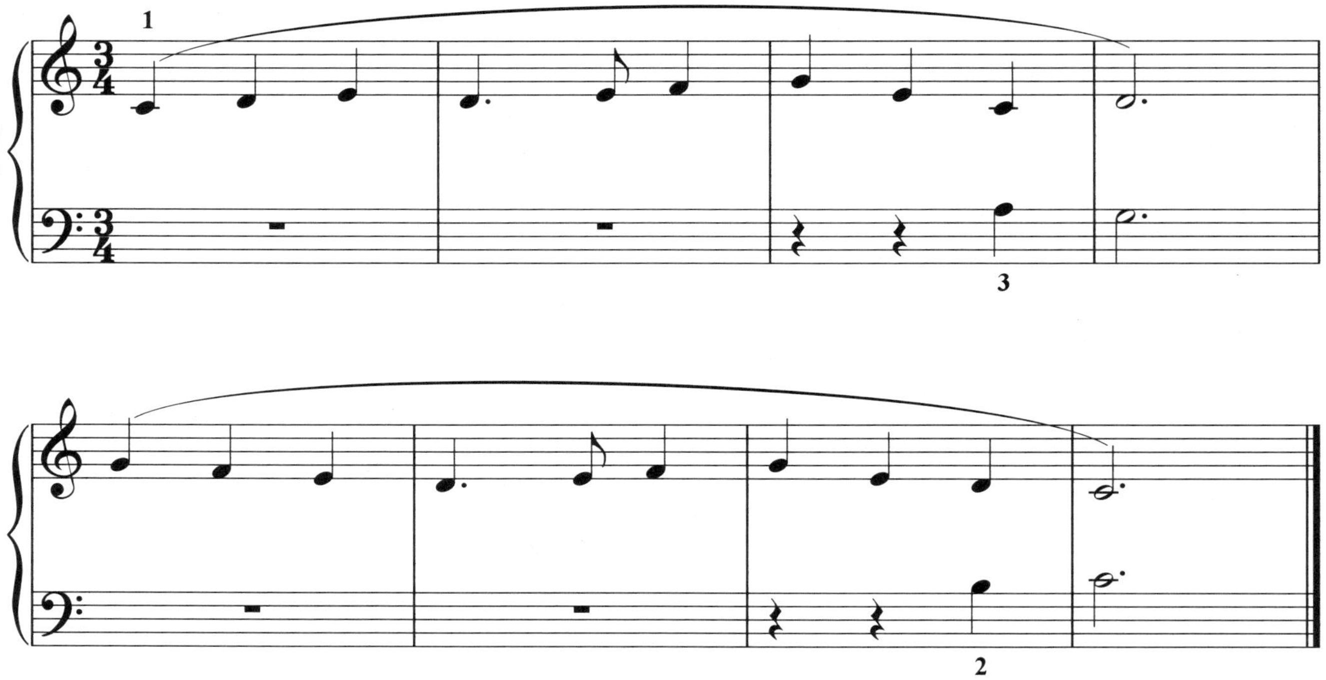

21

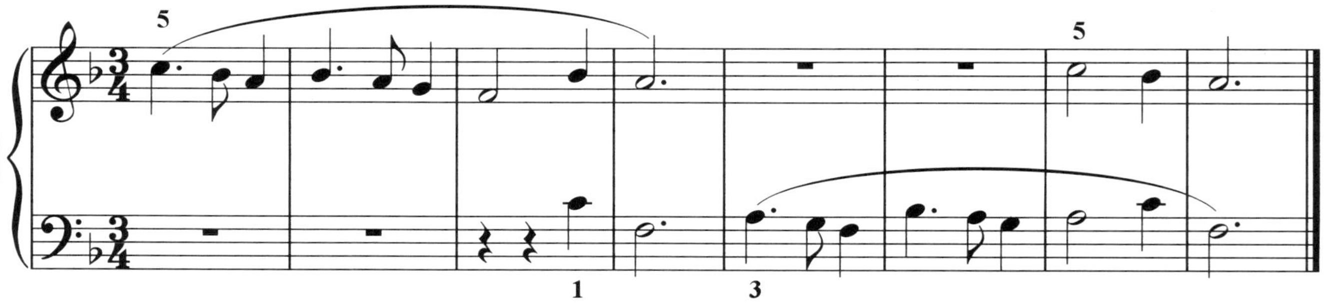

22

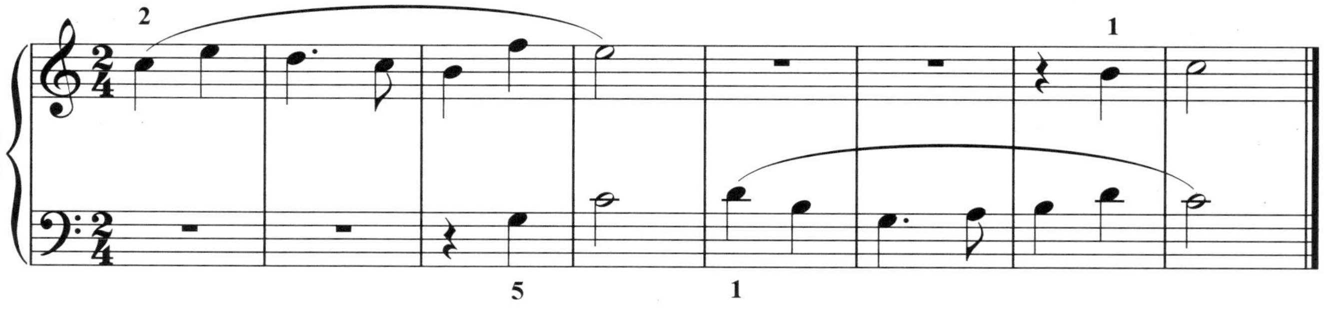

23

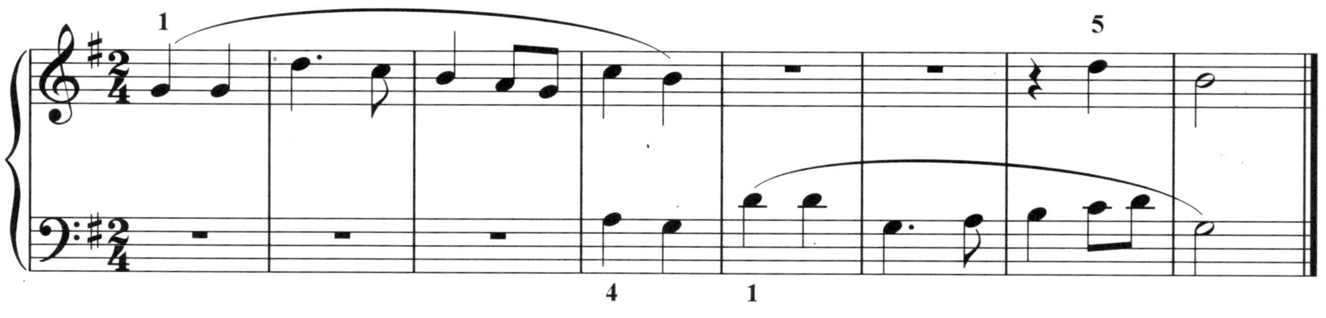

24

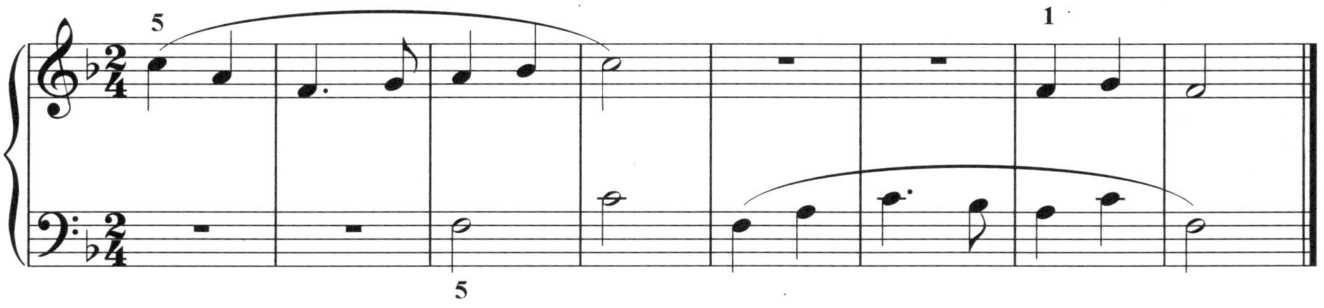

25

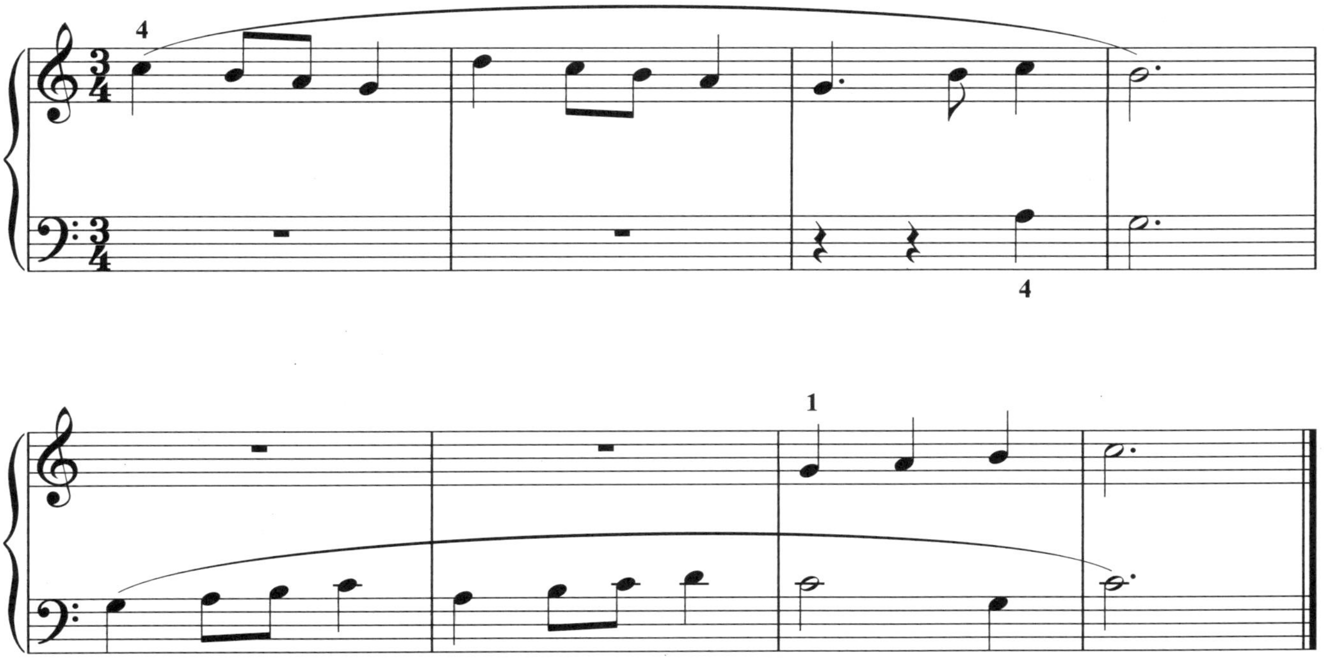

26

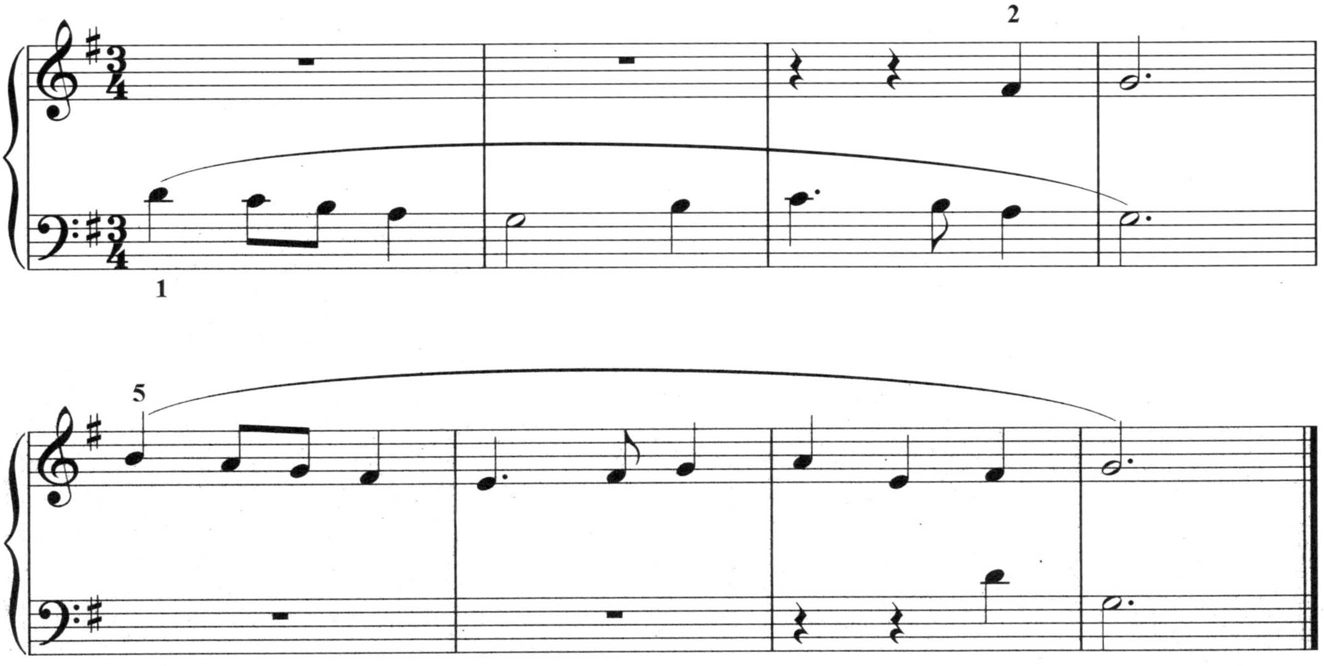

27

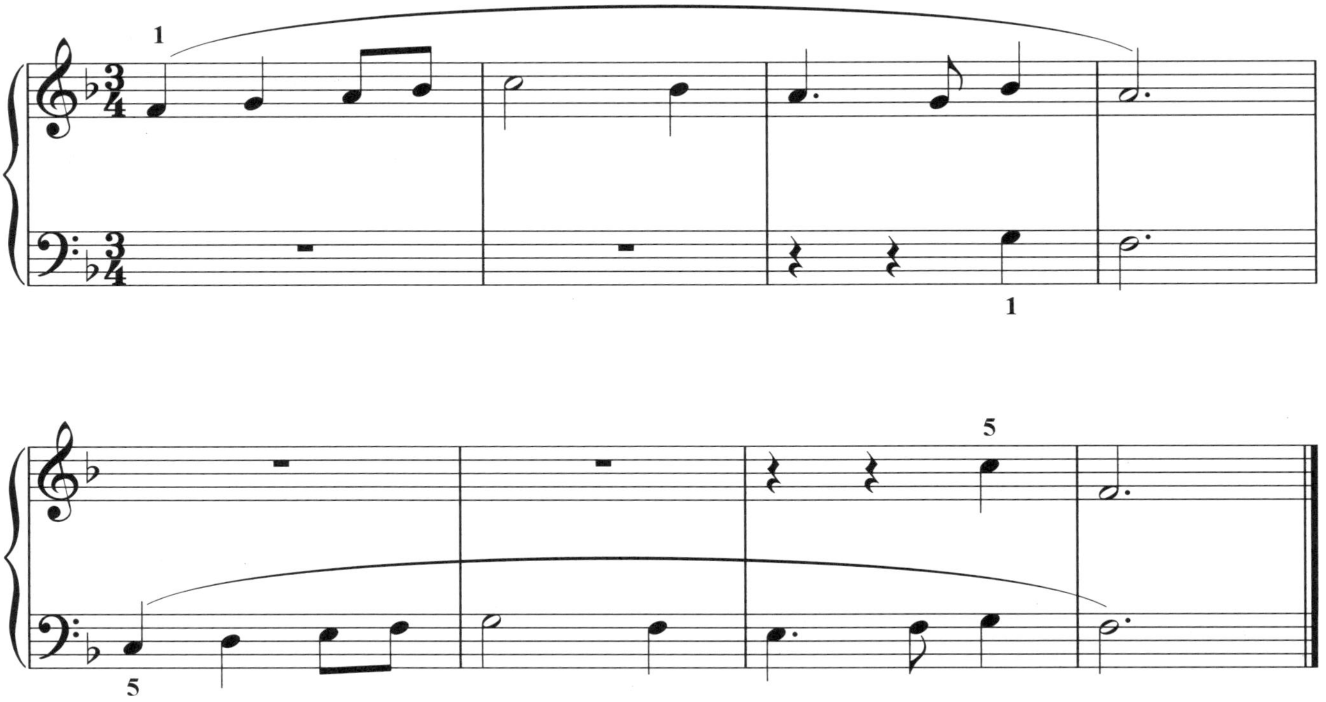

28

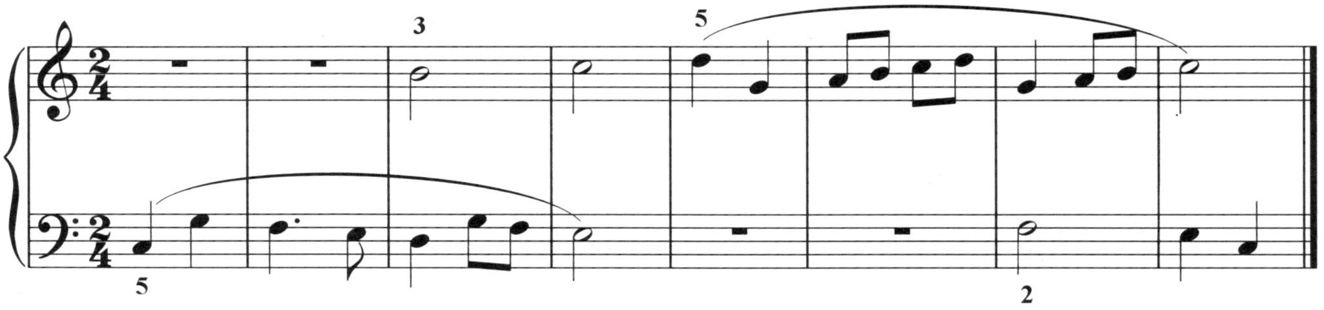

29

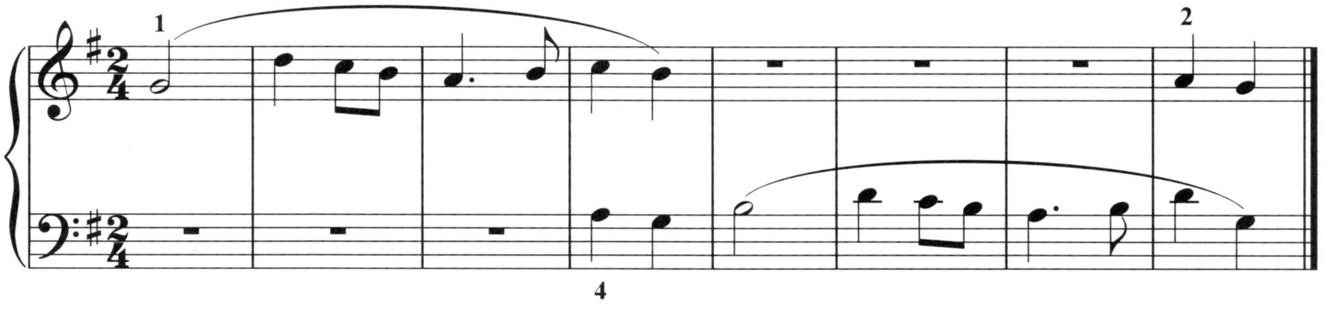

30

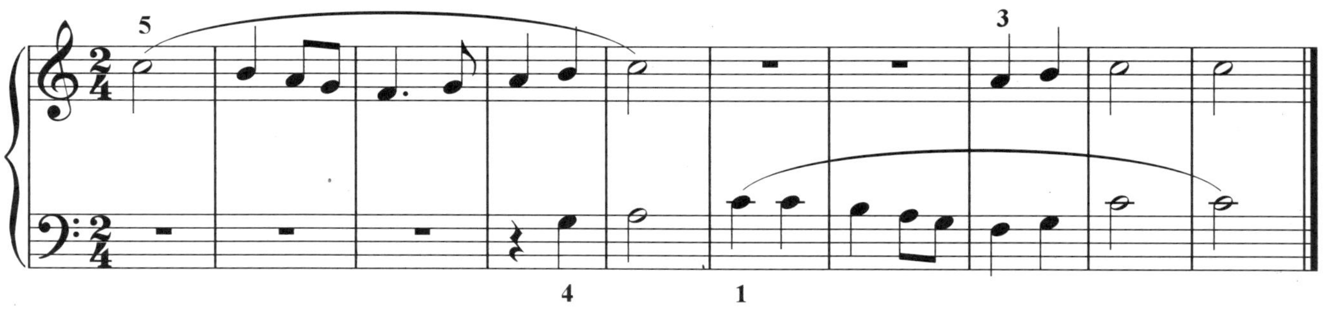

31

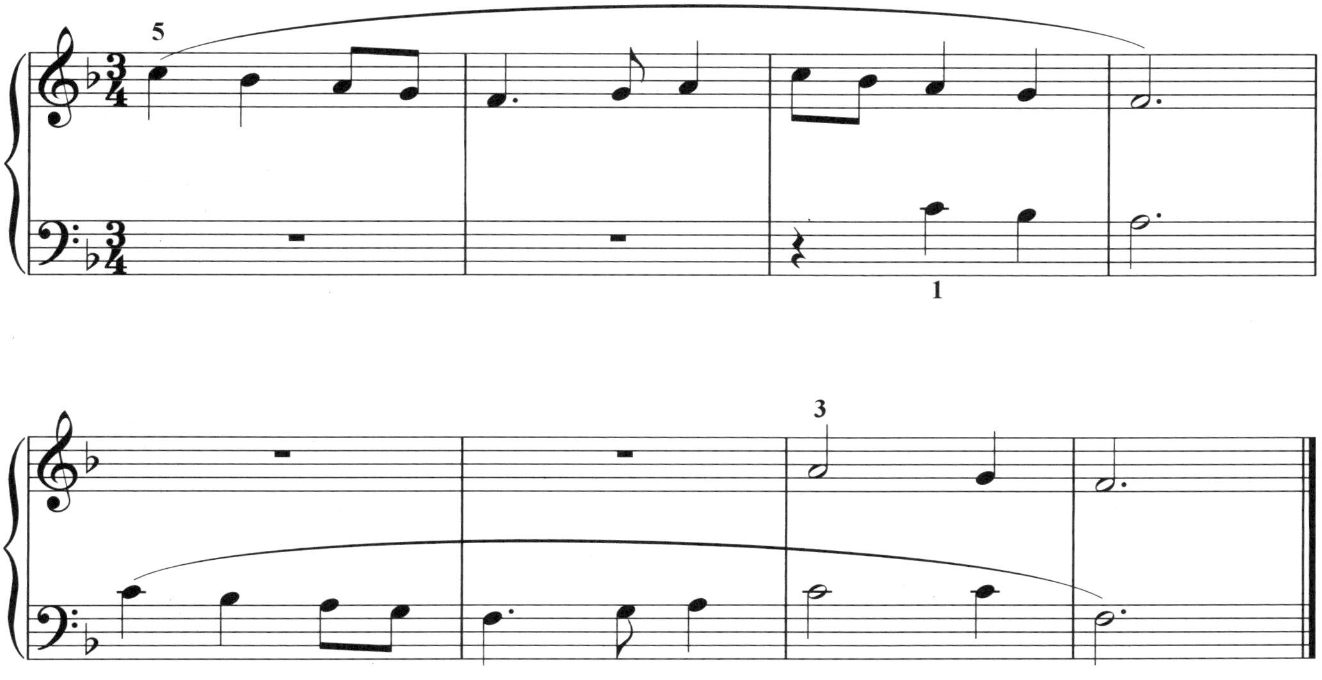

32

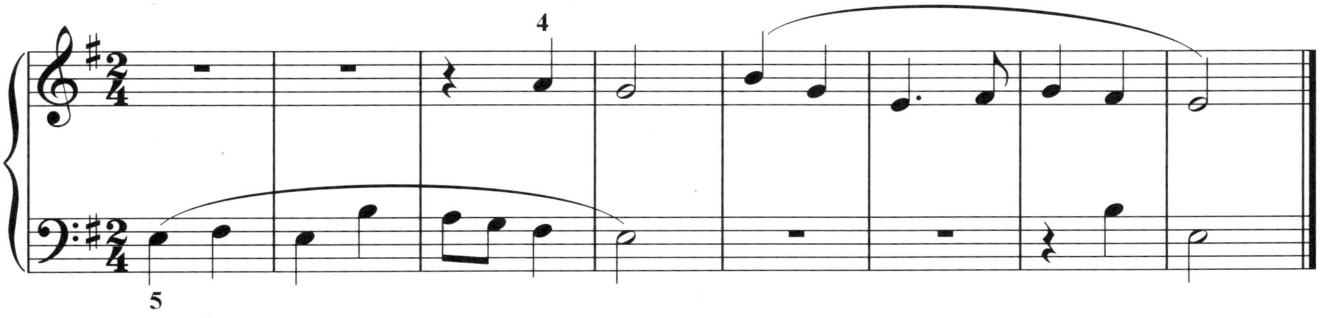

33

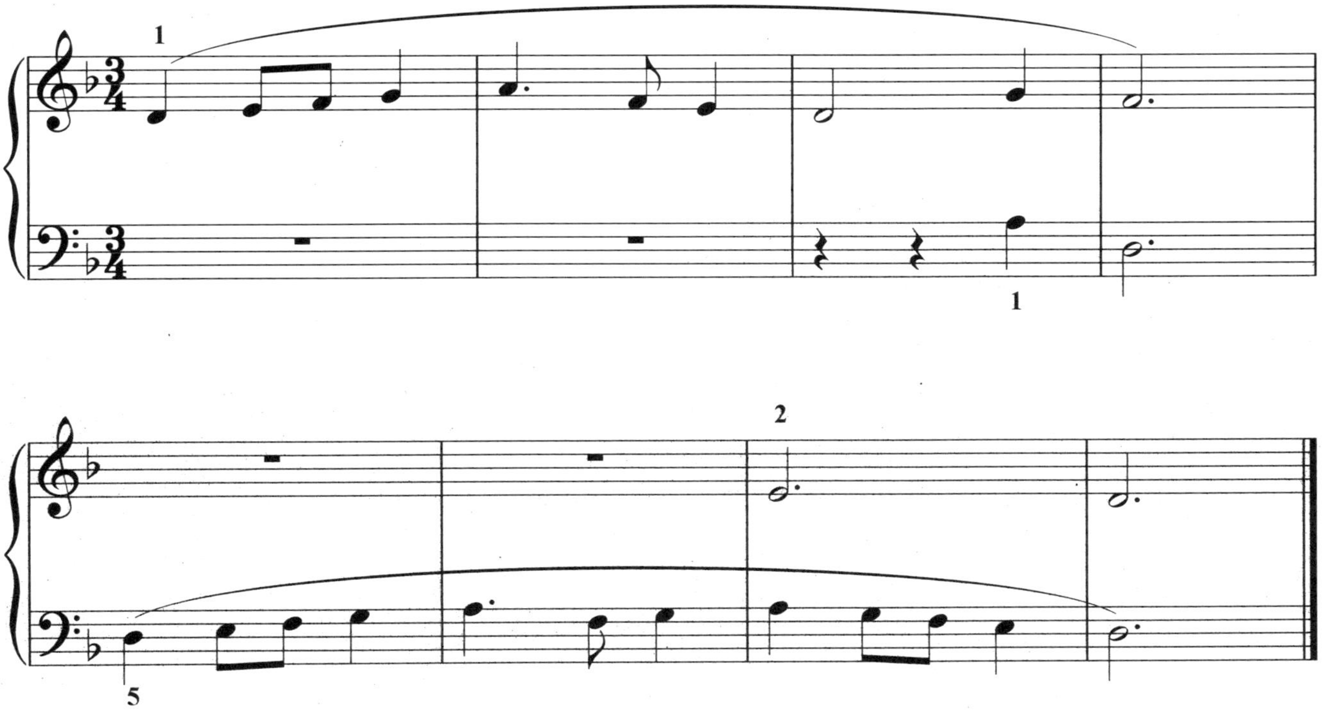

34

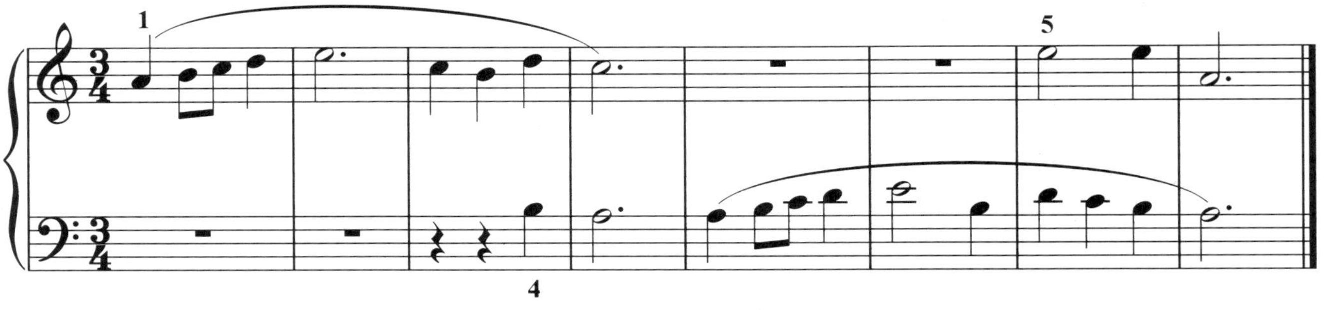

35

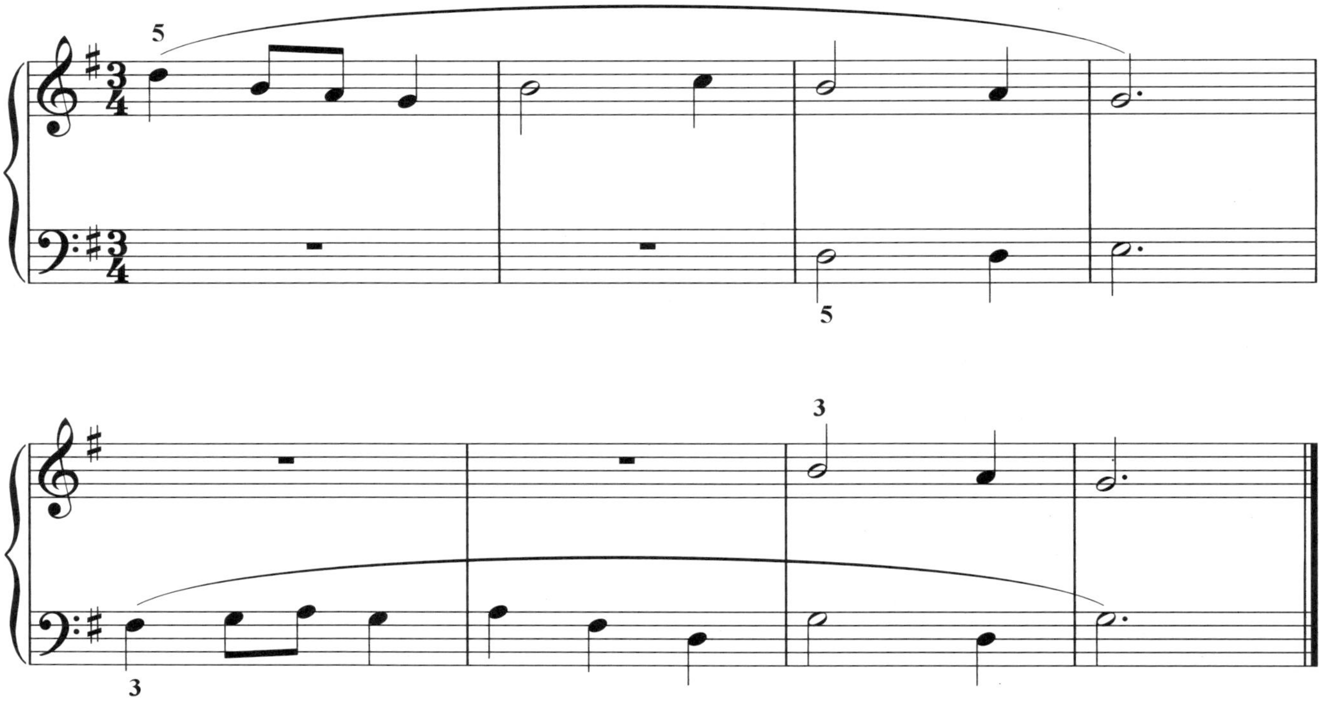

36

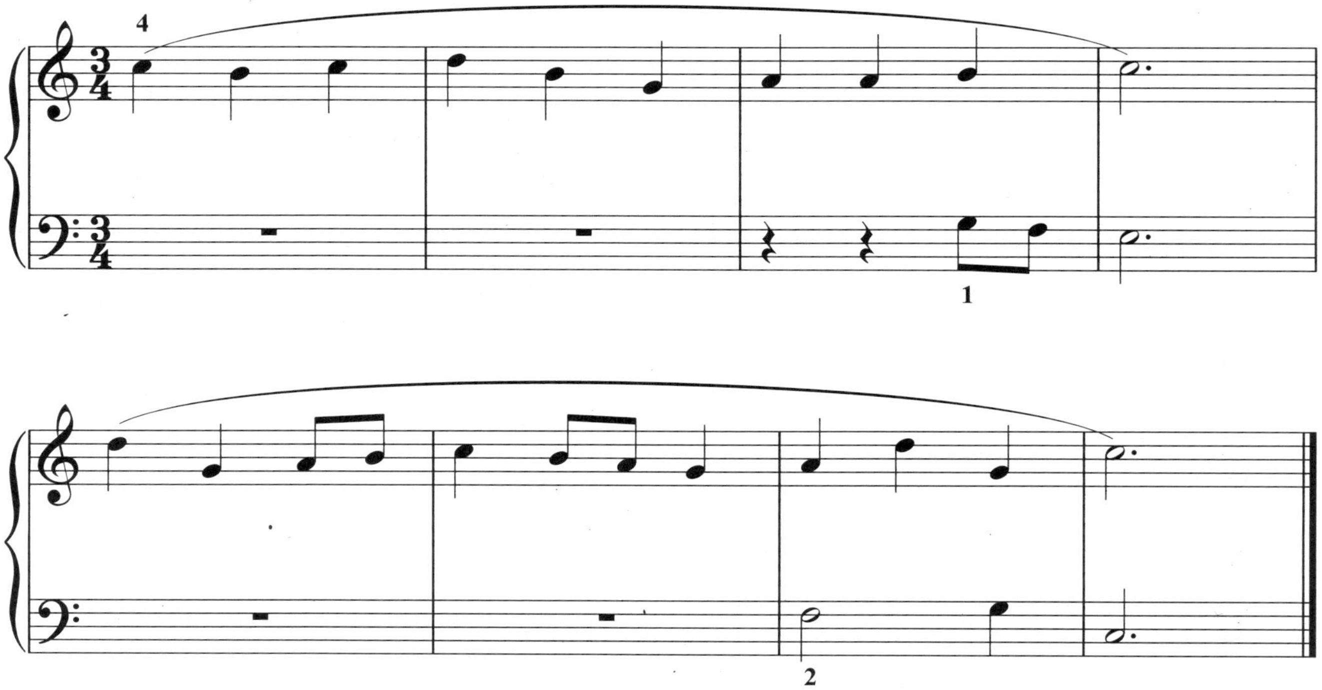

37

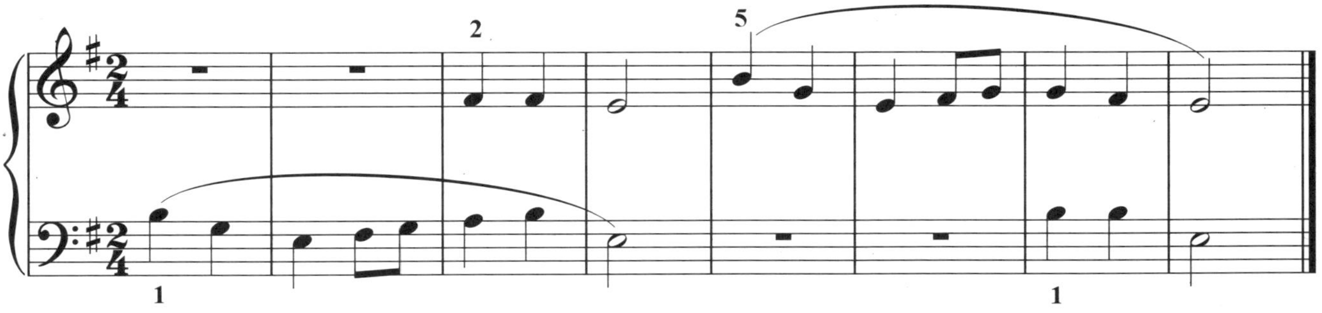

38

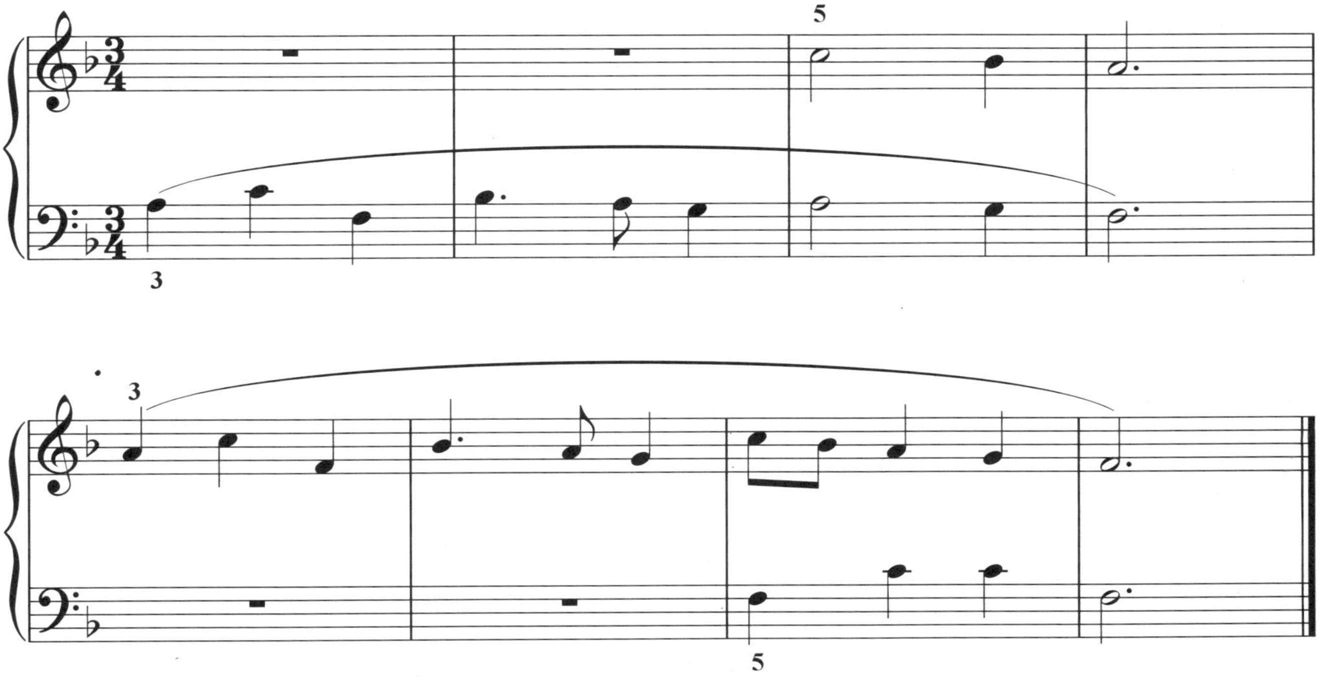

39

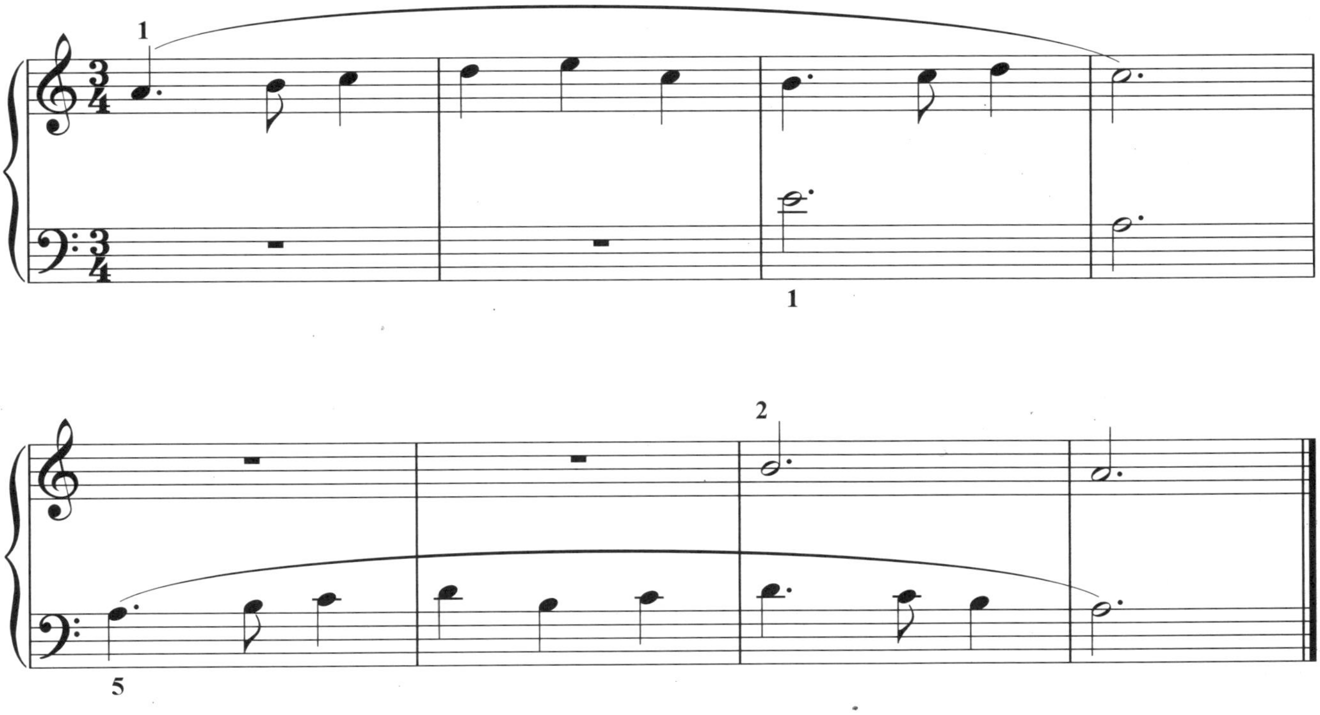

40

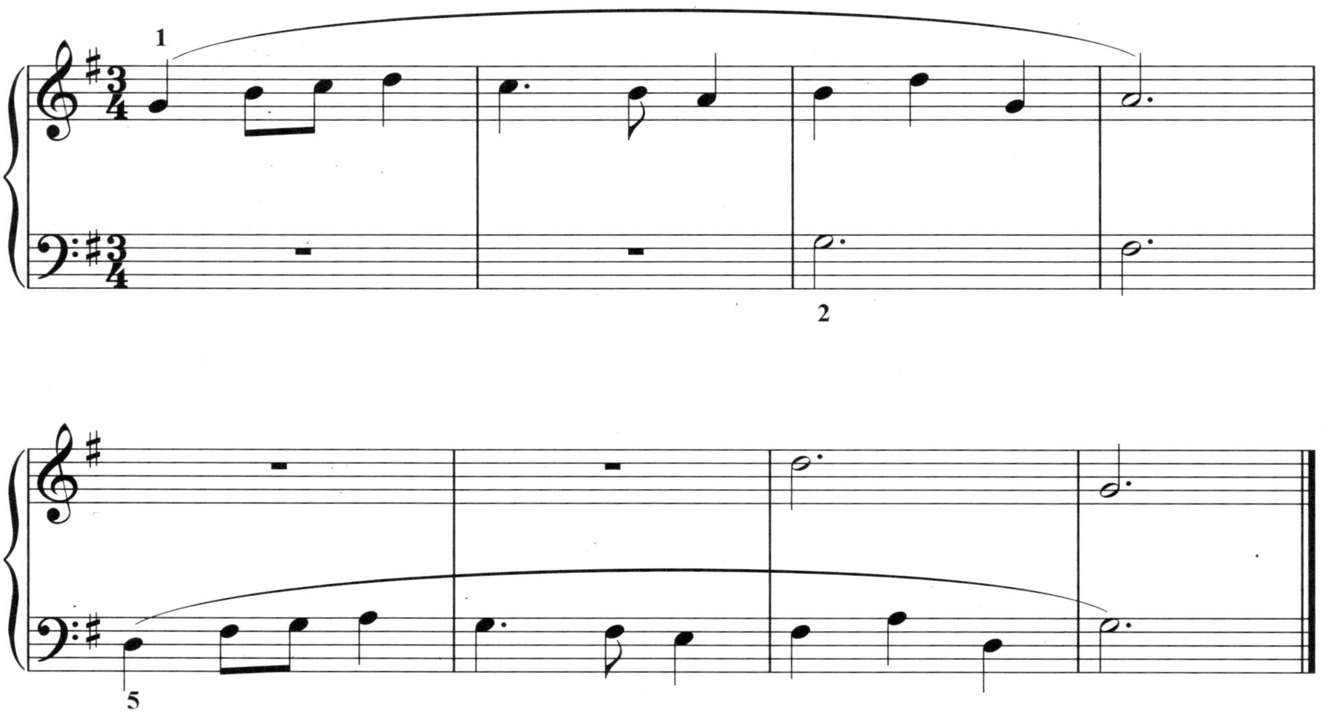

41

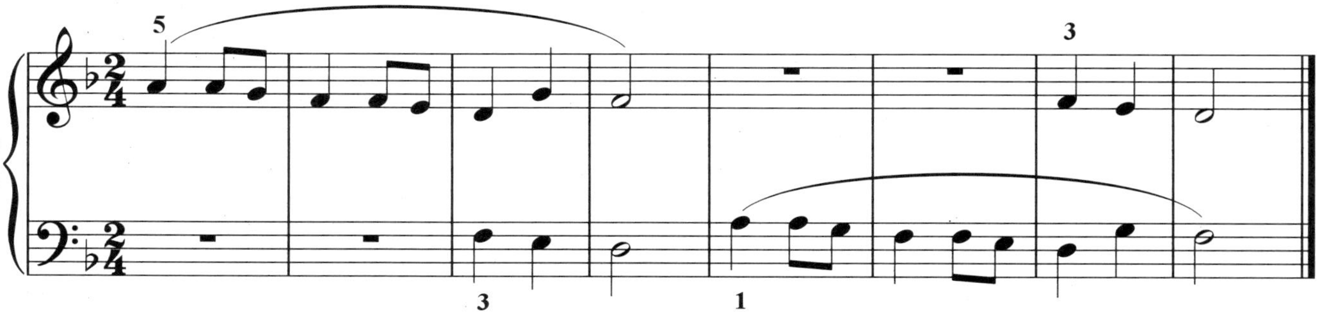

42

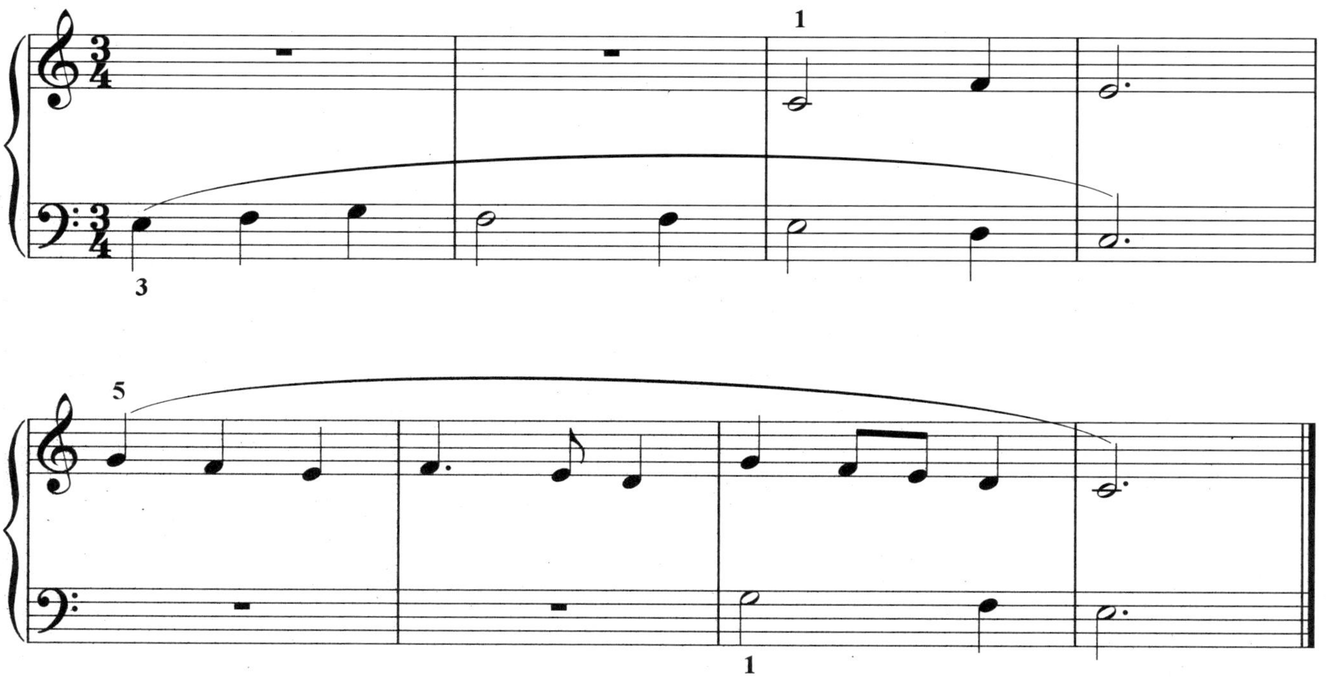

43

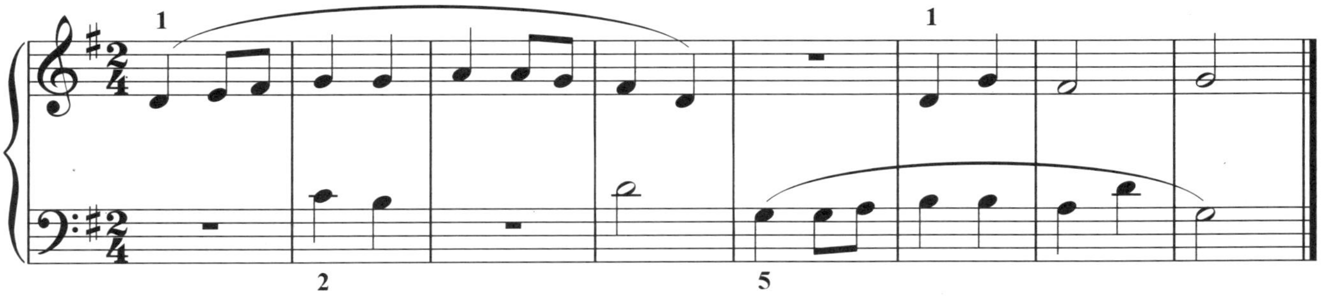

44

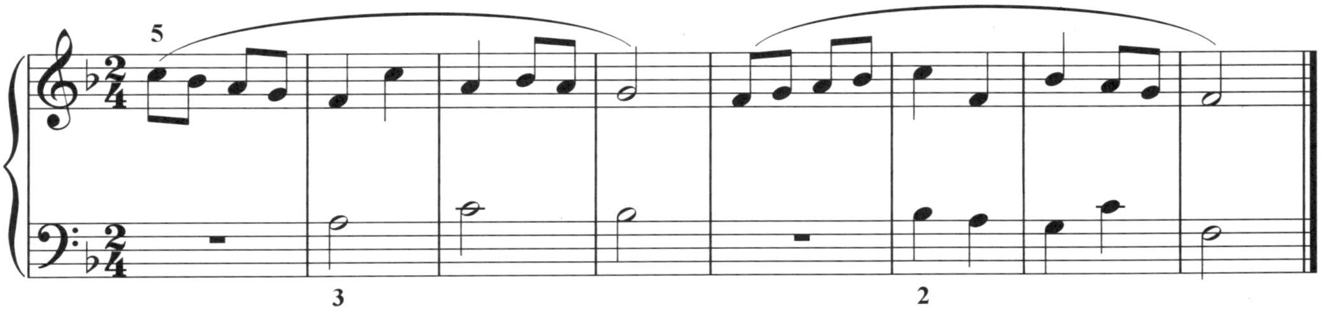

45

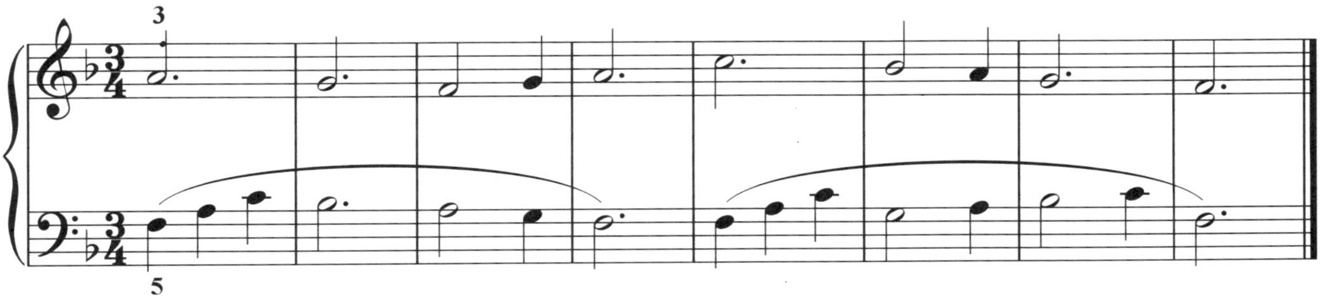

46

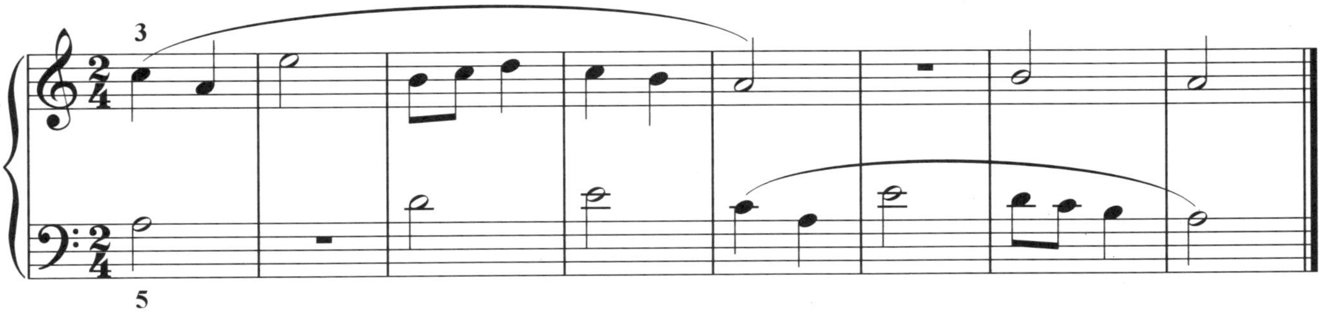

47

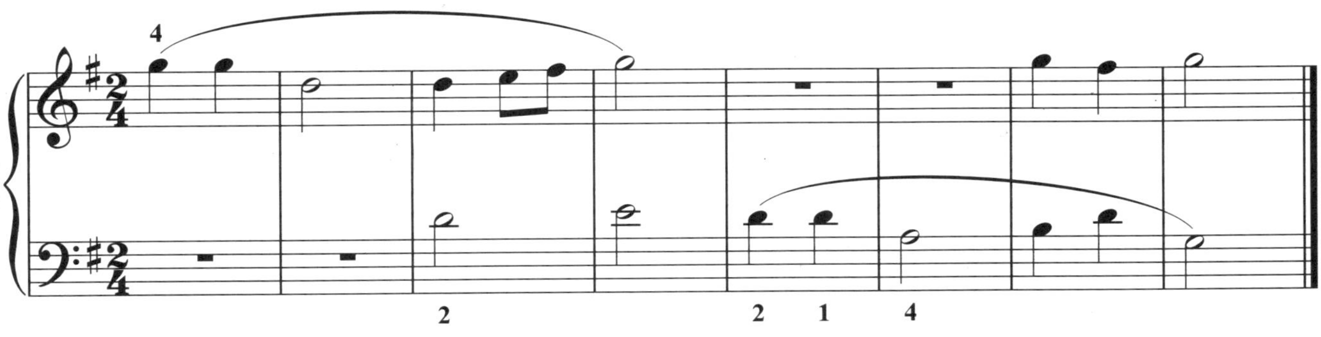

48

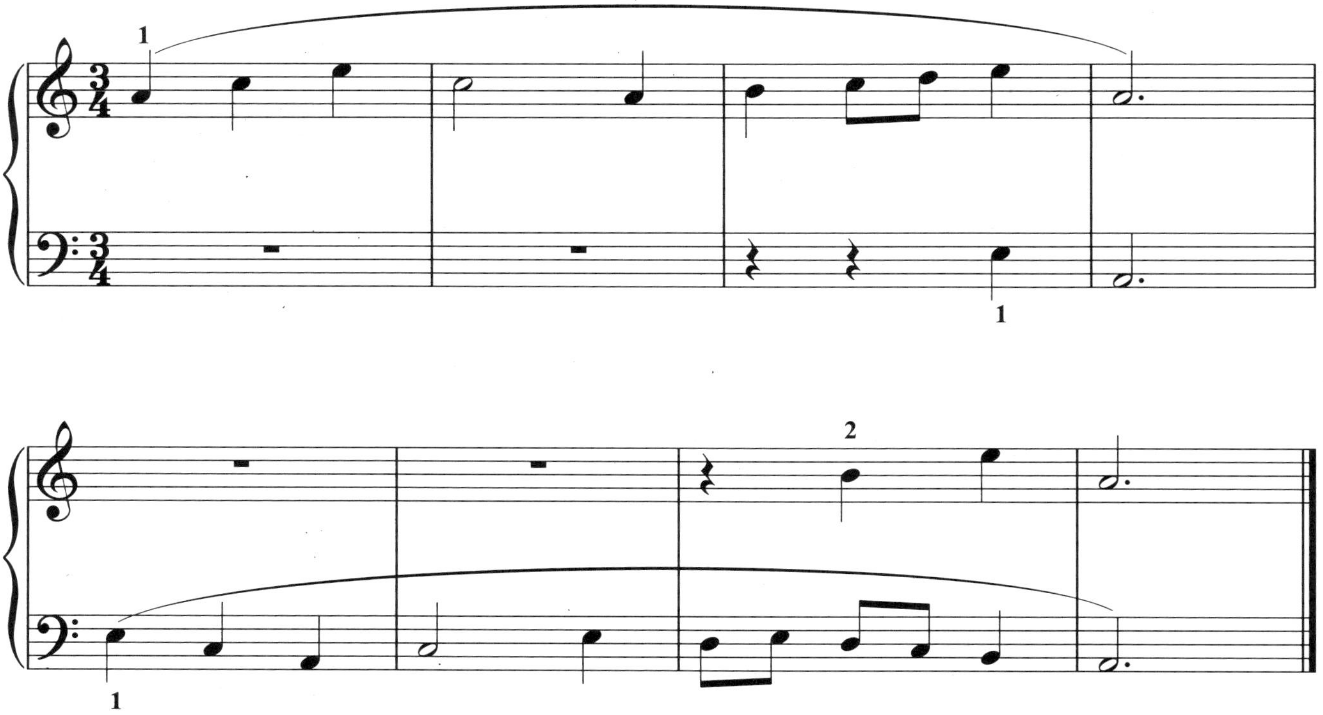

49

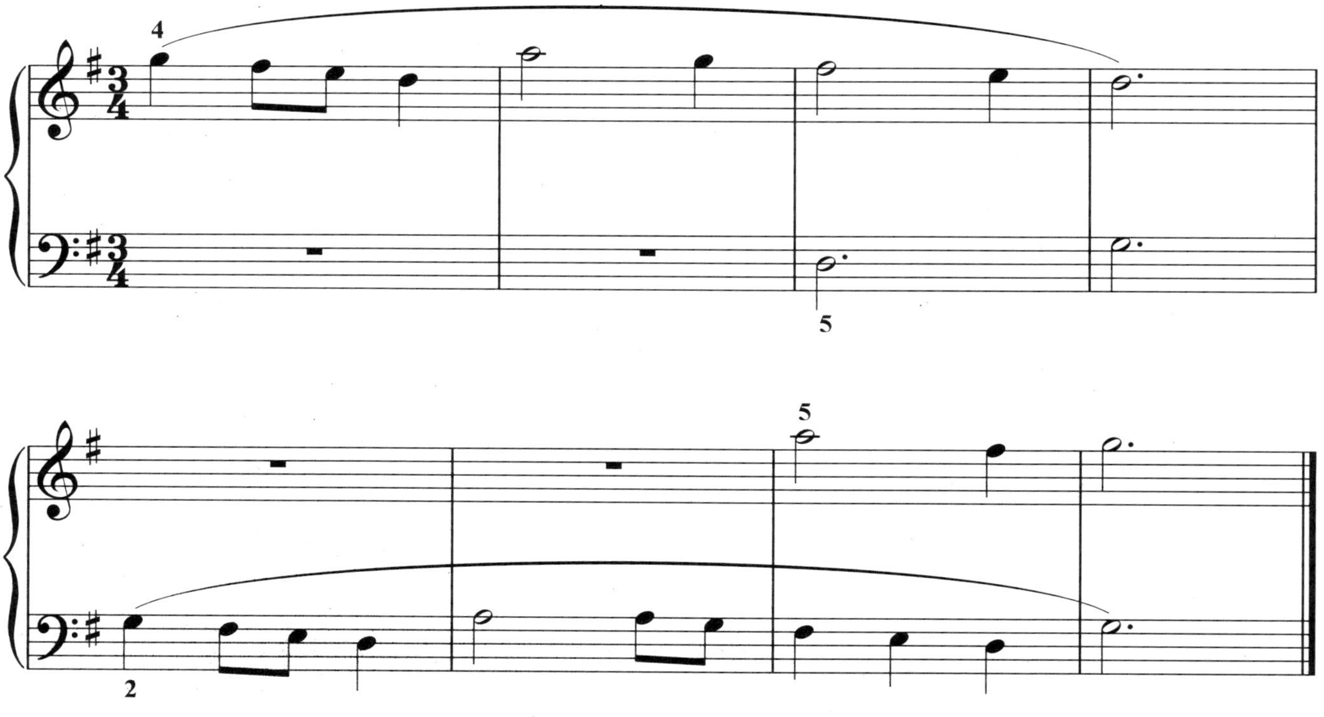

50

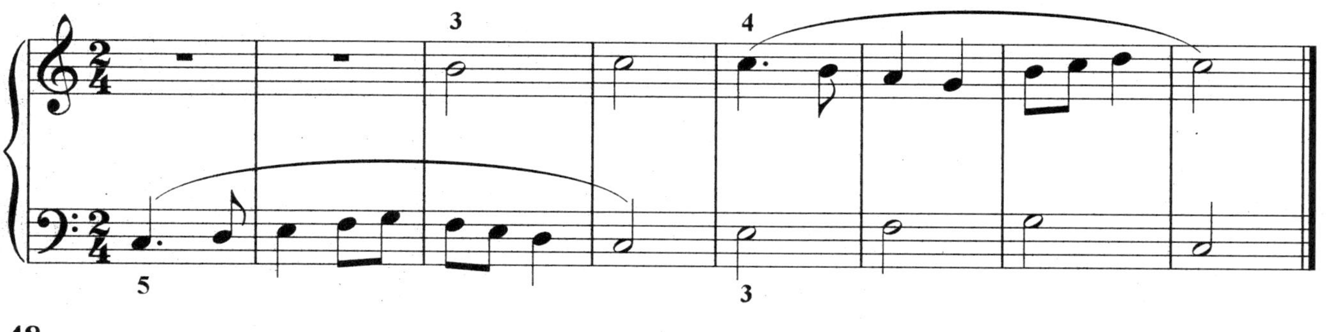

51

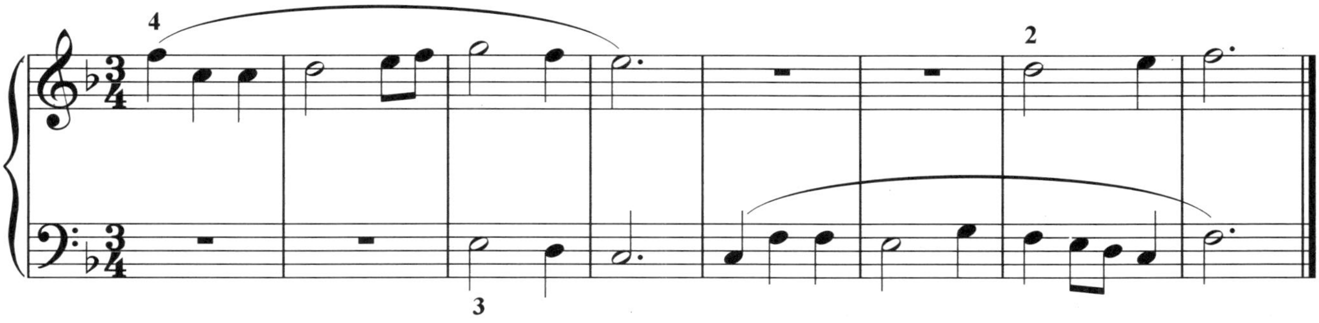

52

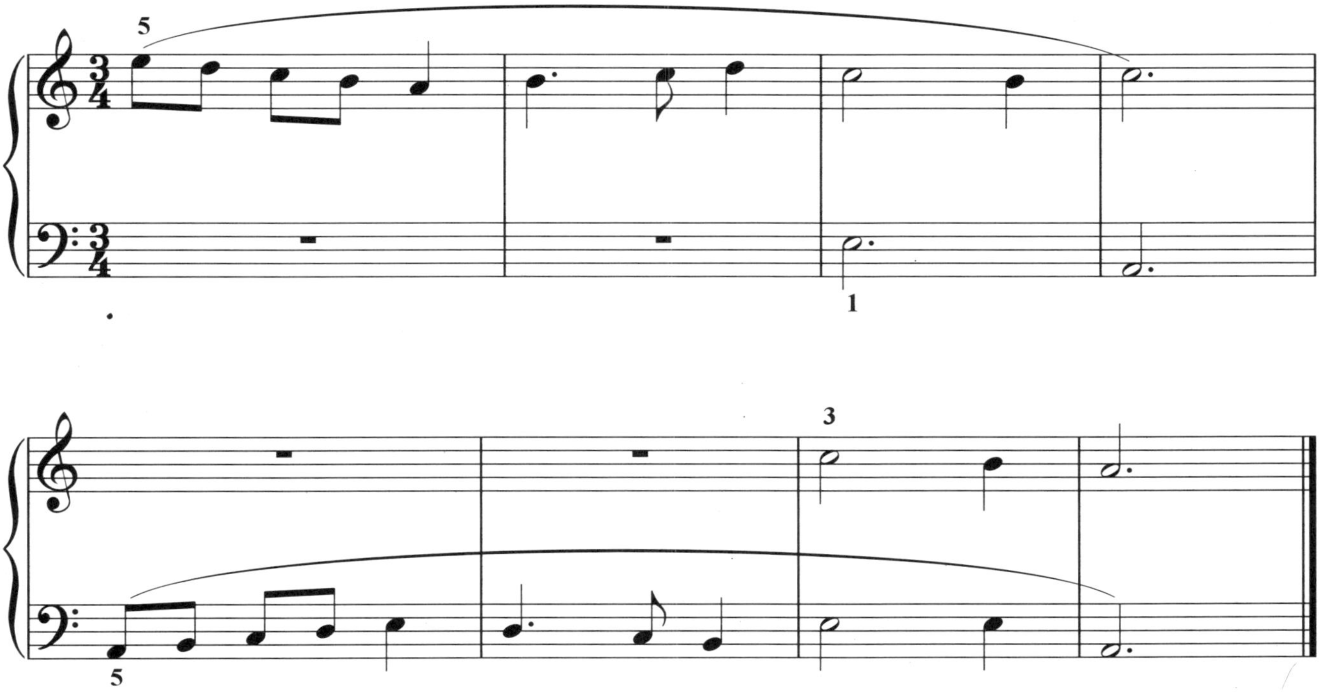

53

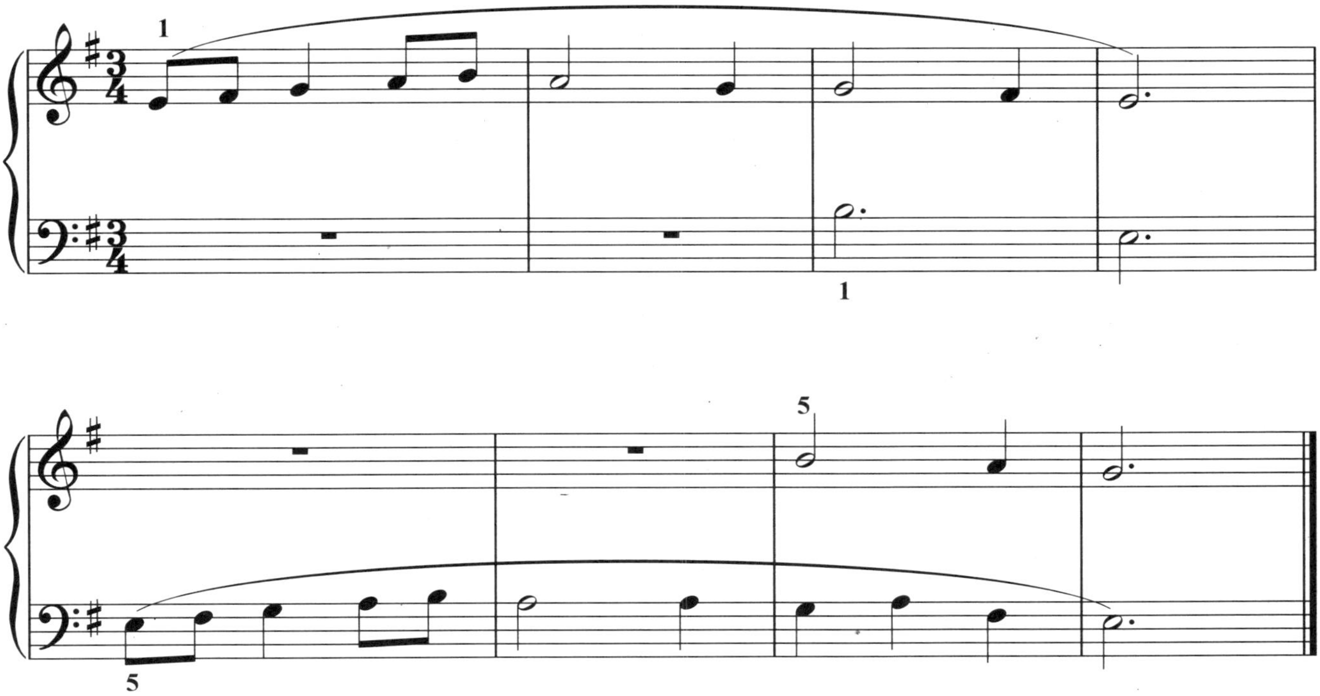

54

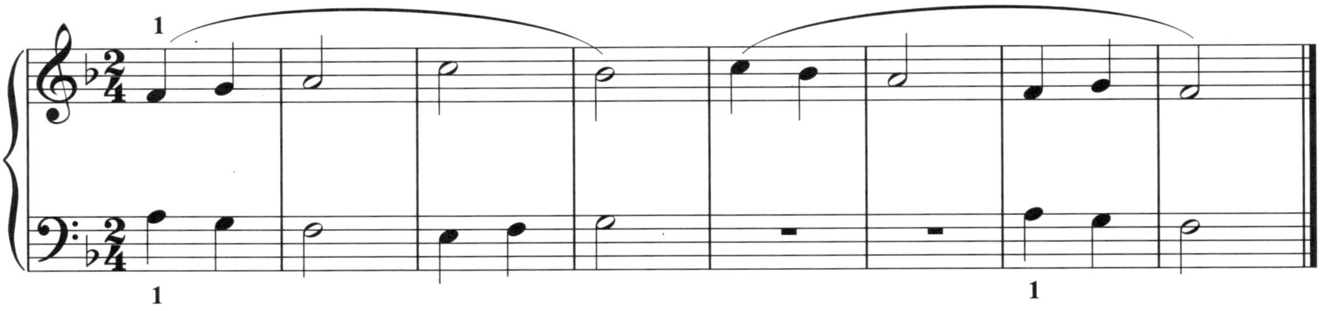

55

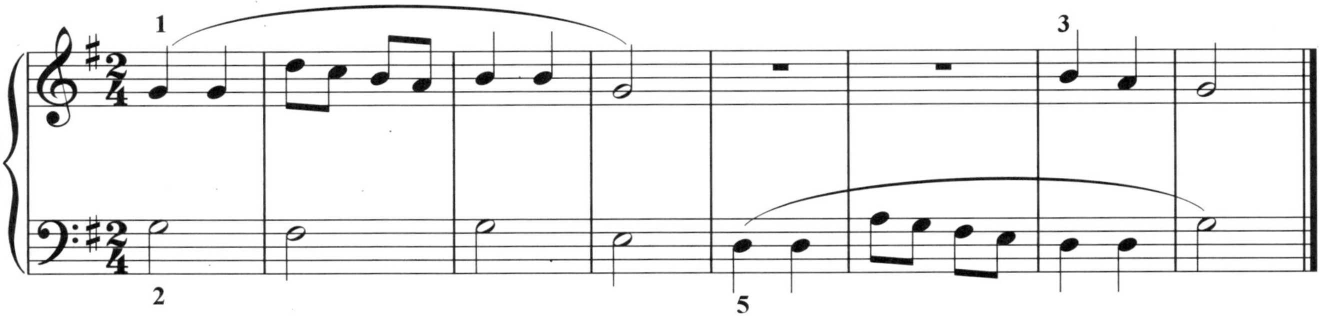

56

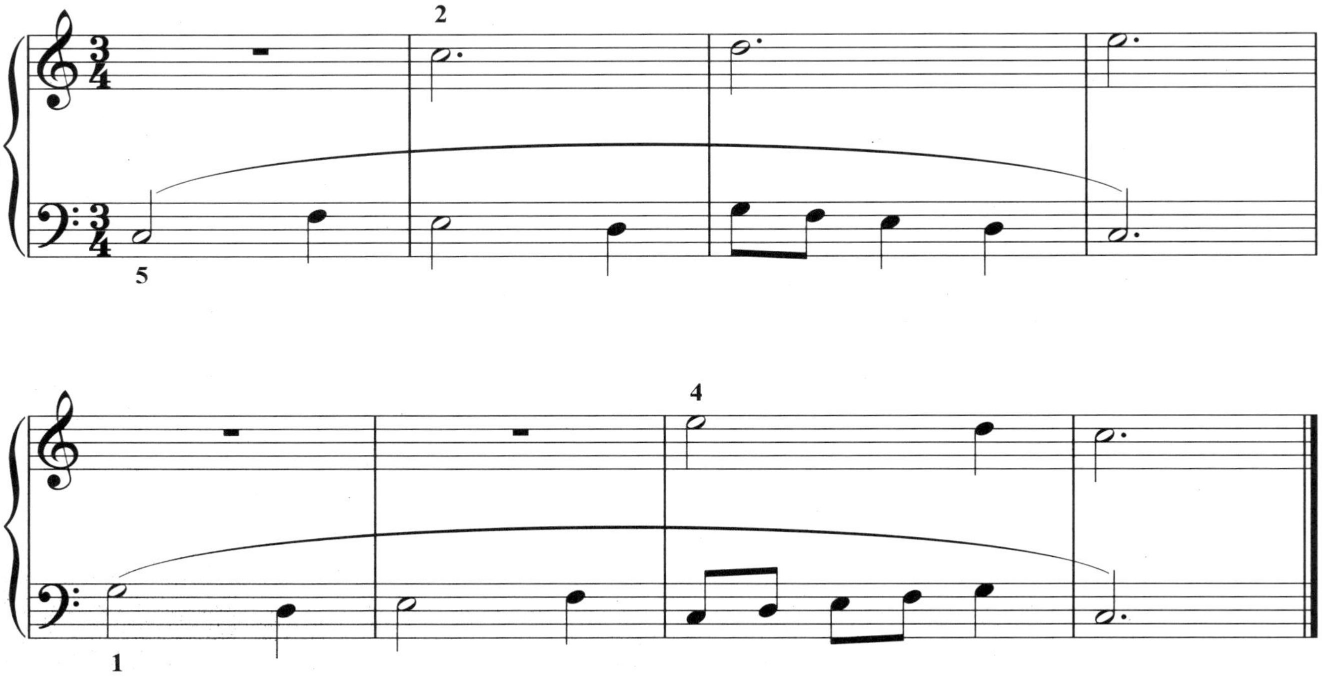

57

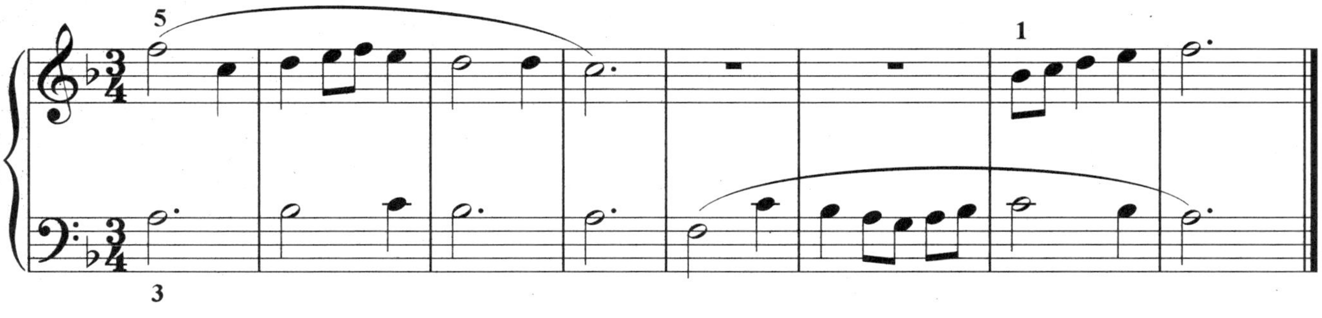

58

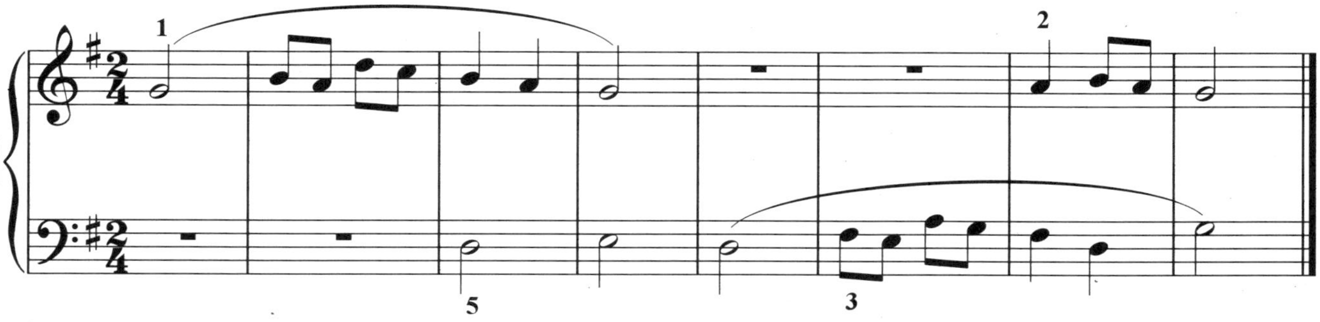

59

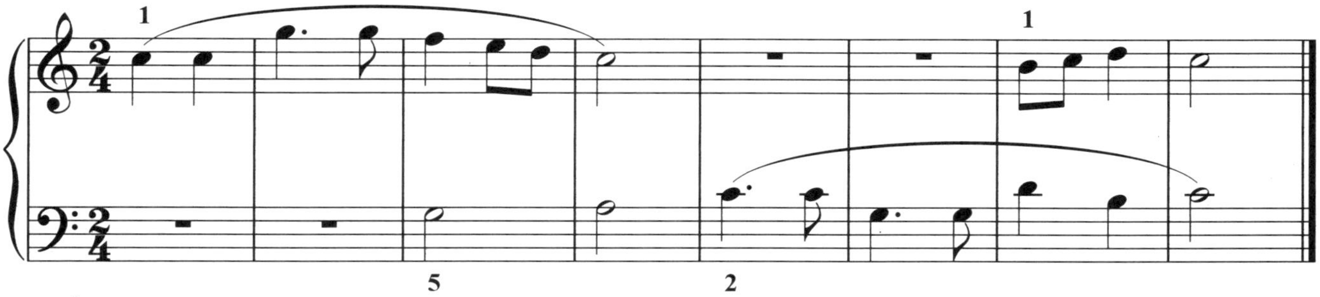

60

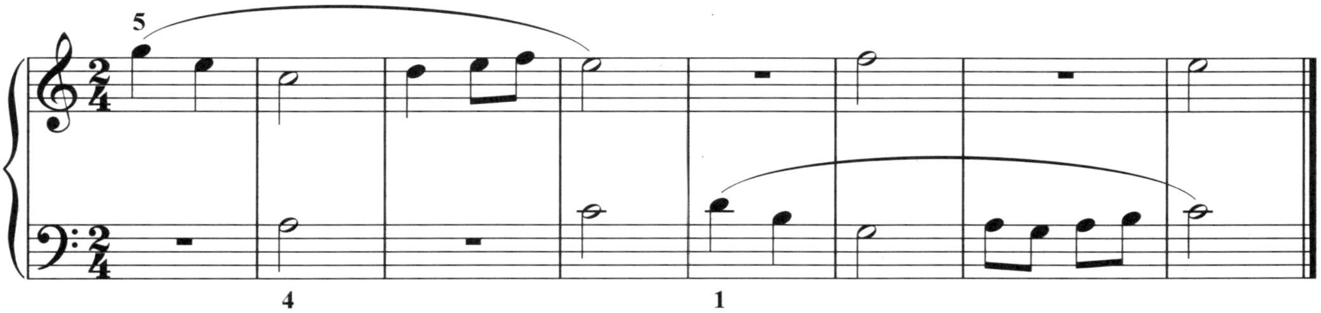

61

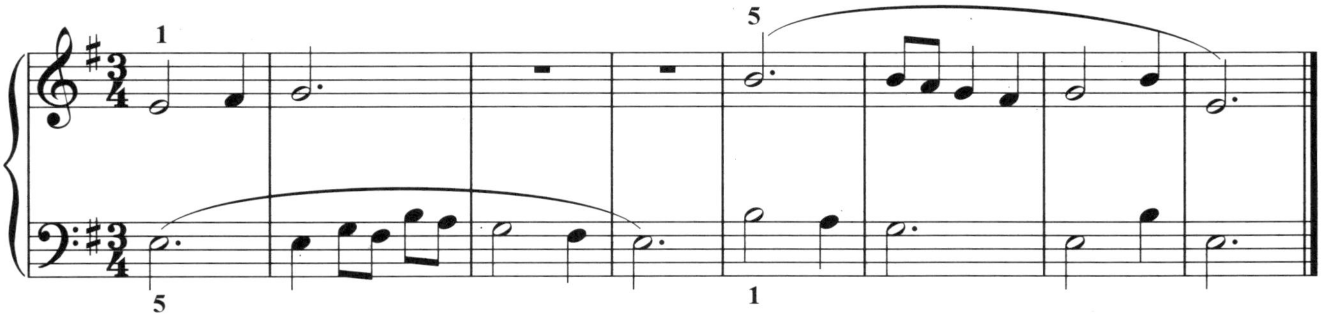

62

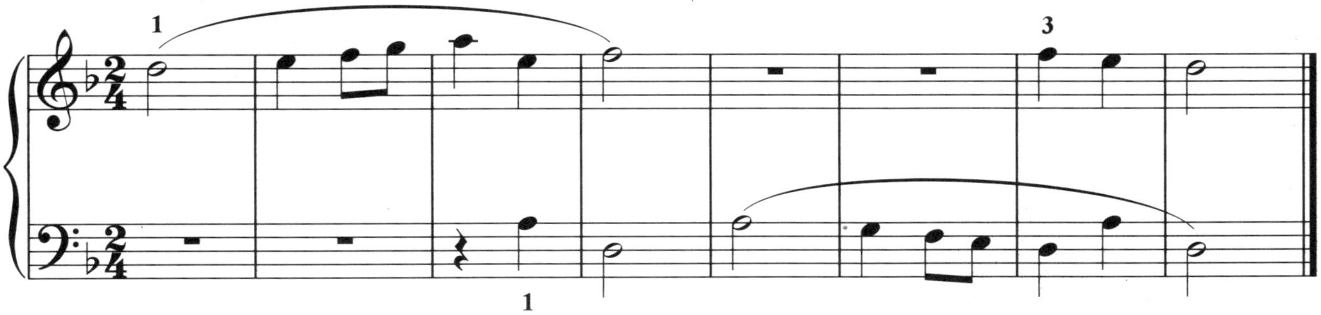

63

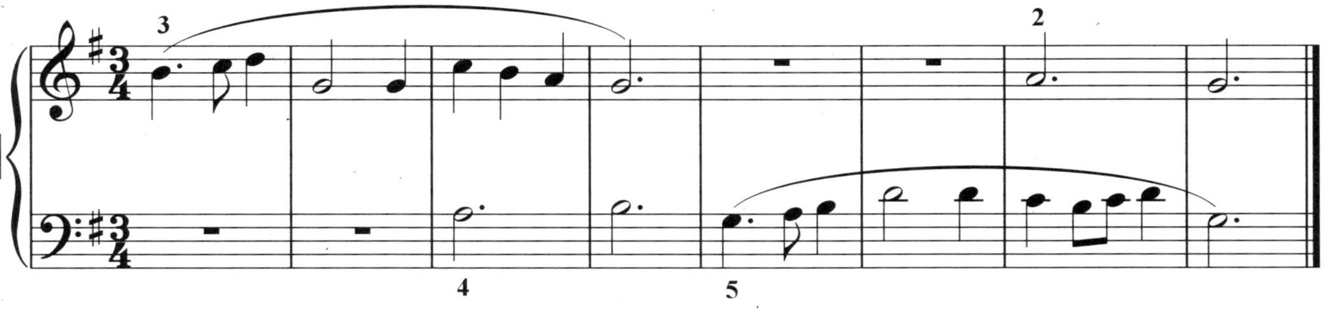

64

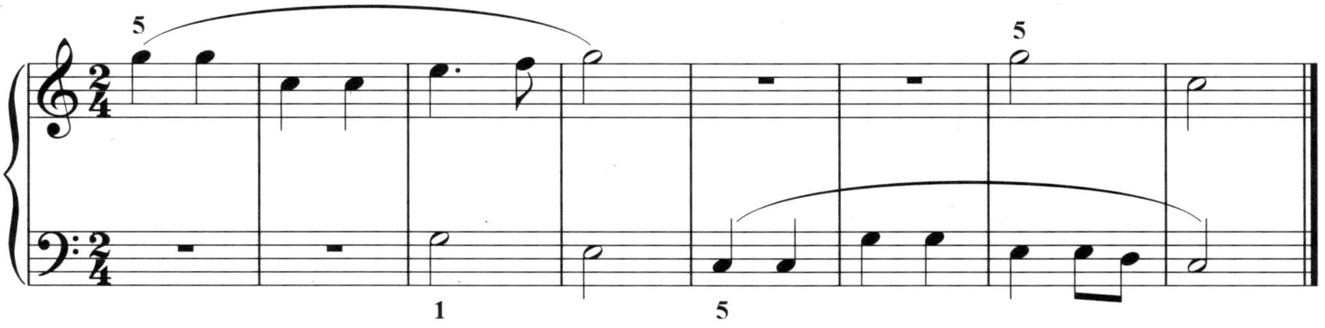

65

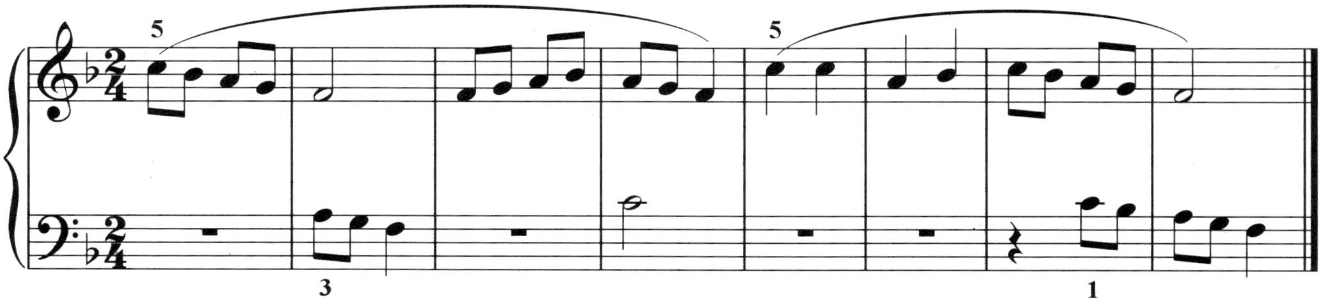

66

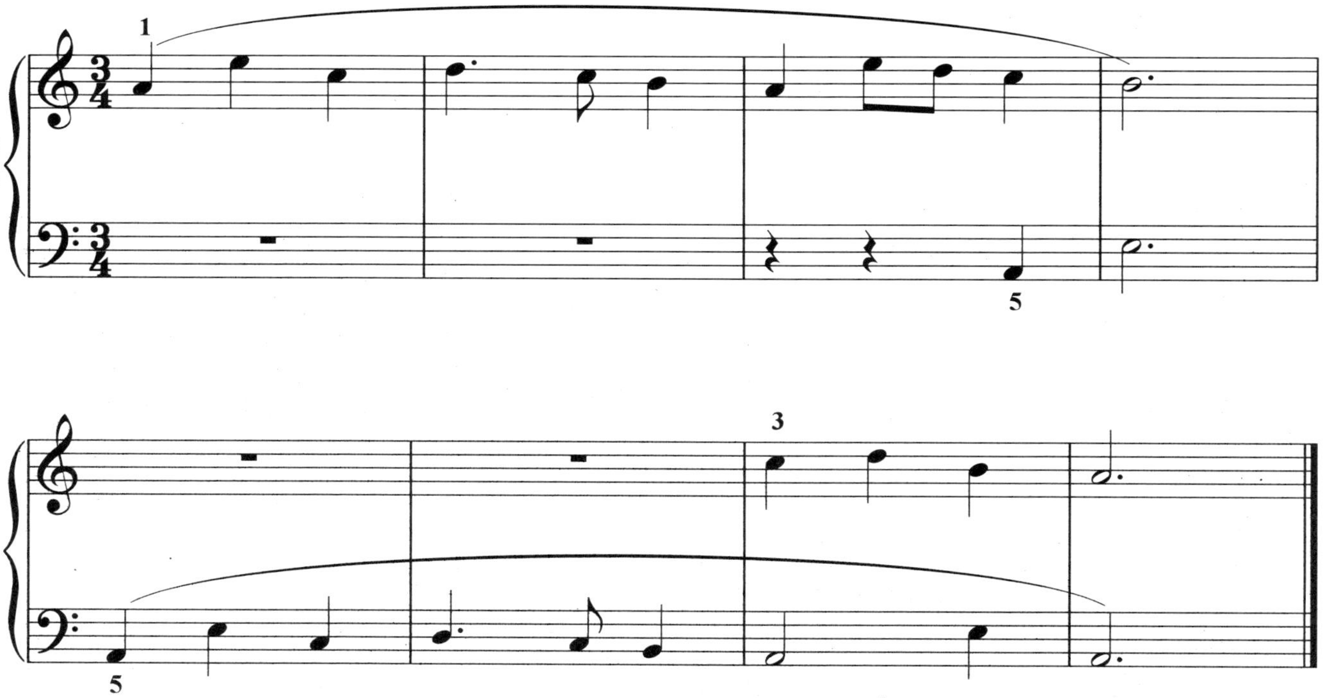

67

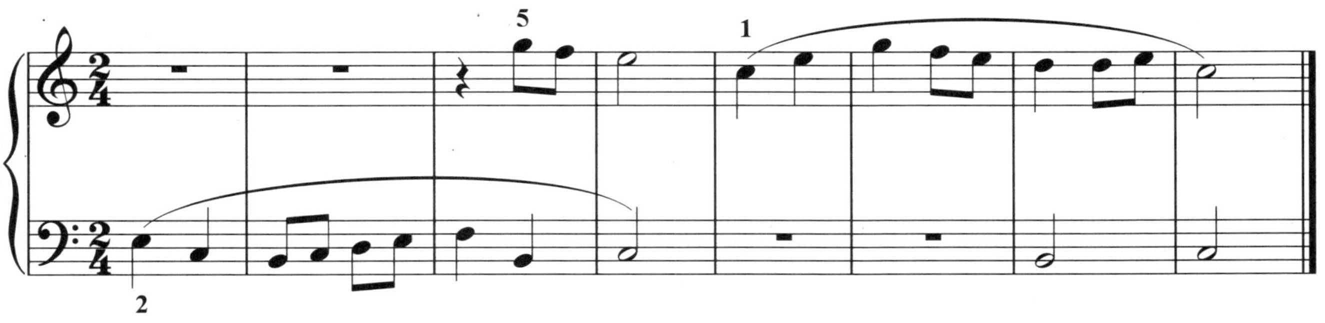

68

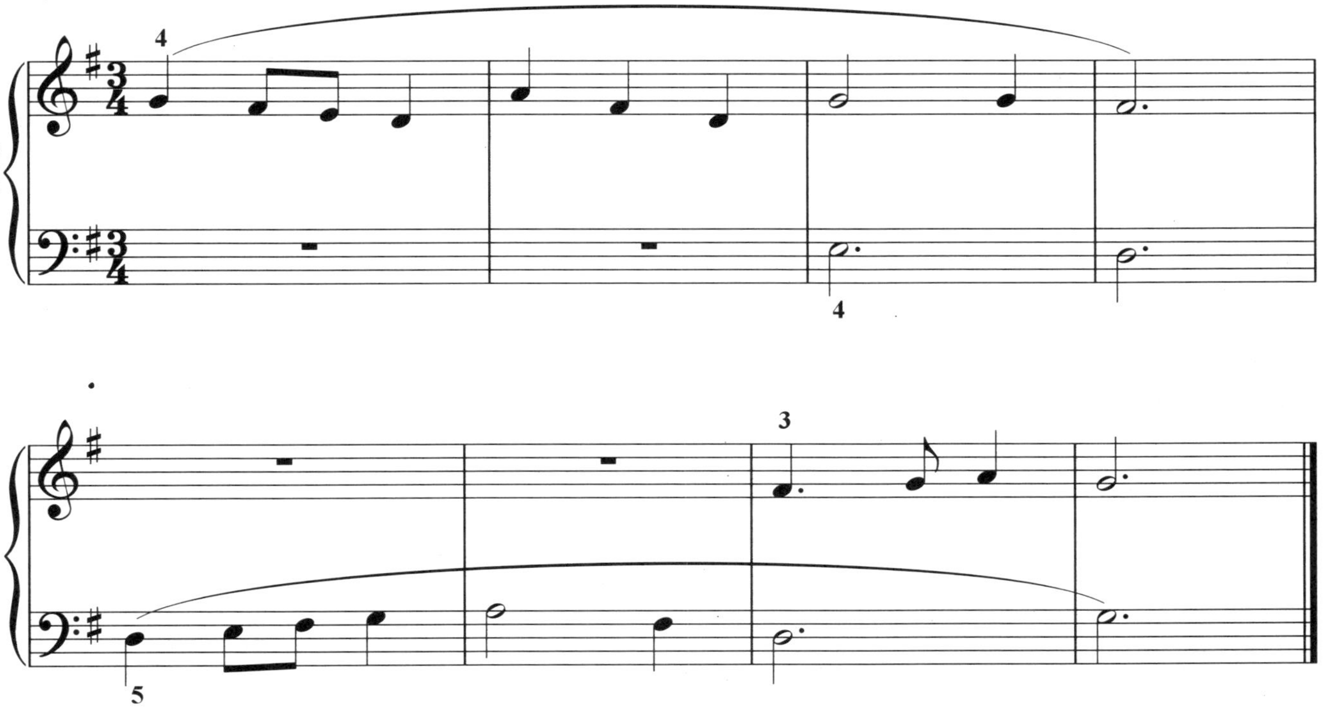

69

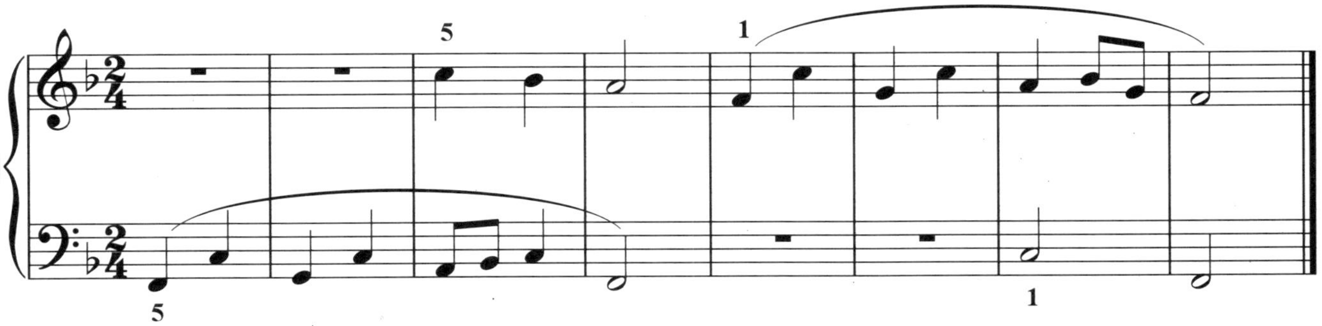

70

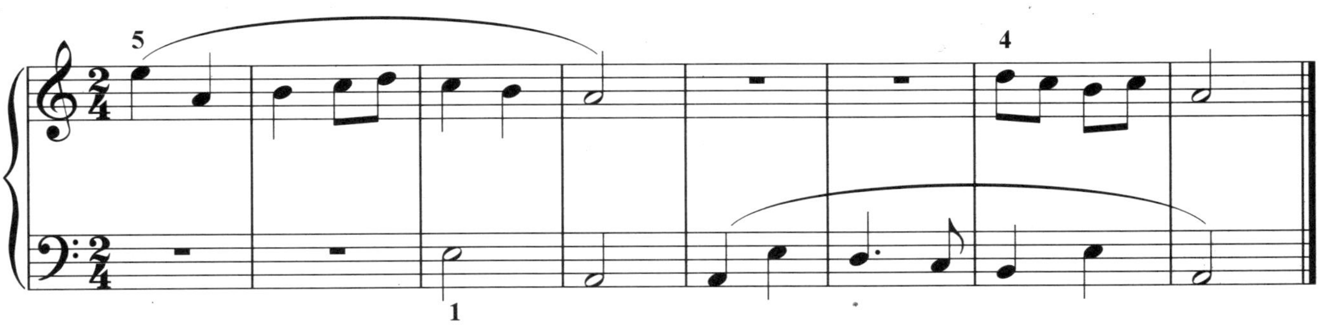

71

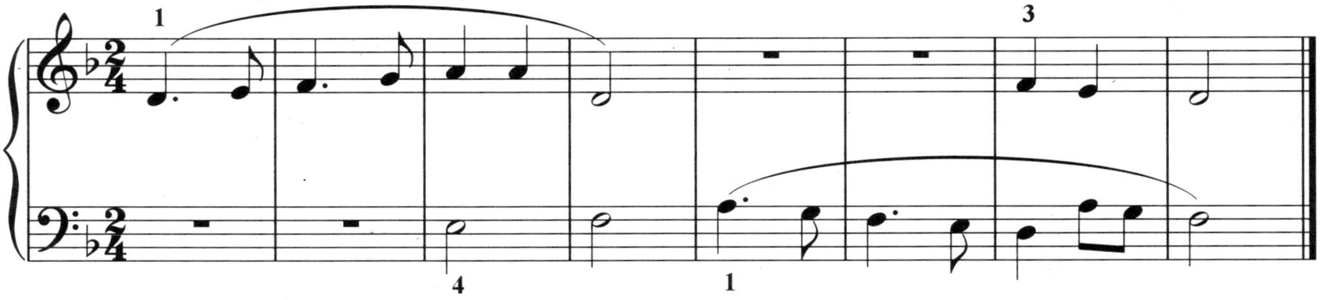

72

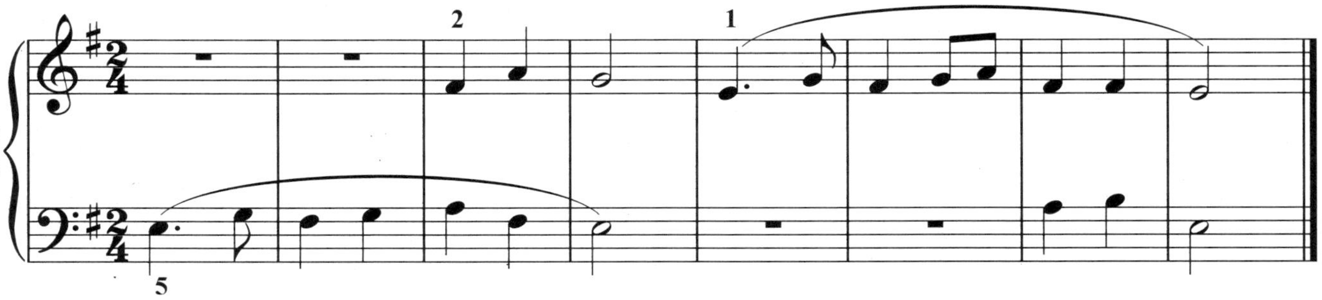

73

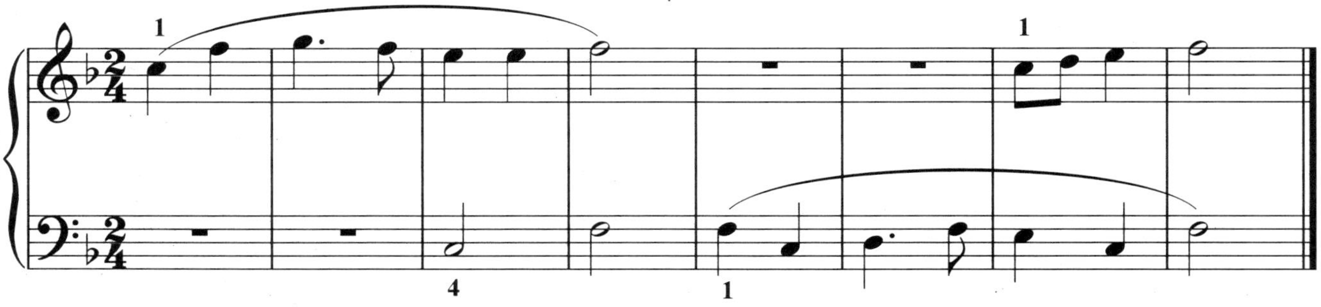

74

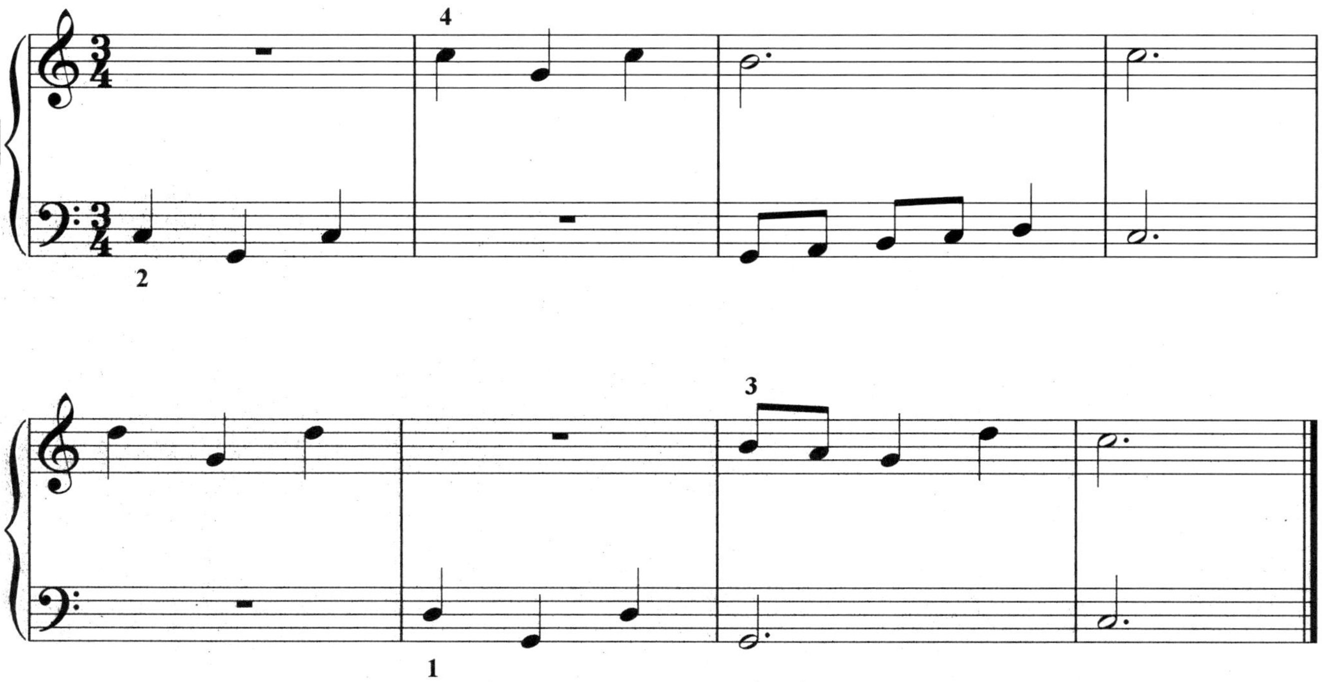

This piece begins on the upbeat

Section Four

Introducing $\frac{6}{8}$ time

Here are words to help you count $\frac{6}{8}$ time:

Galloping

Trot-ting

Stay

Stay-there

$\frac{6}{8}$
Gal–lo-ping Trot-ting   Stay   Stay   Stay-there

Piece 10 onwards

Here we will sometimes extend our hand-shape to one note beyond the five-finger group, making a range of six notes. Before playing, see that there are no note problems. If you are uncertain, check with the nearest 'Landmark' note. Where there is more than one 'skip' in a row (see beginning of each hand in Nos. 10 and 11) it is a help to play the three notes as a chord, silently, before you play to get the feeling of the shape. Additional fingering in these pieces helps with the bigger intervals.

Piece 26 onwards

Changes of hand position are shown like this: //
These are marked in pieces 26 – 32; thereafter check them out yourself before playing.

Piece 32 $\frac{4}{4}$ appears for the first time.

Piece 45 onwards introduces accidentals.

Piece 66 onwards

Hand-shape is extended to seven notes.

Section 4

3

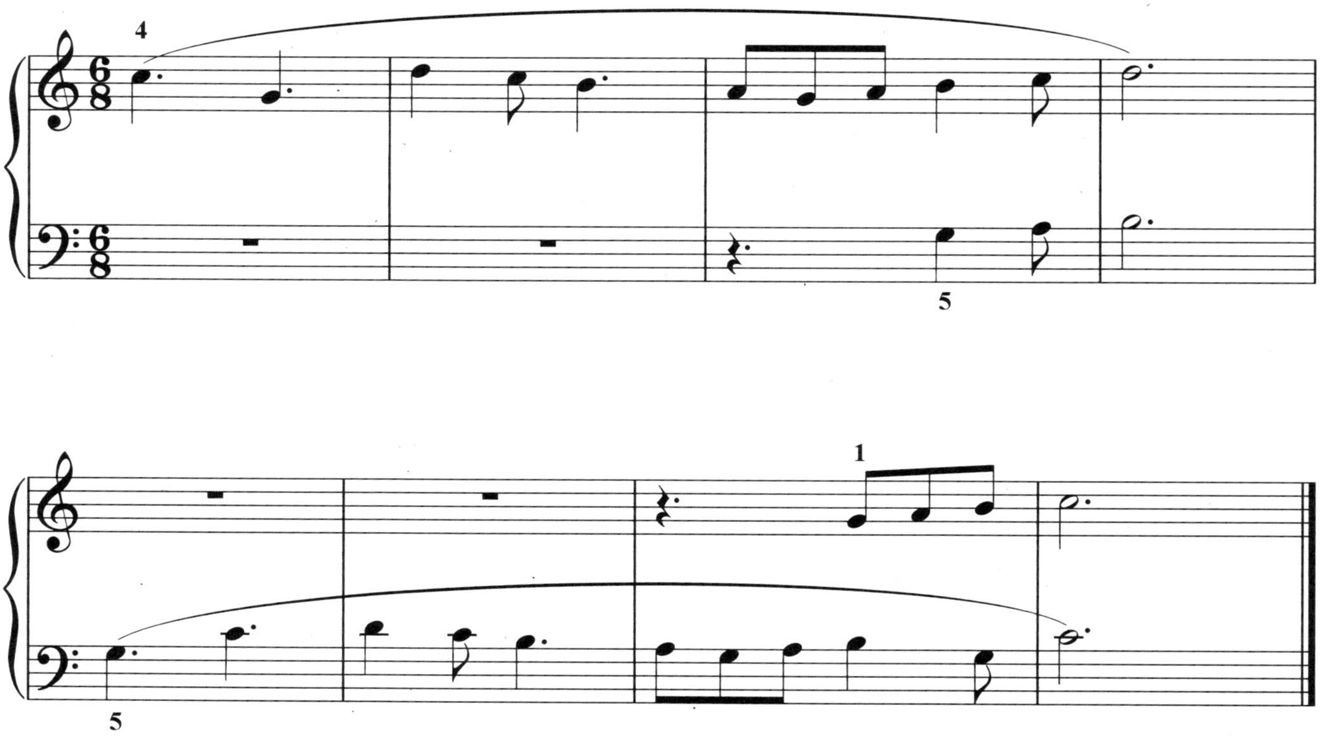

4

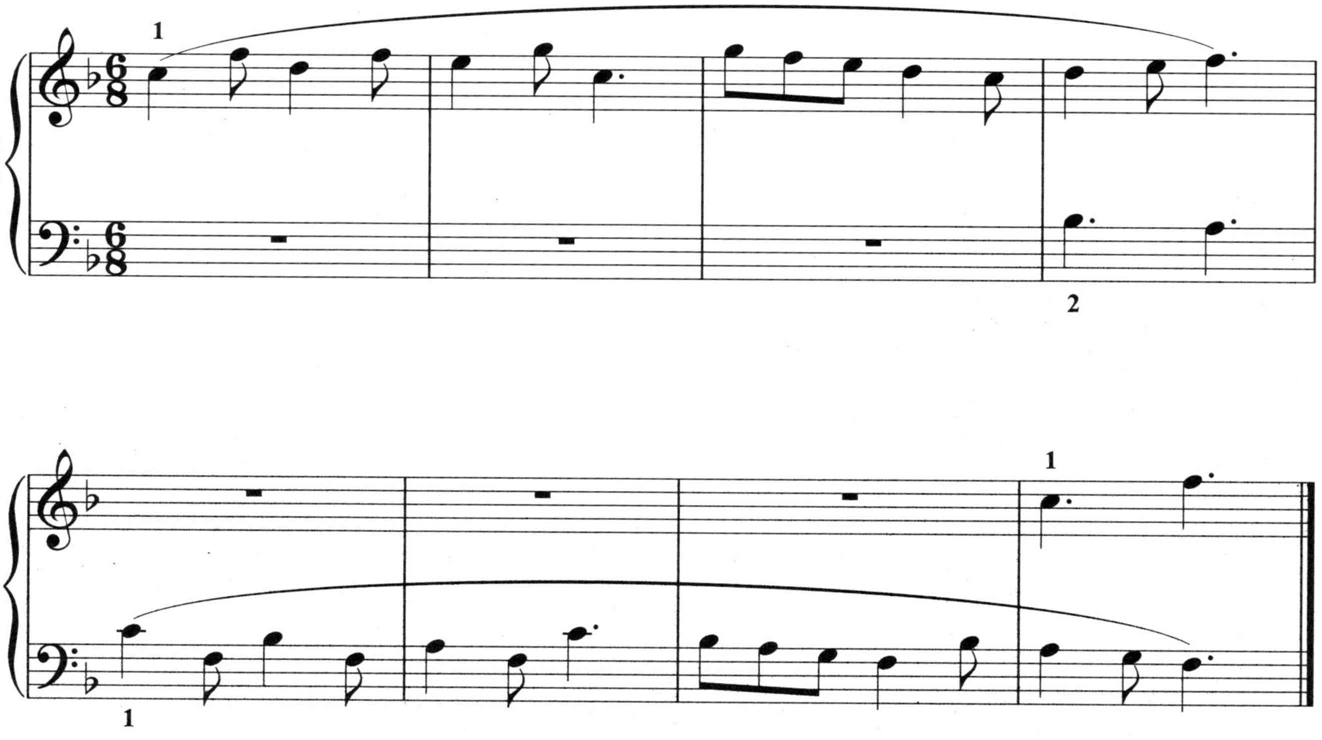

59

7

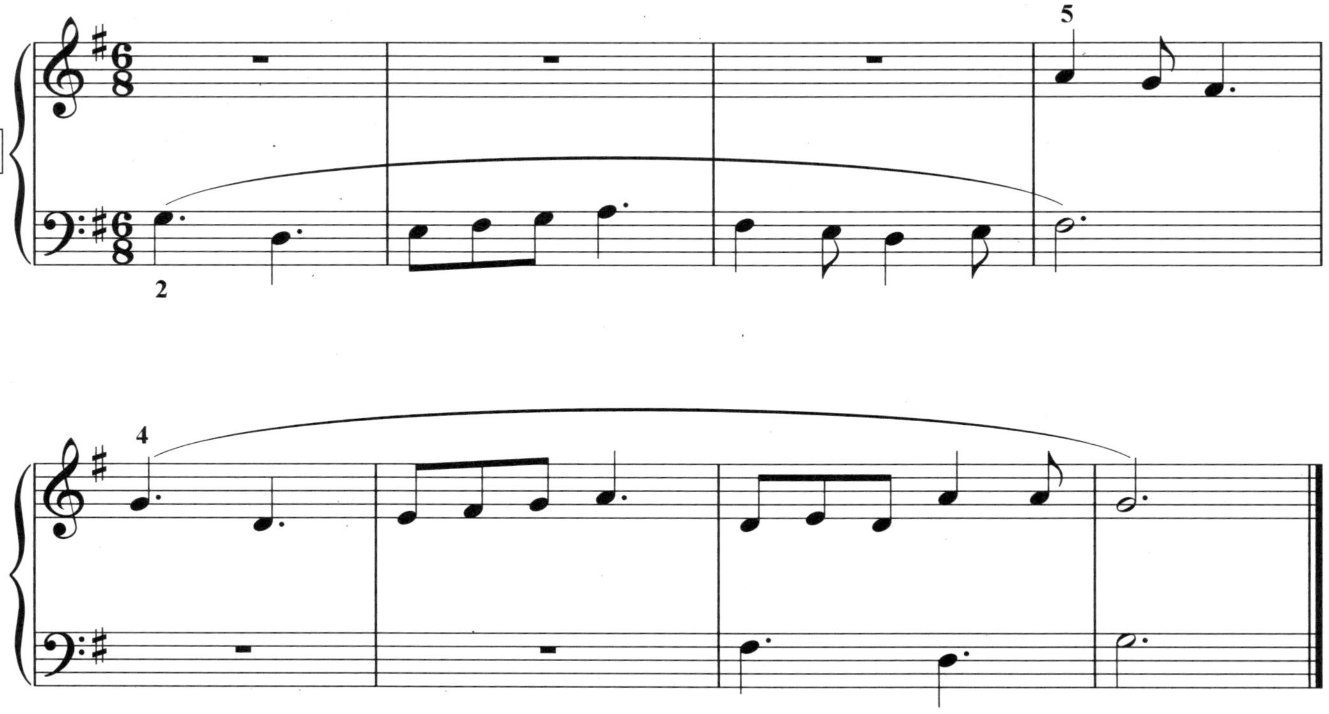

8

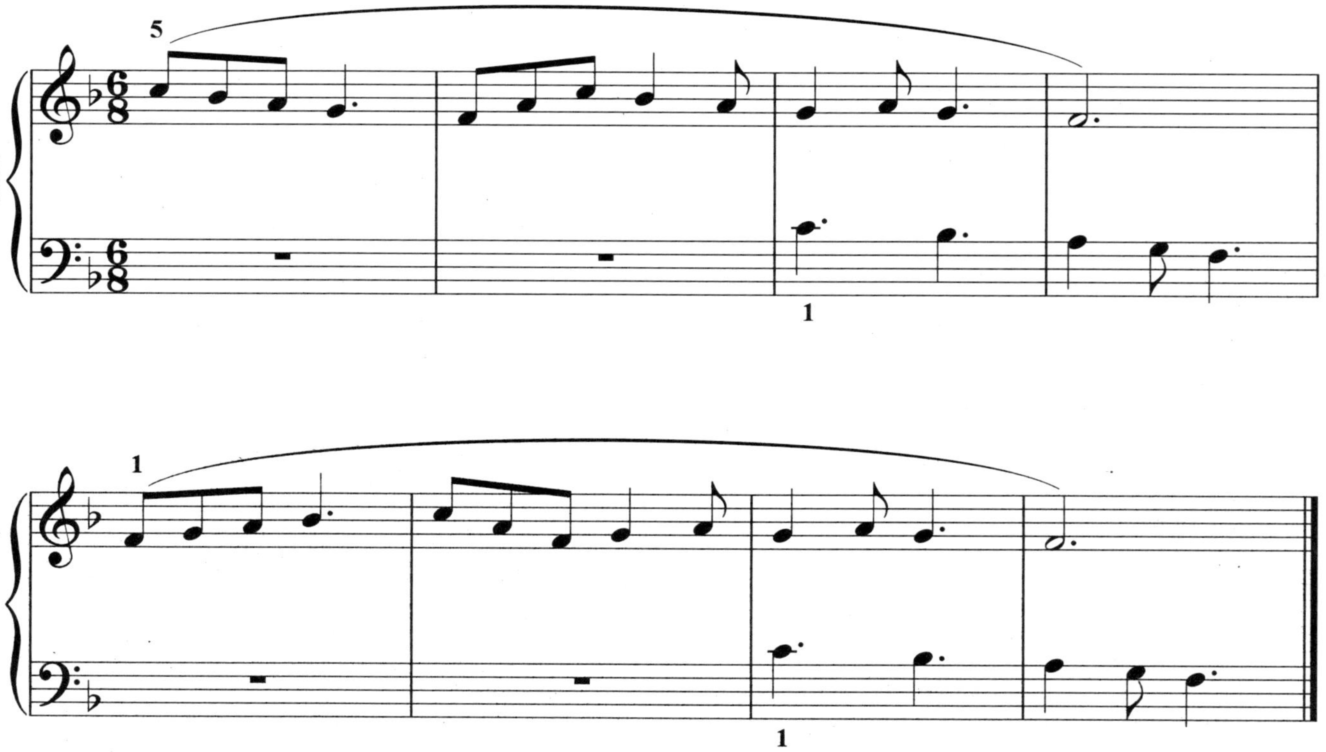

Hand shape extension (stretch) to 6ths

12

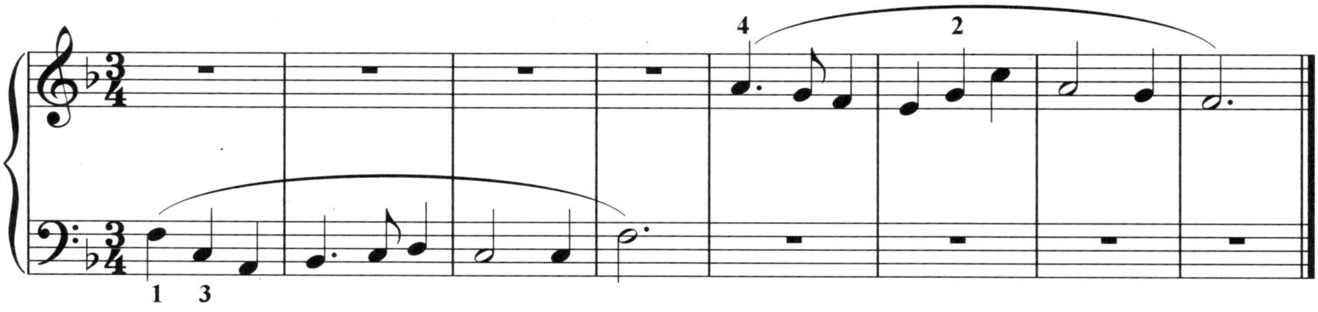

13

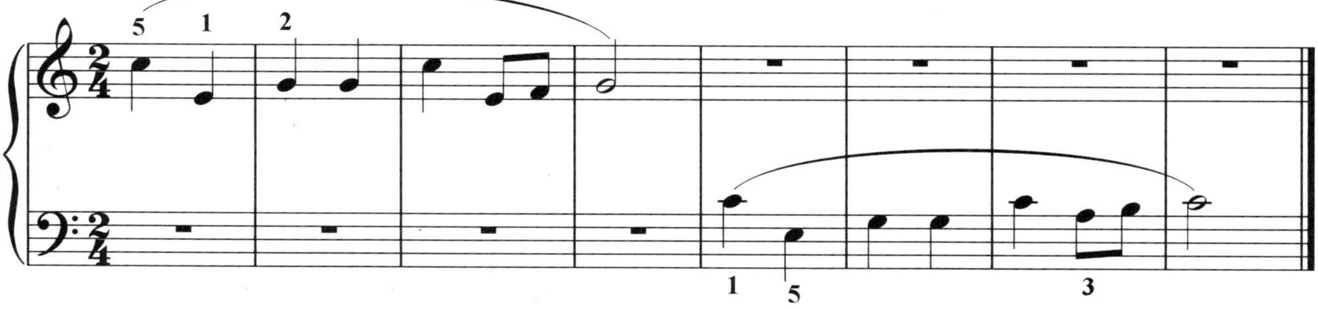

14

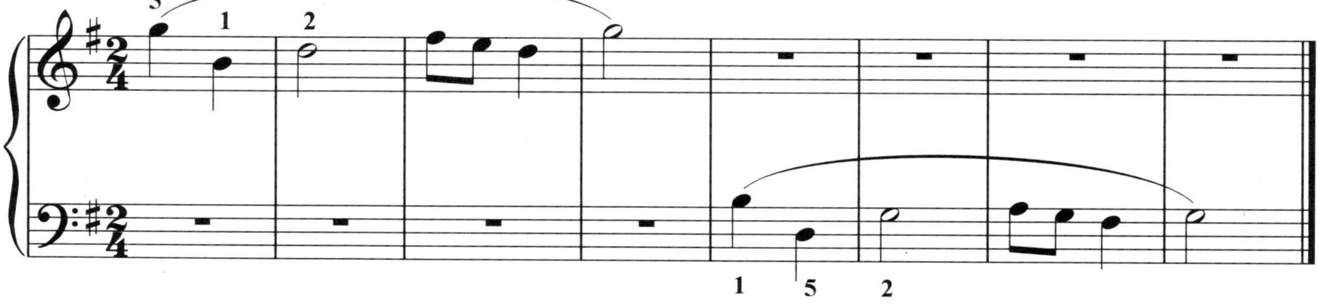

15

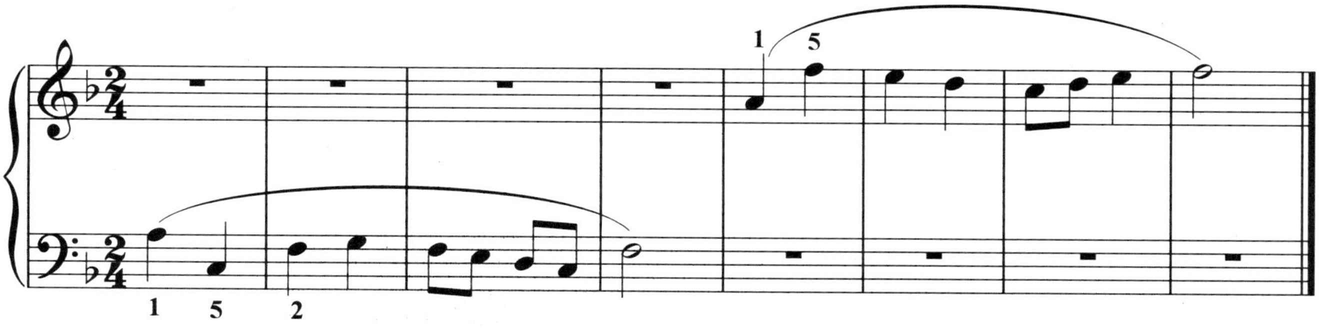

16

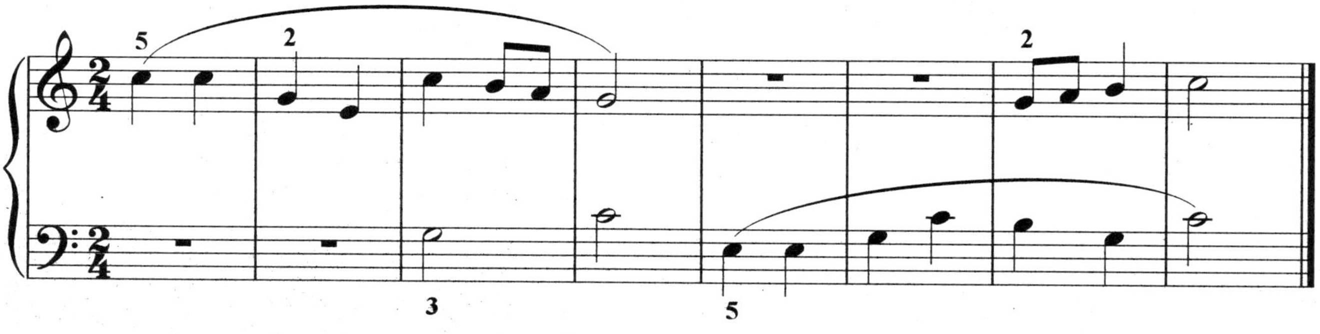

17

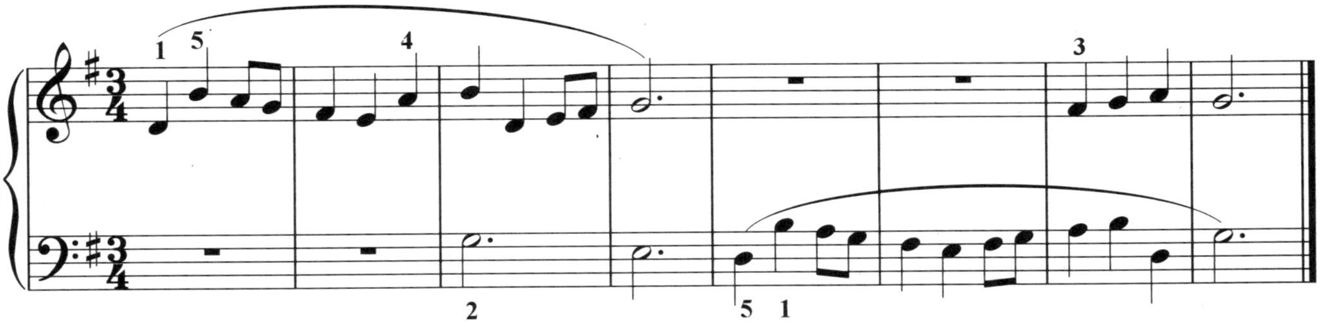

18

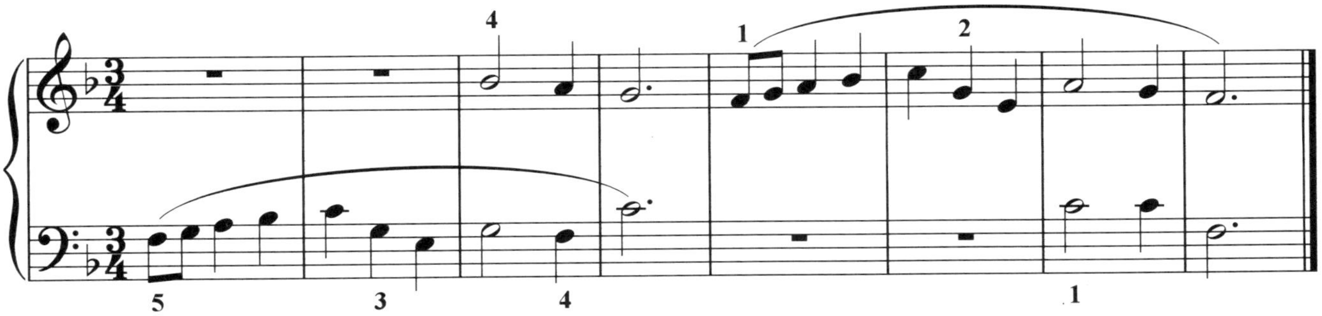

19

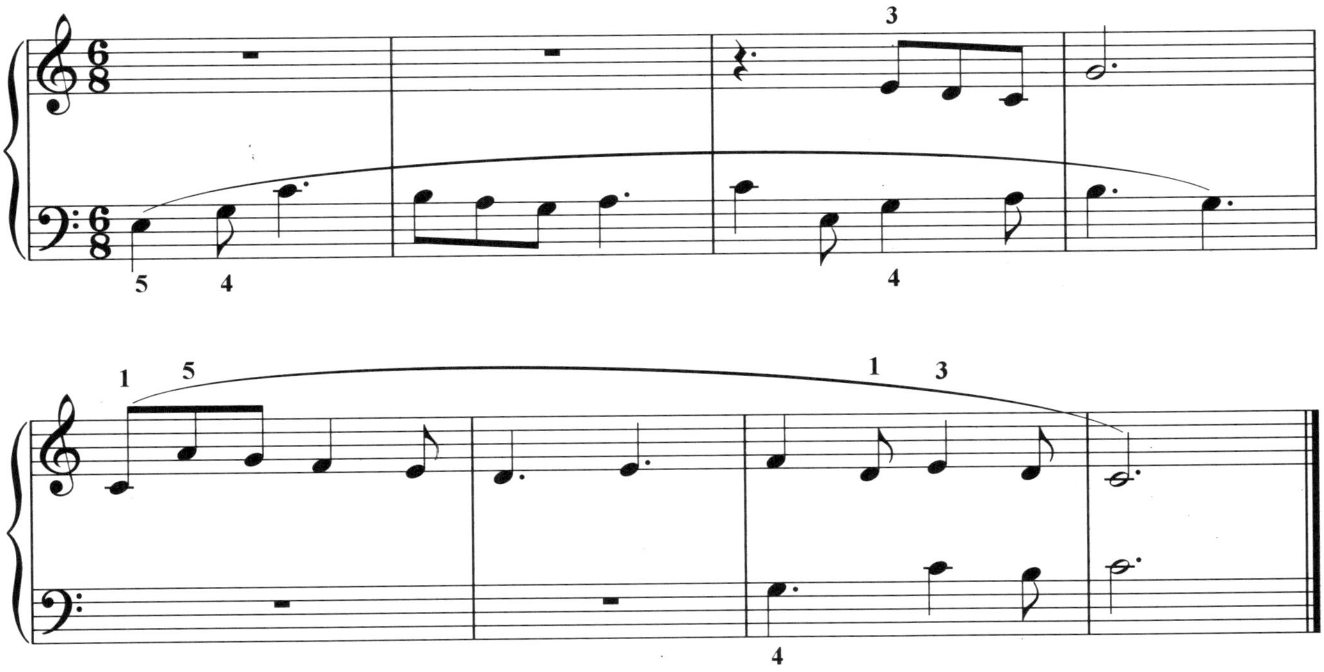

20

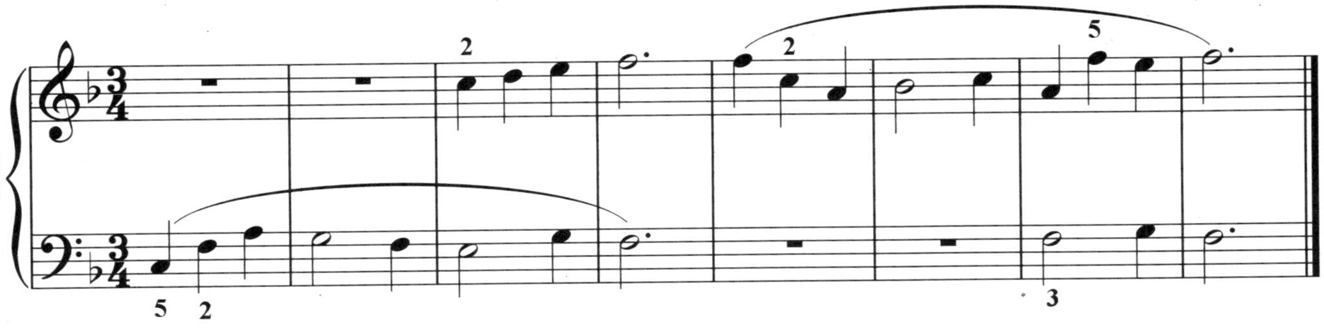

21

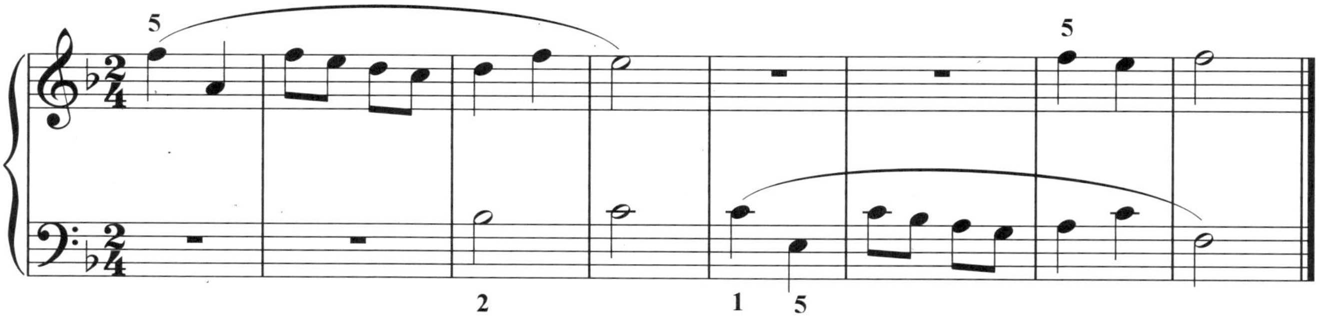

22

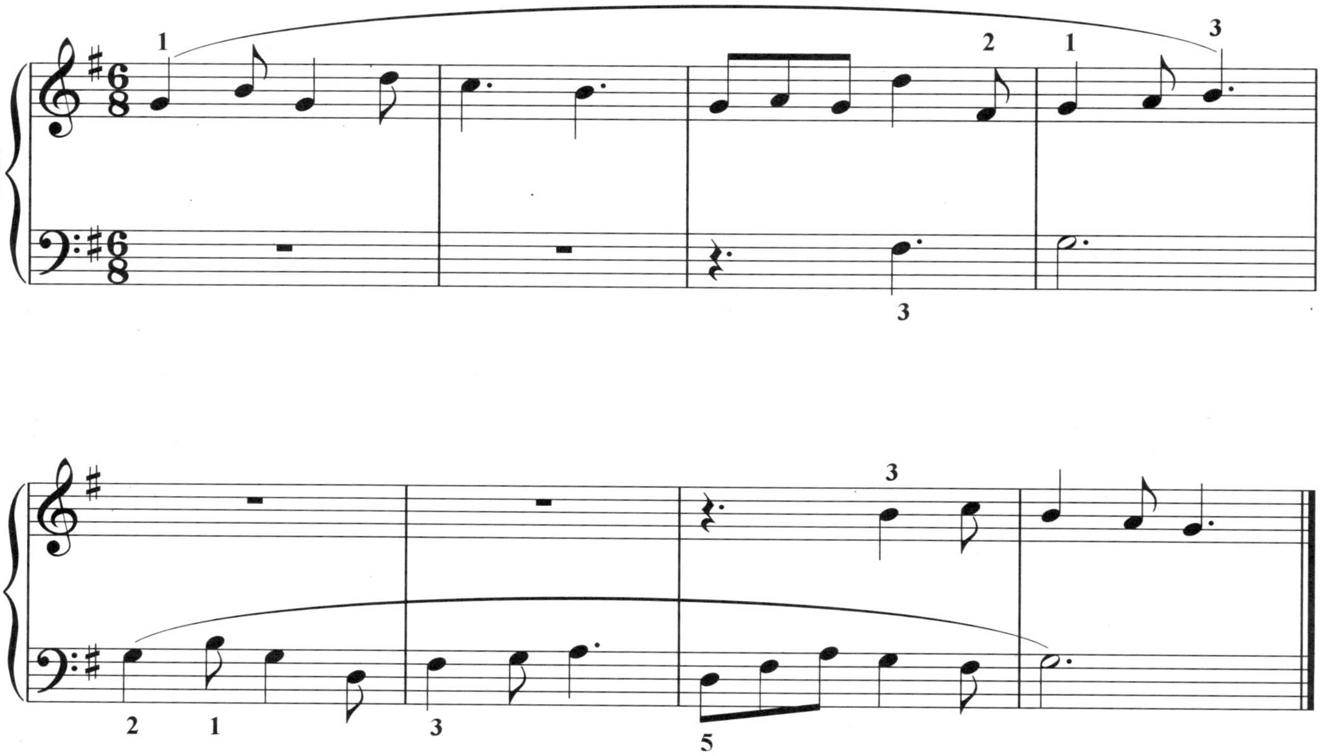

23

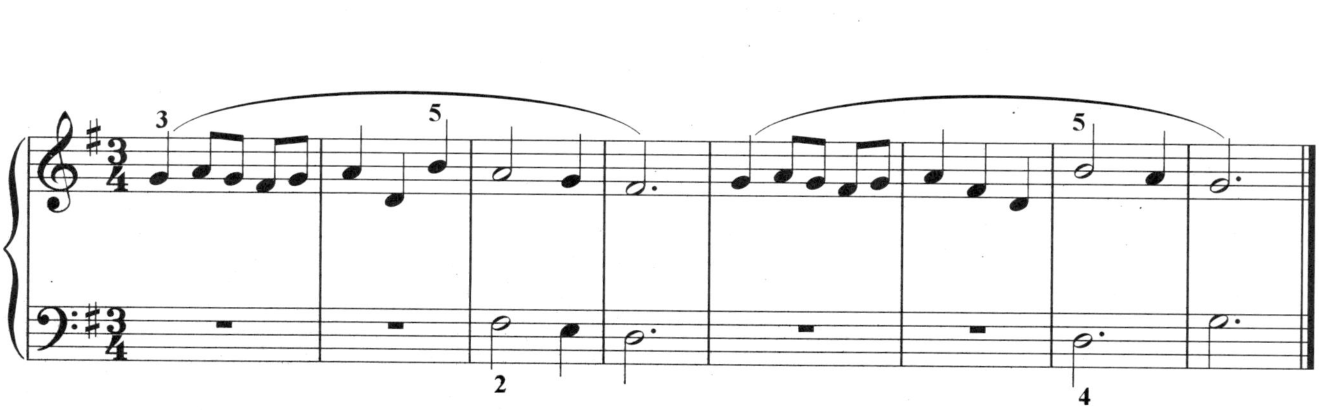

24

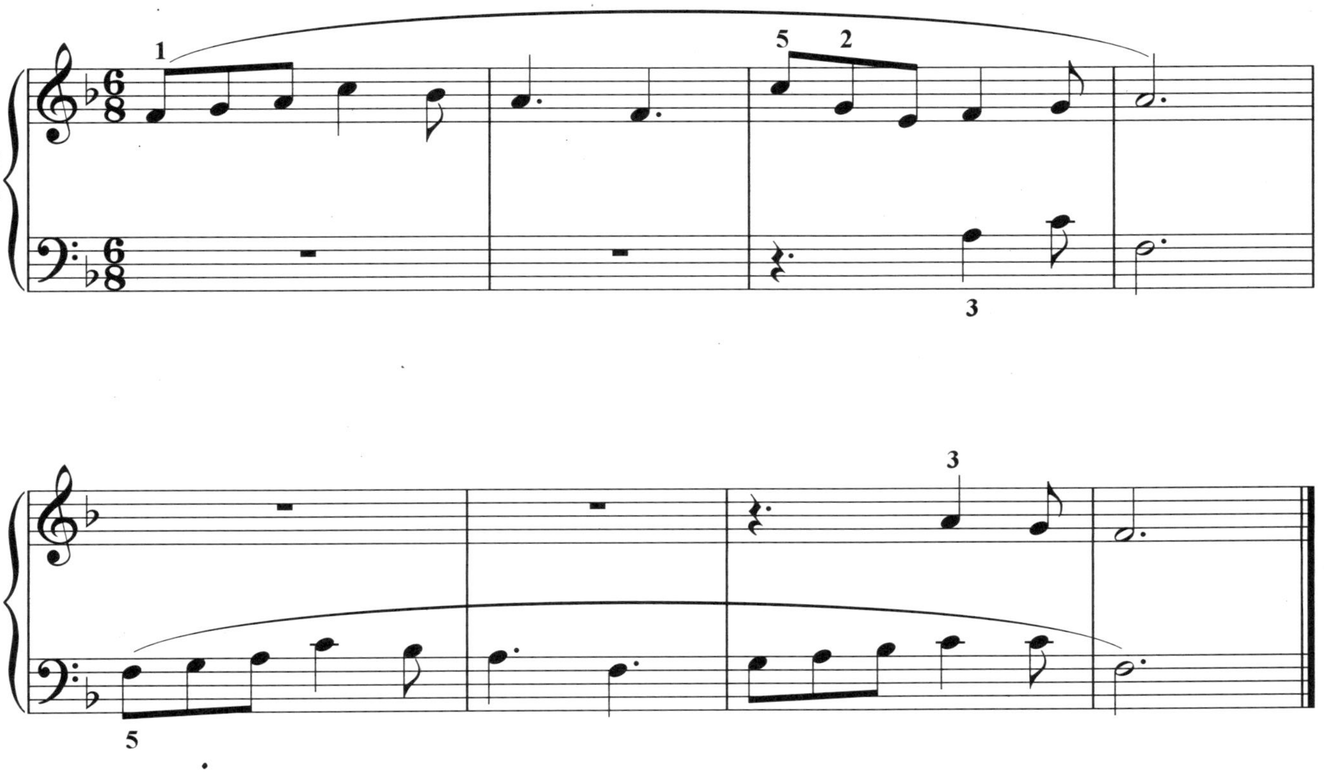

25

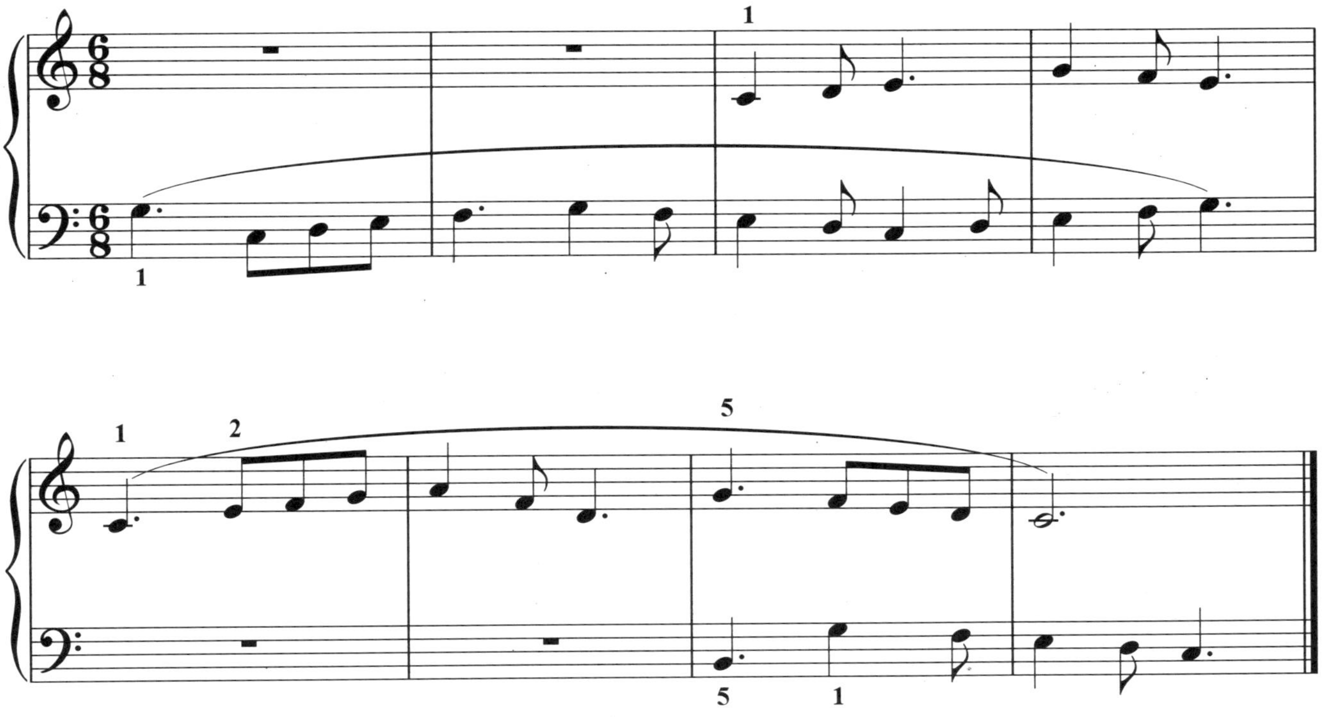

Change of hand position

29

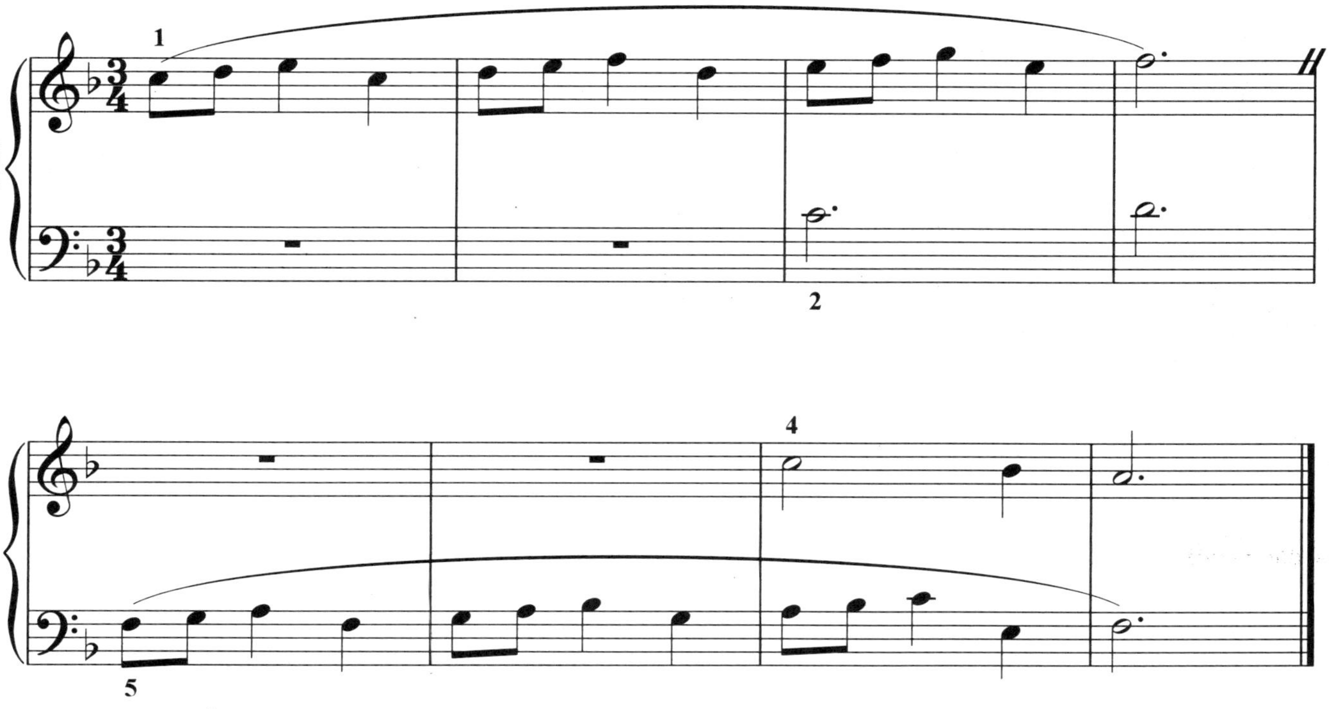

30

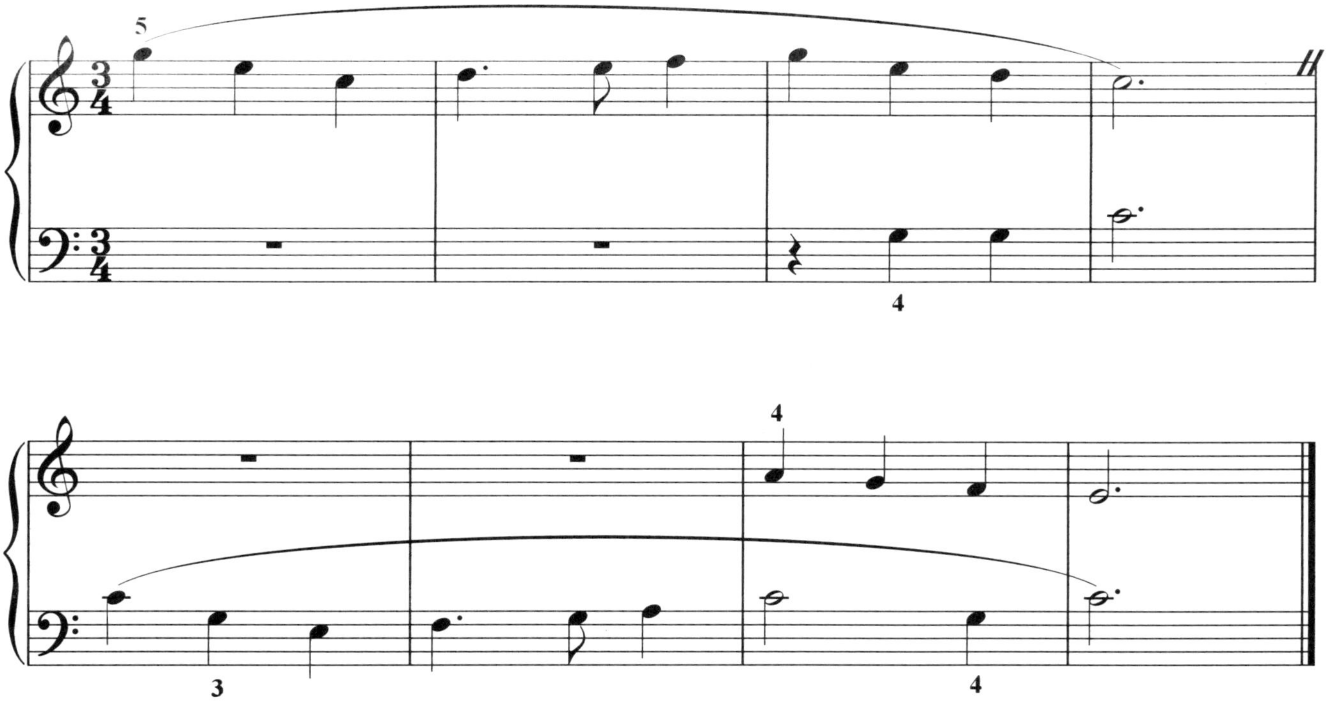

31

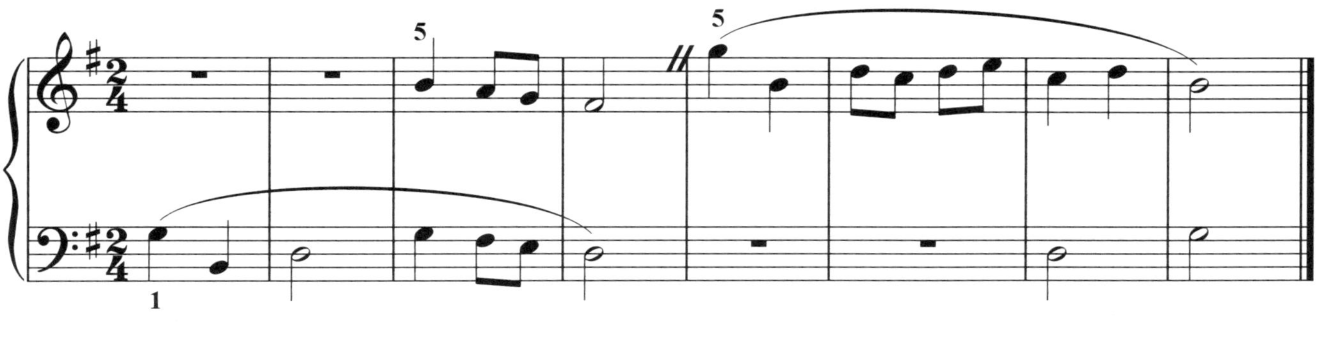

Introducing $\frac{4}{4}$

32

Find the changes of hand position before you play

33

68

34

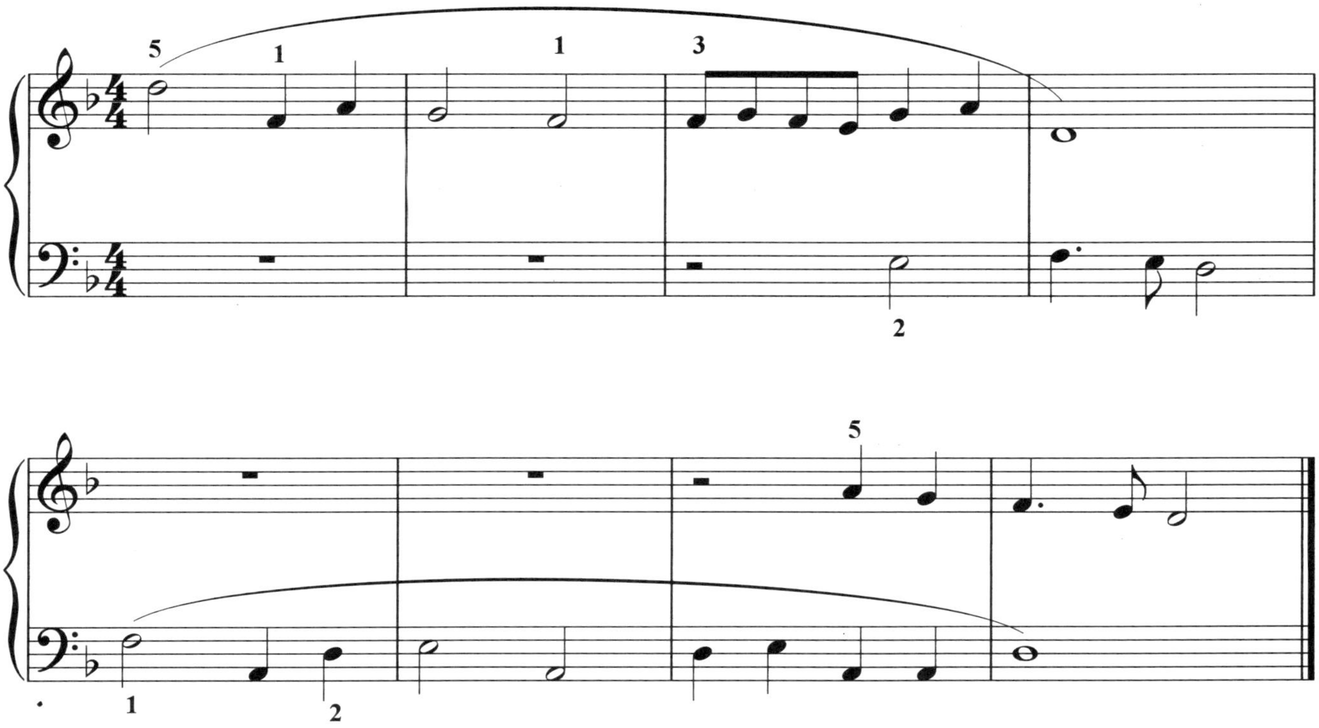

35

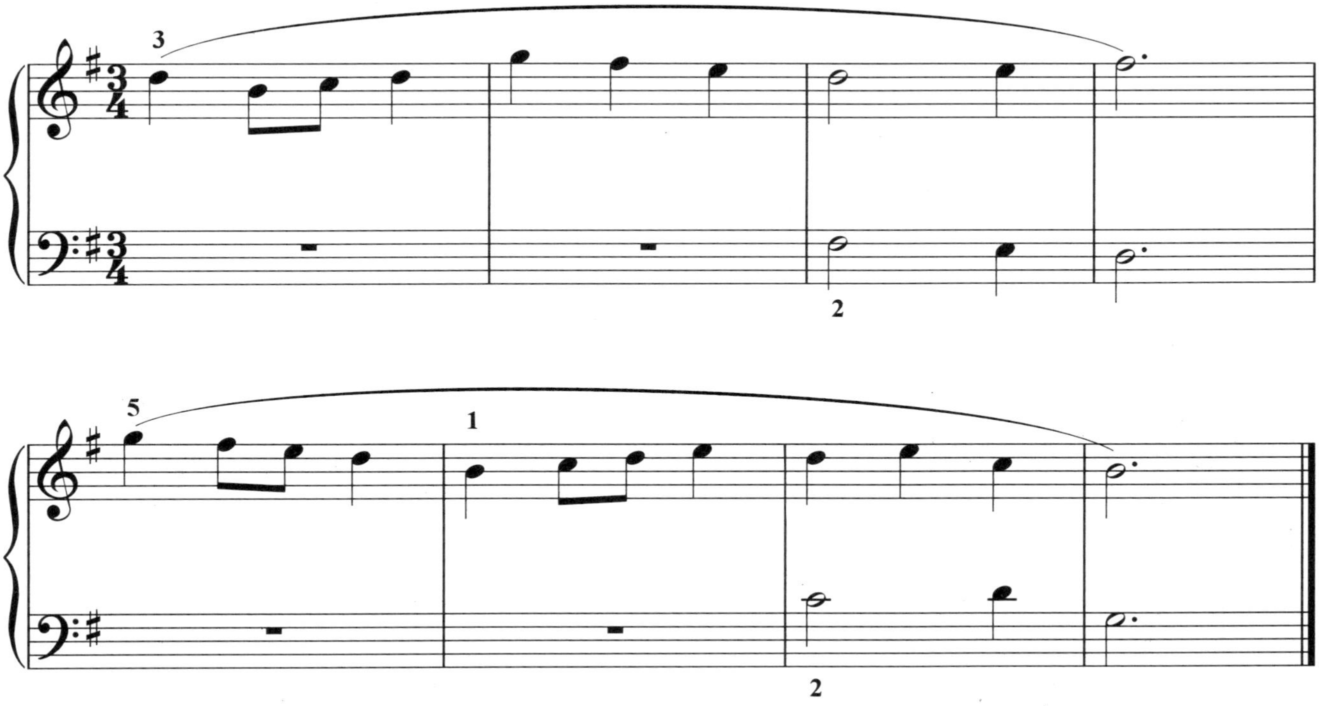

36

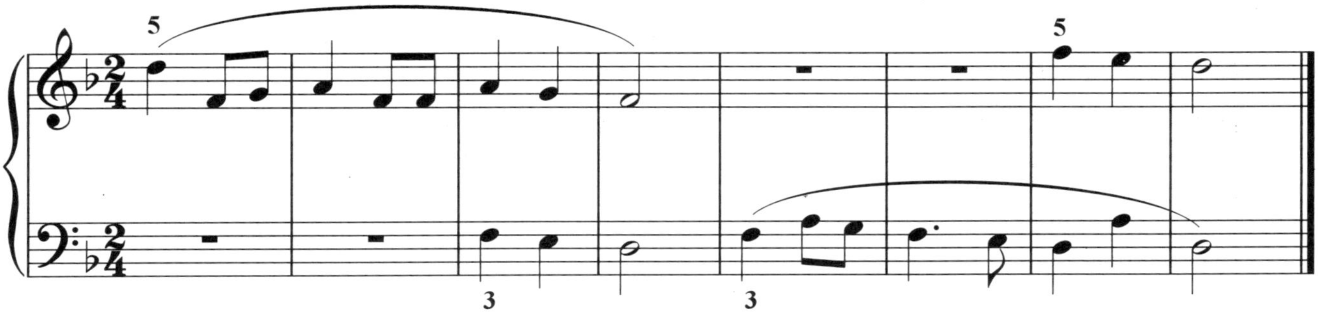

37

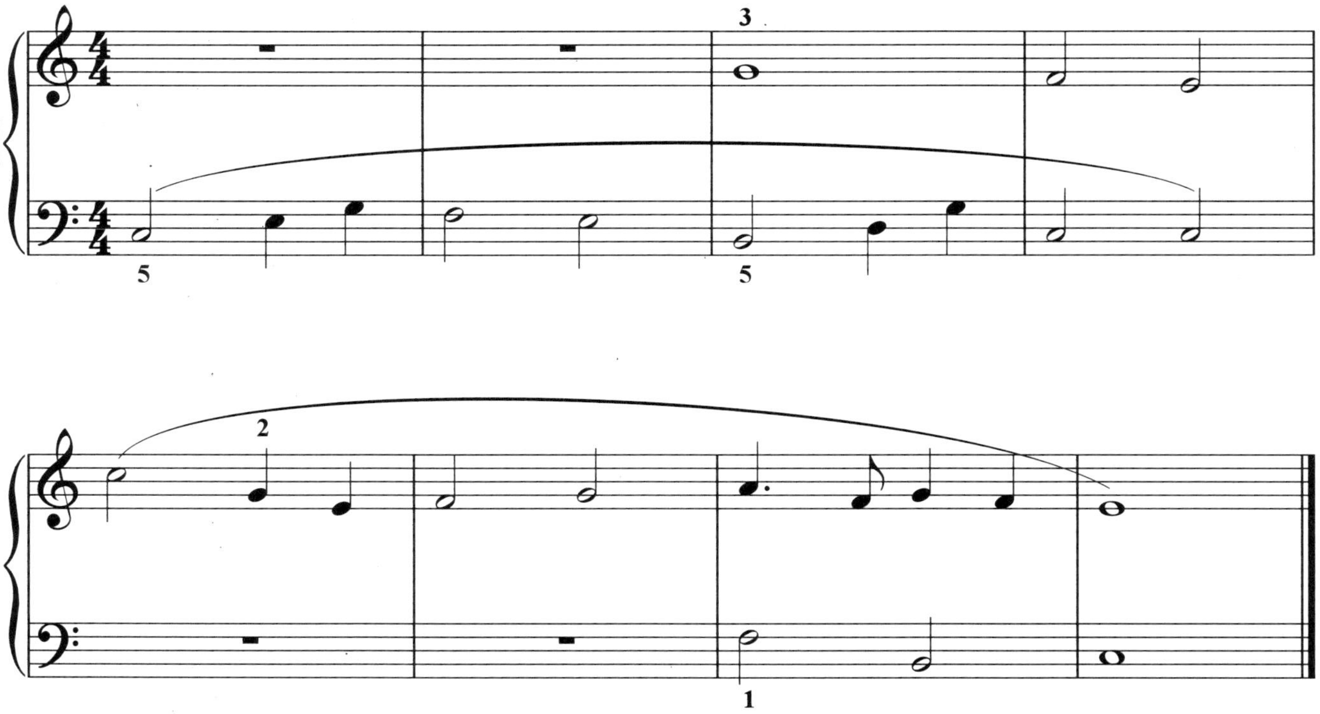

38

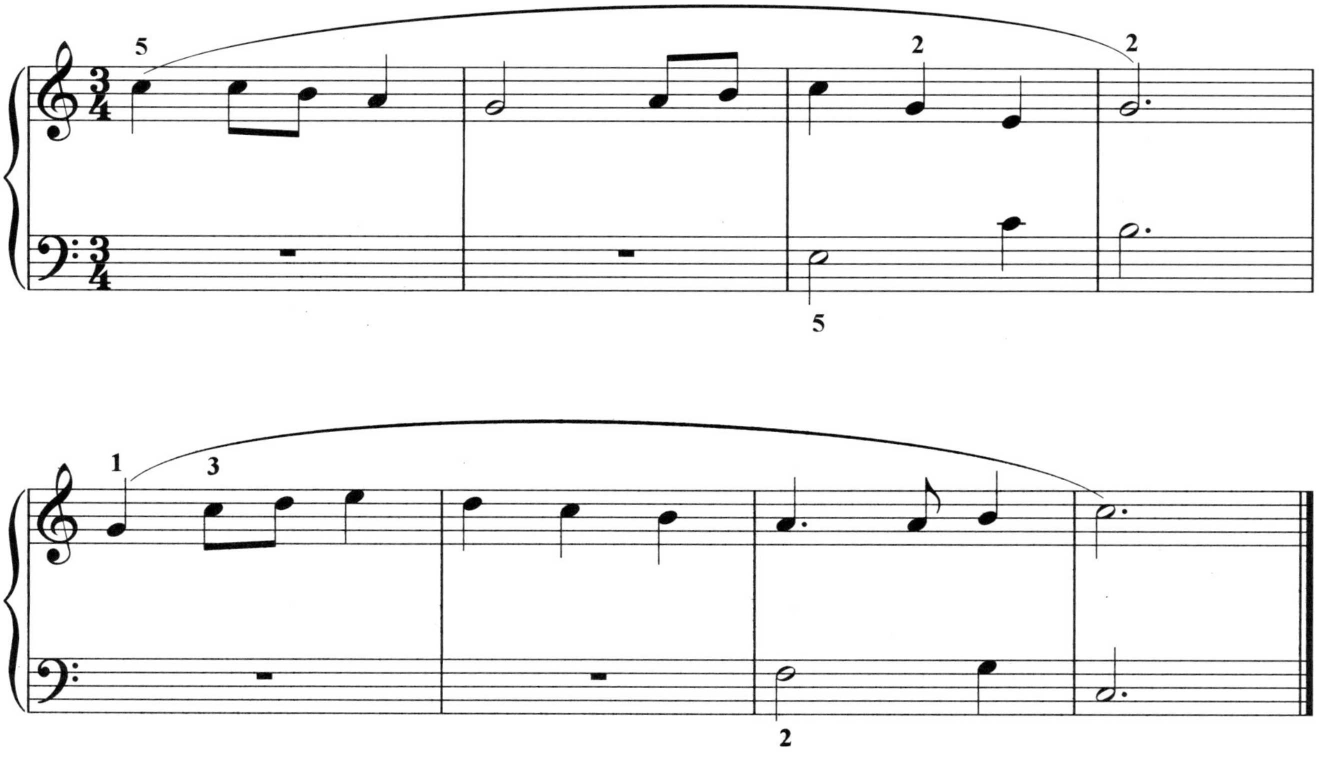

71

42

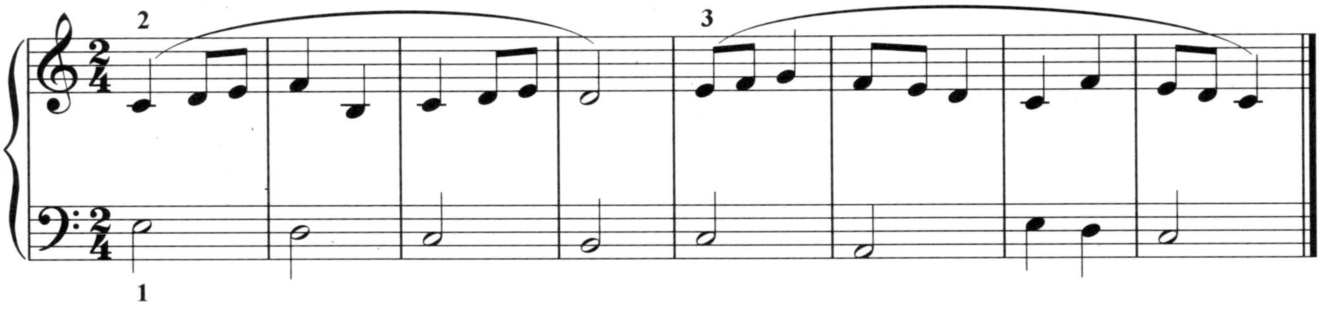

43

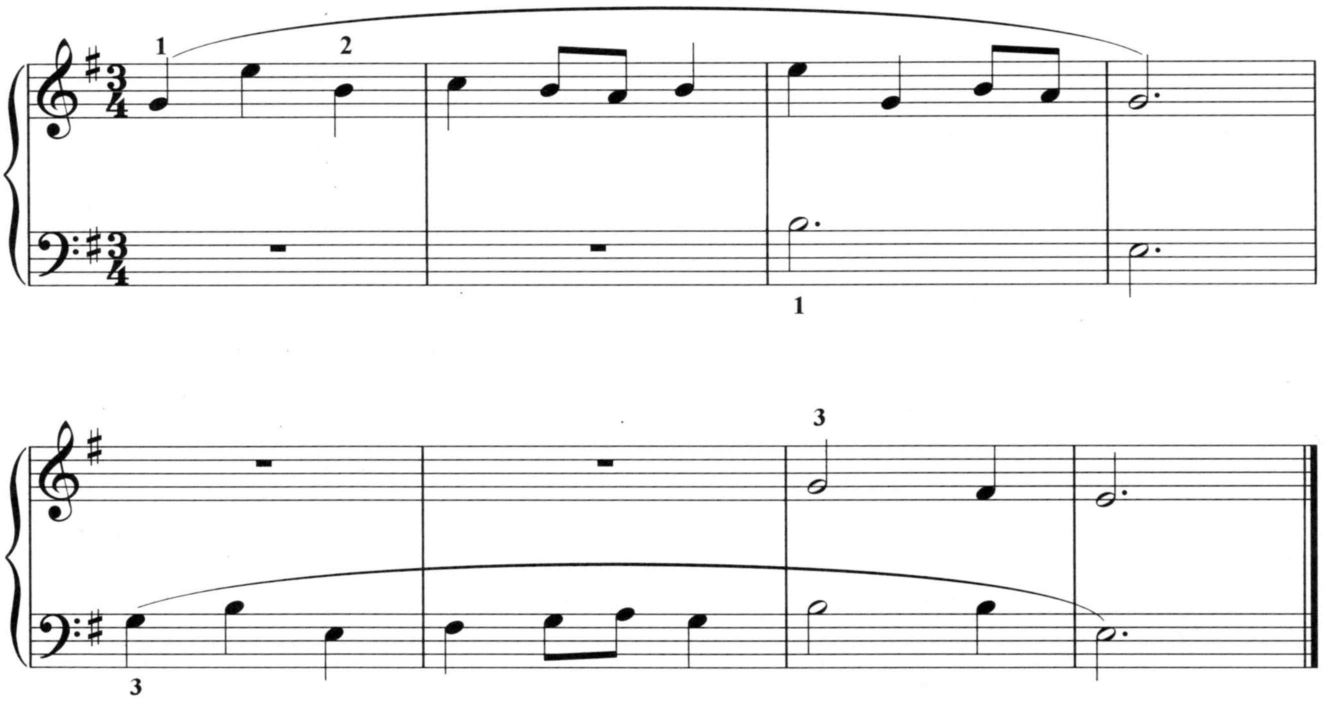

44

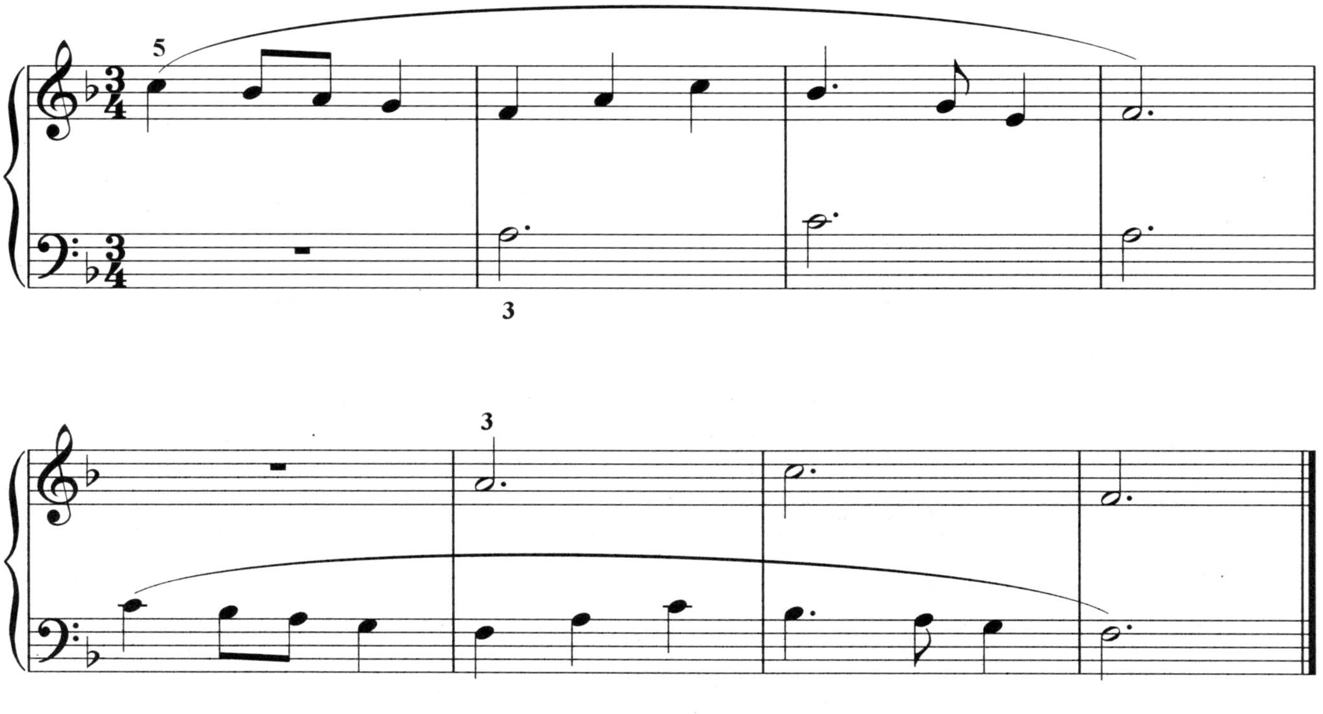

Introducing accidentals

49

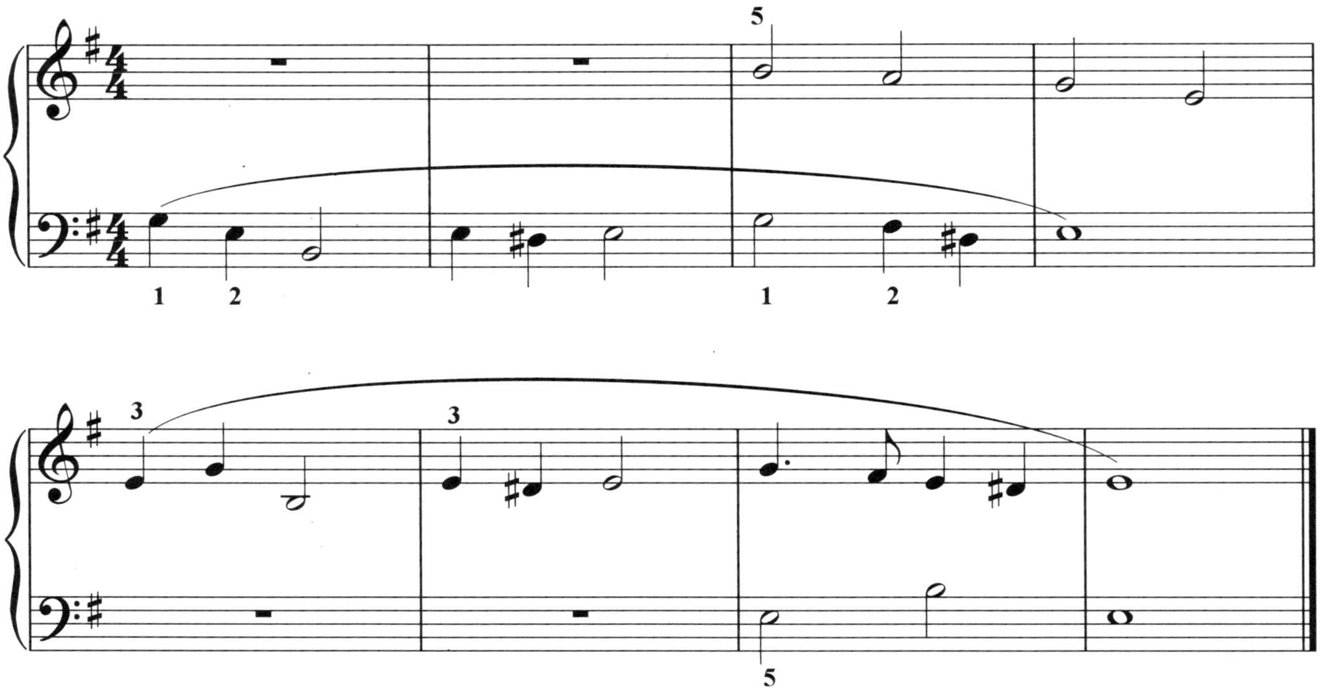

50

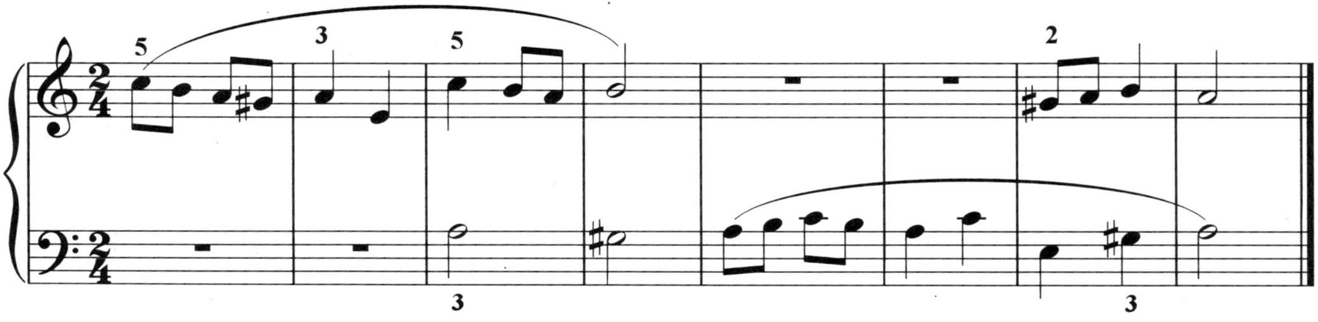

51

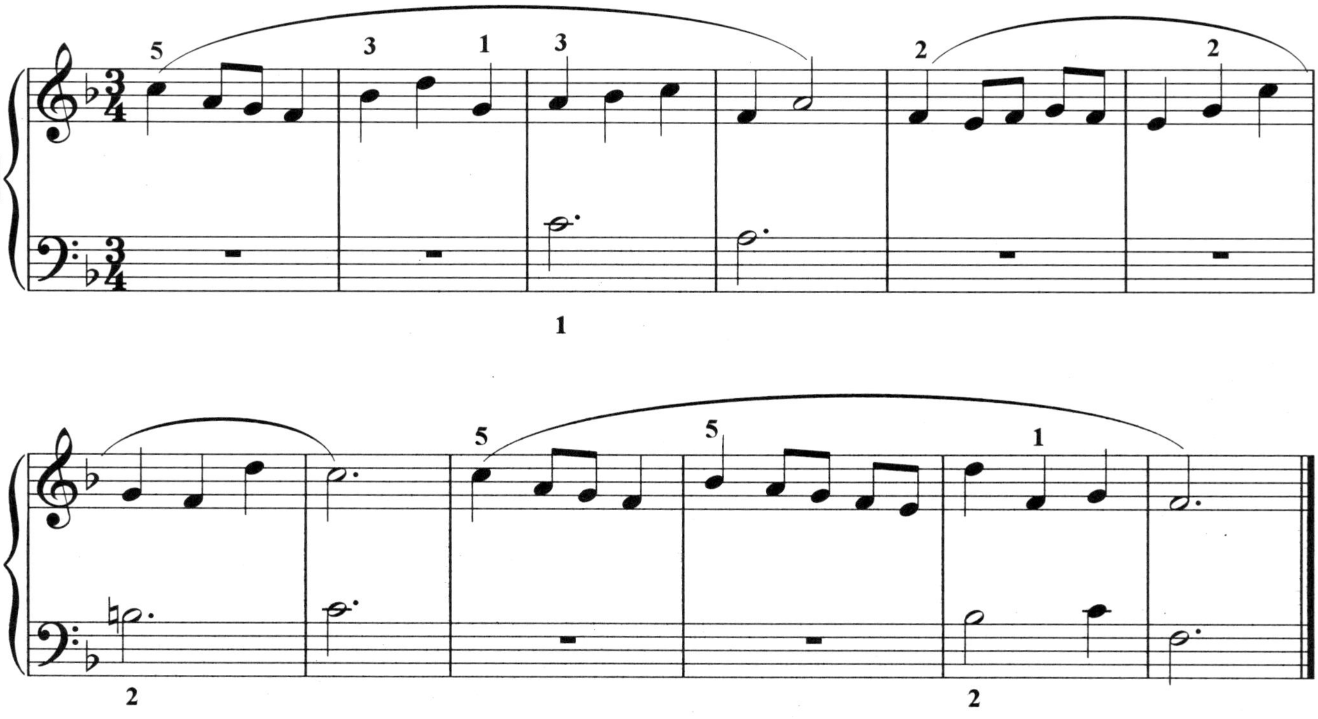

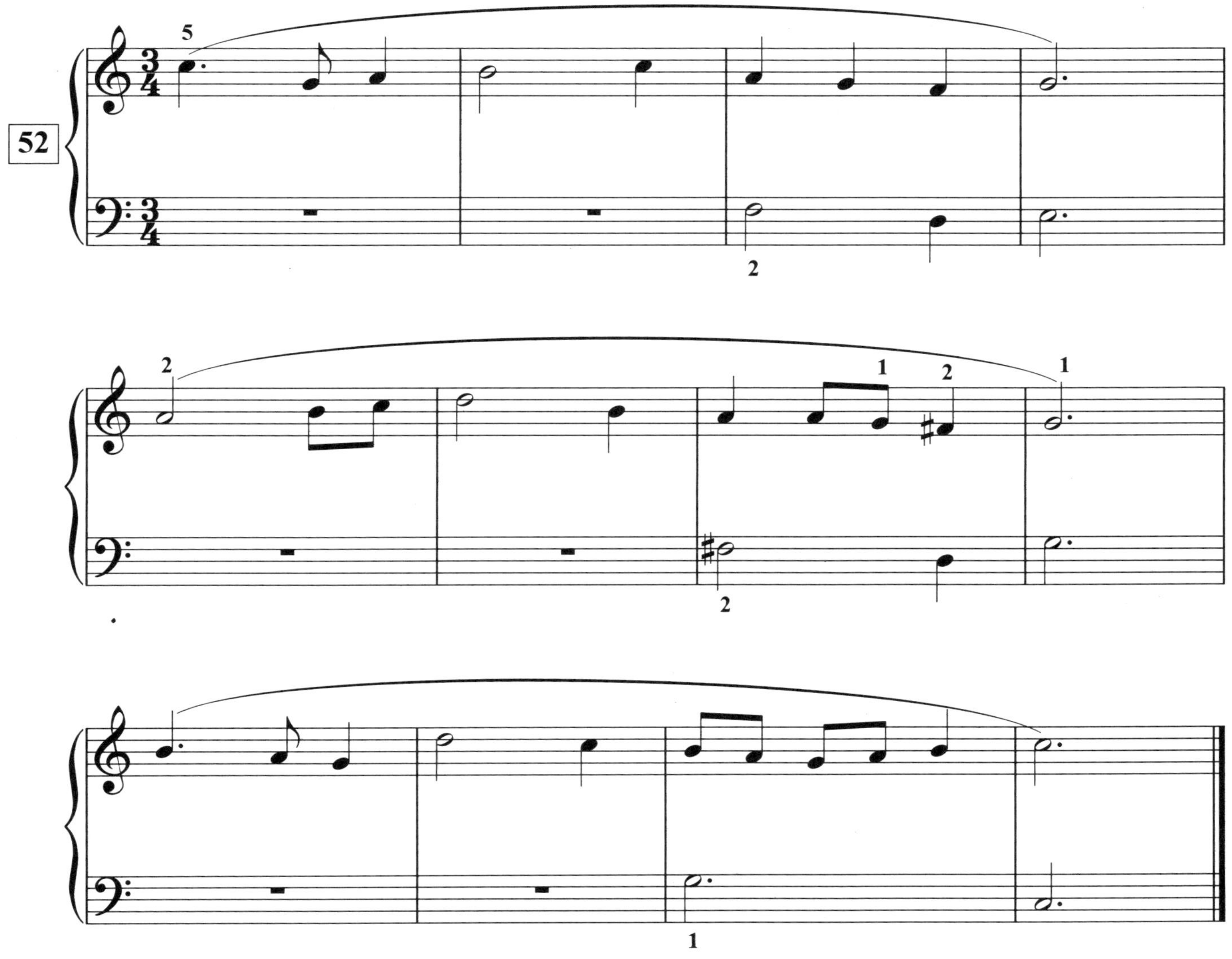
52

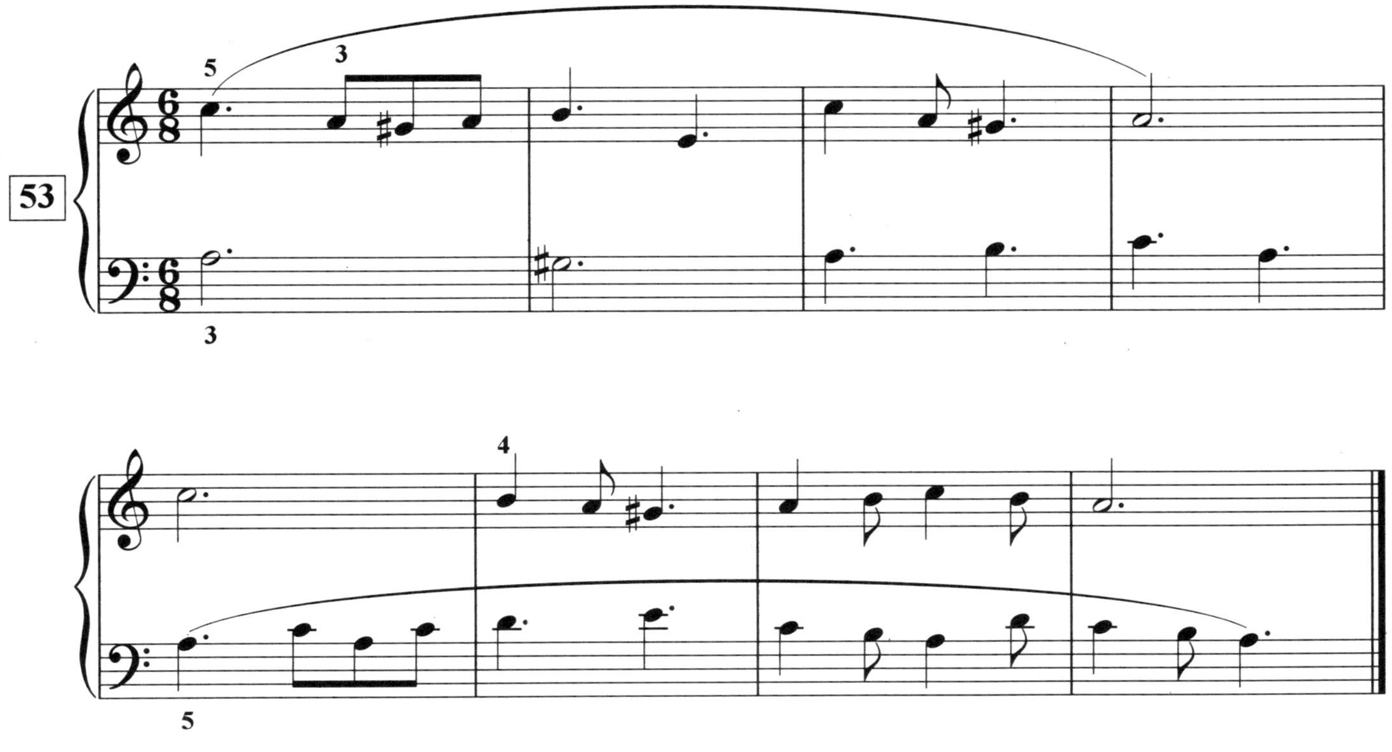
53

54

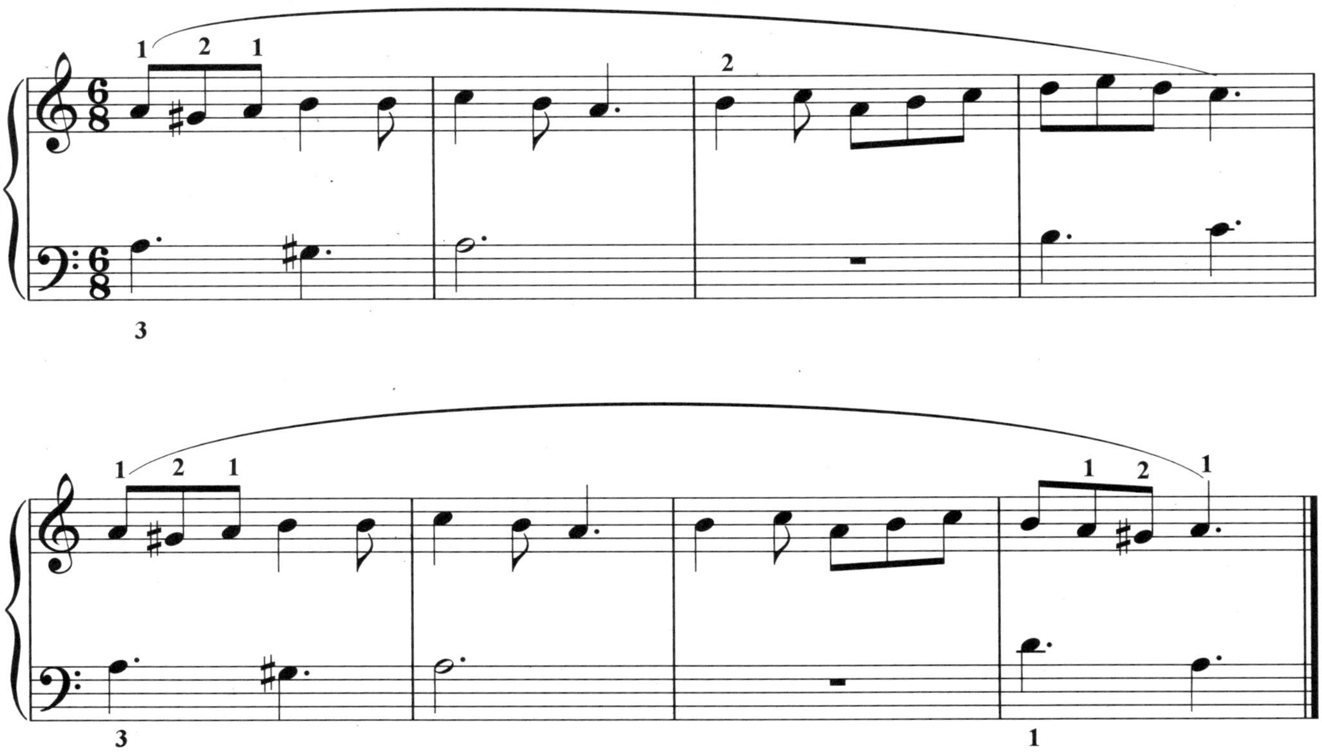

55

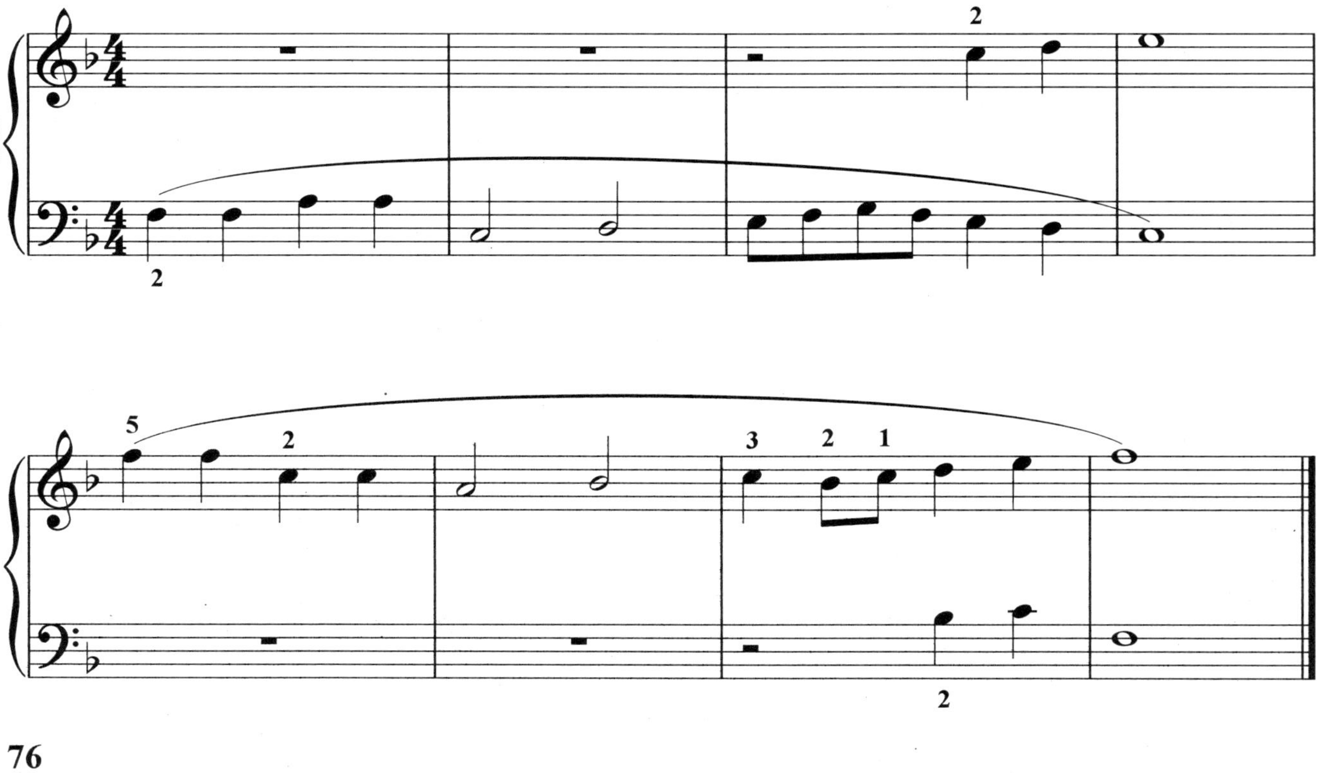

56

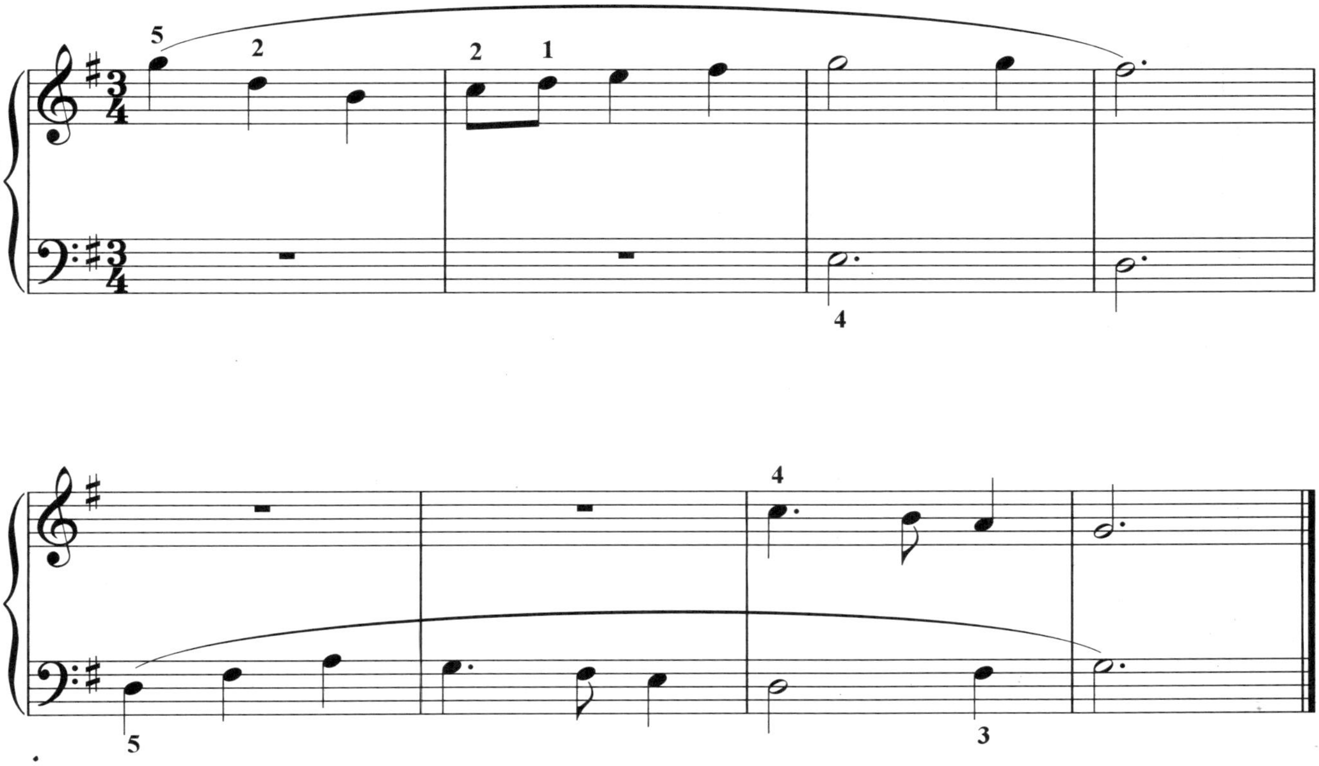

57

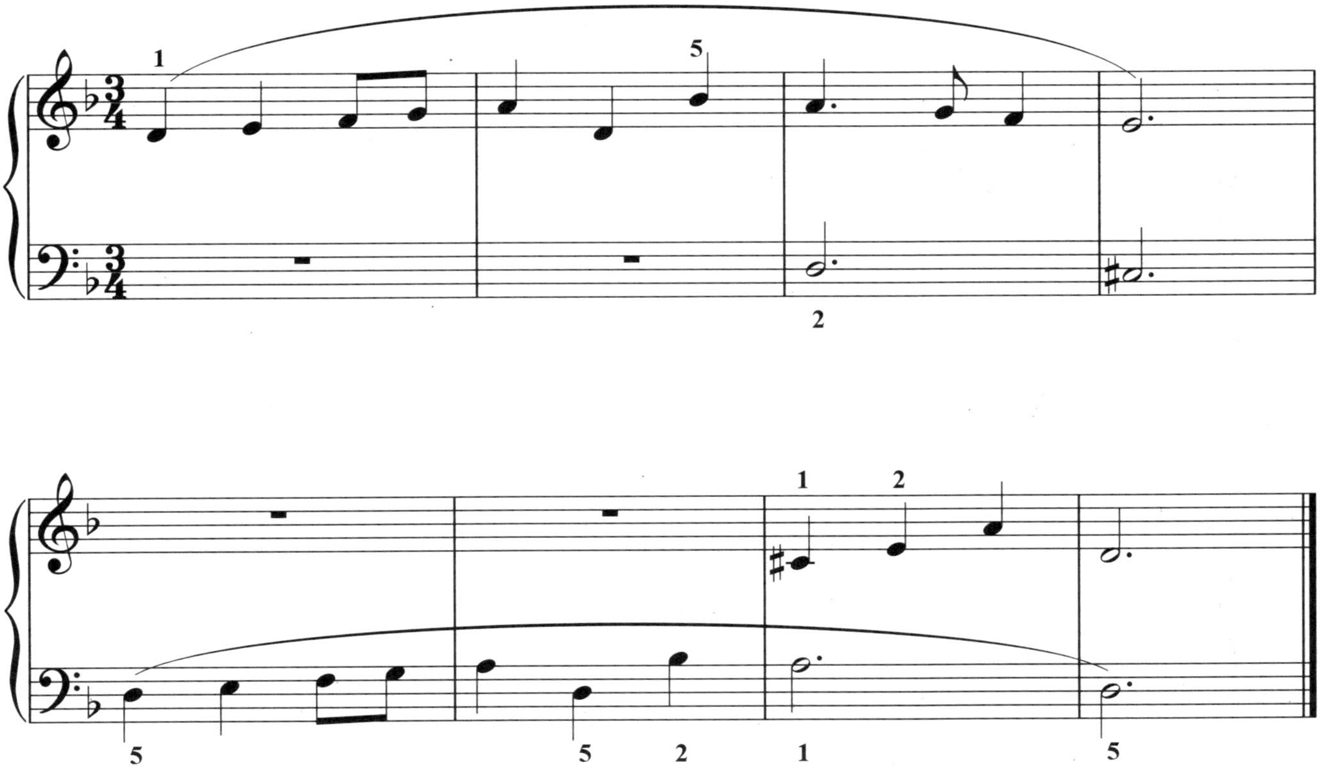

58

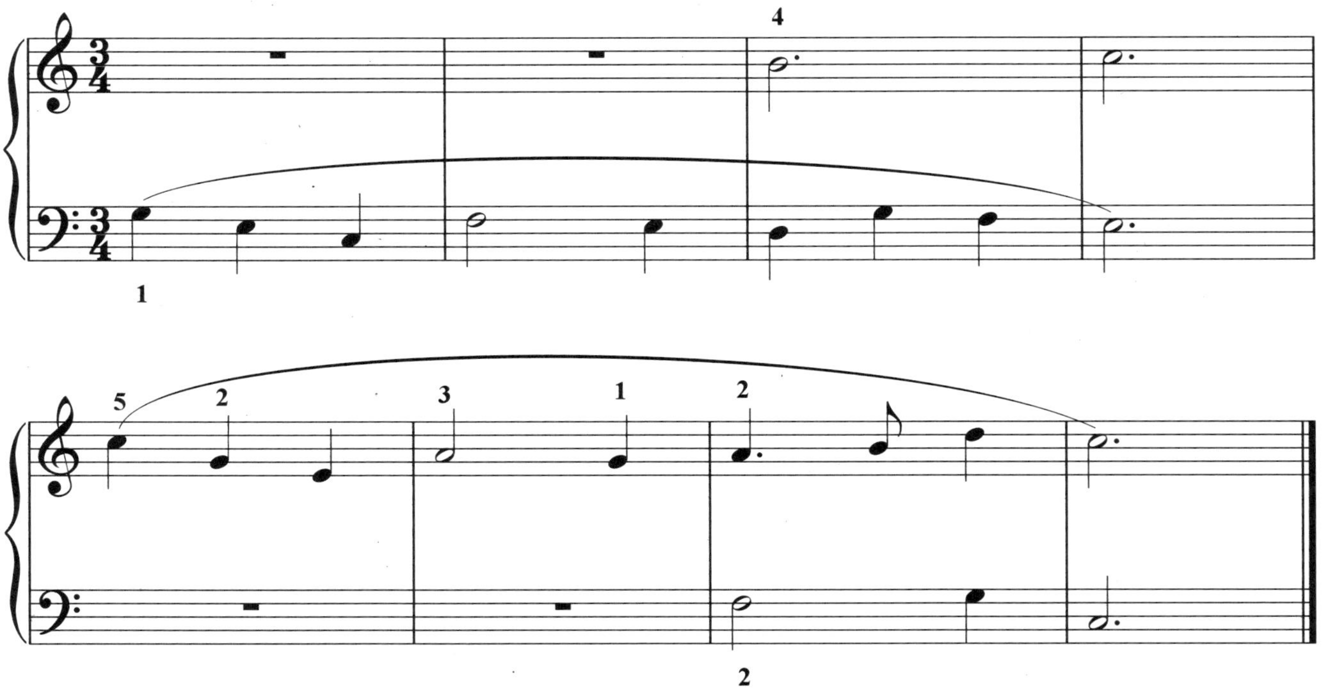

59

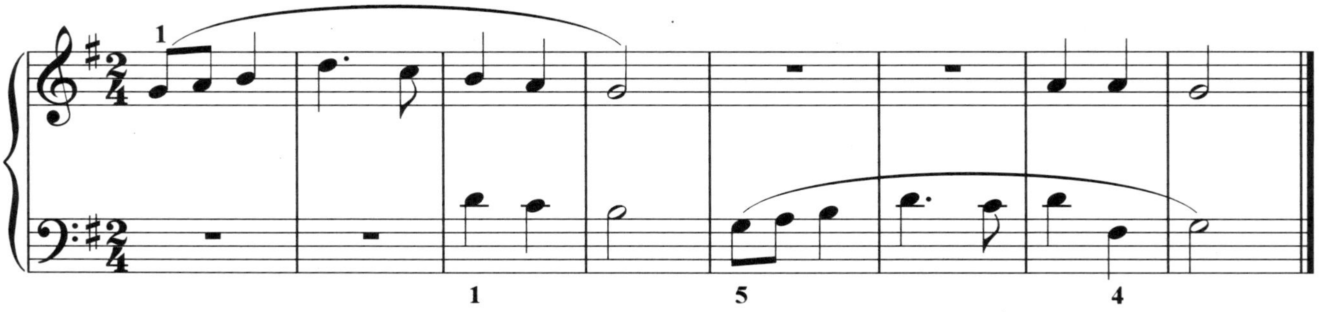

60

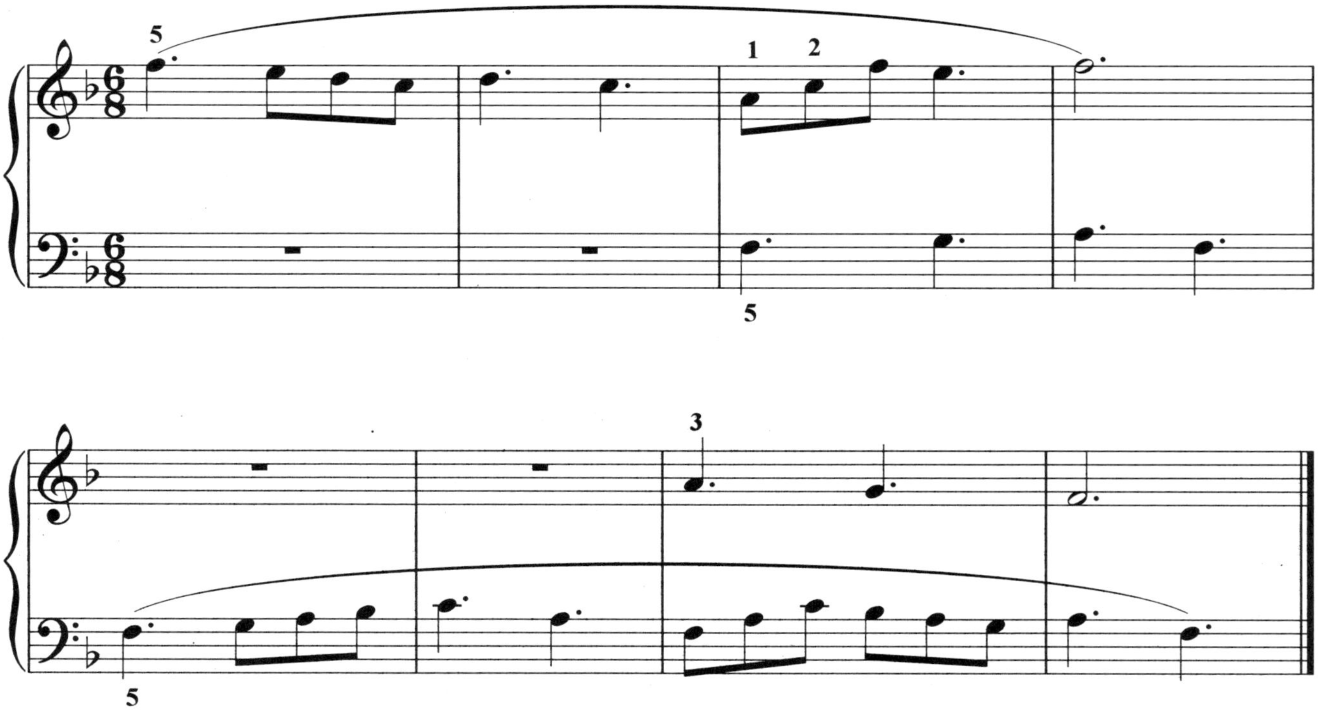

61

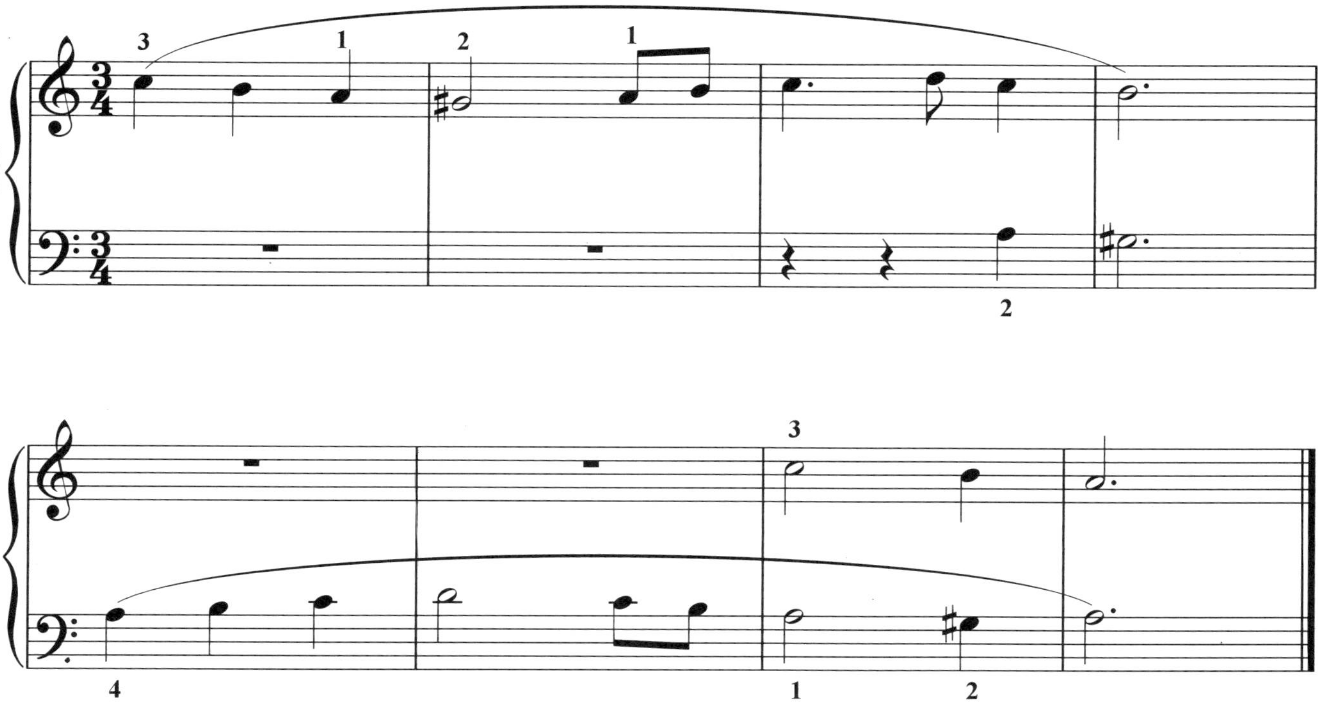

62

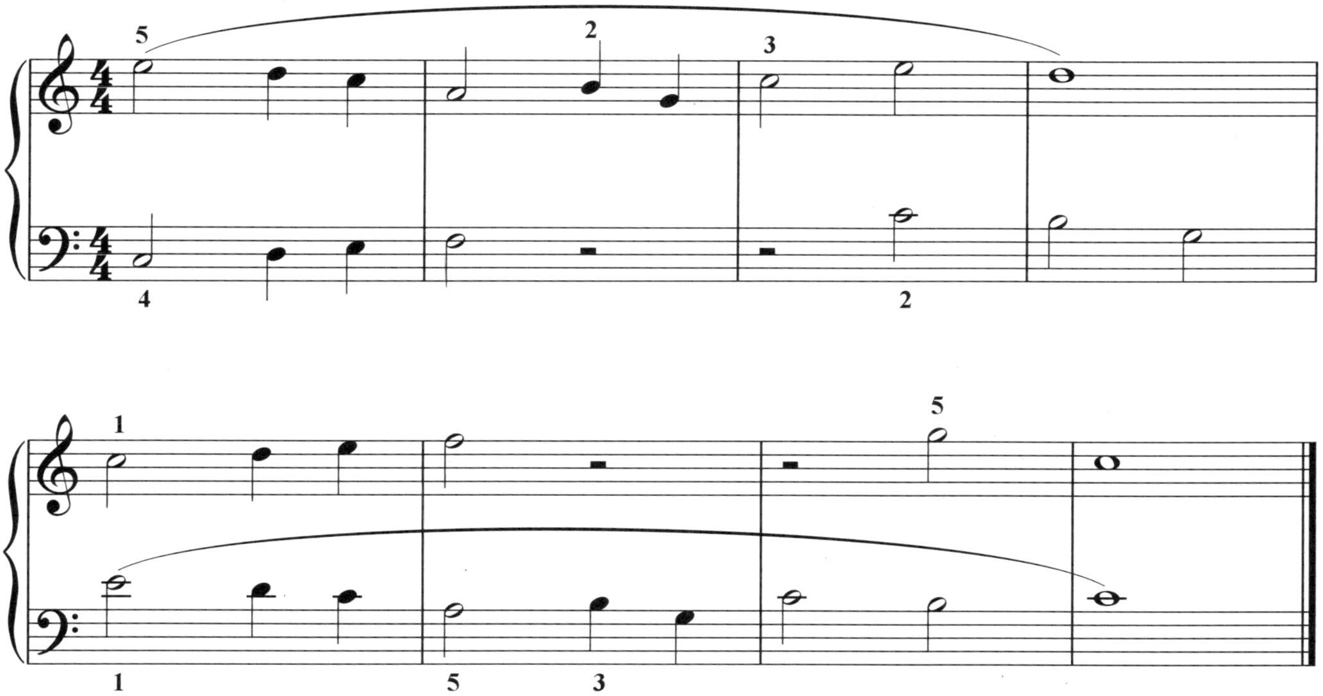

63

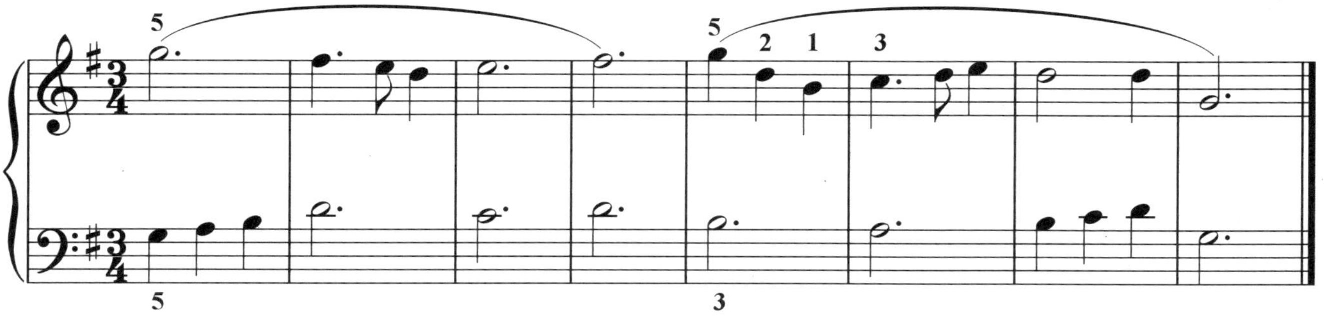

Extension to 7ths

67

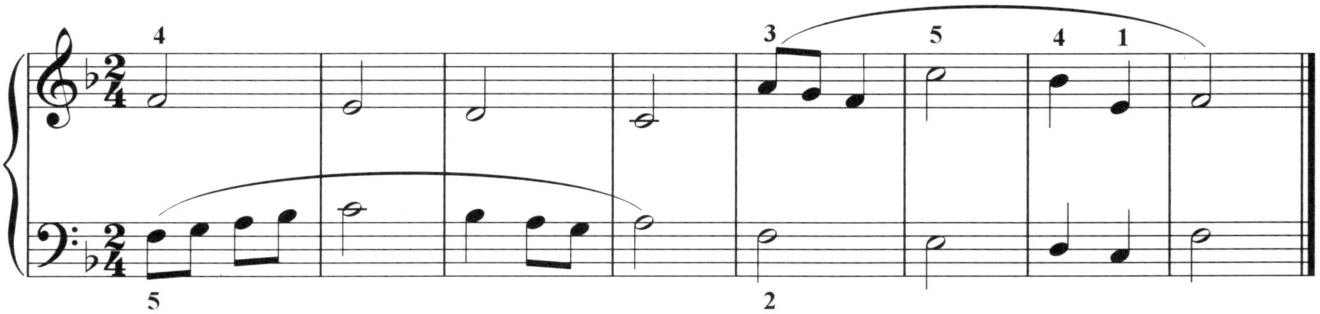

68

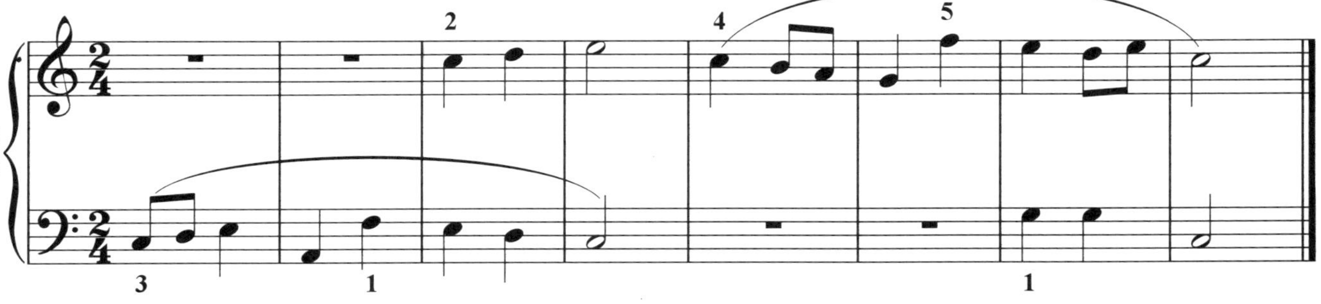

69

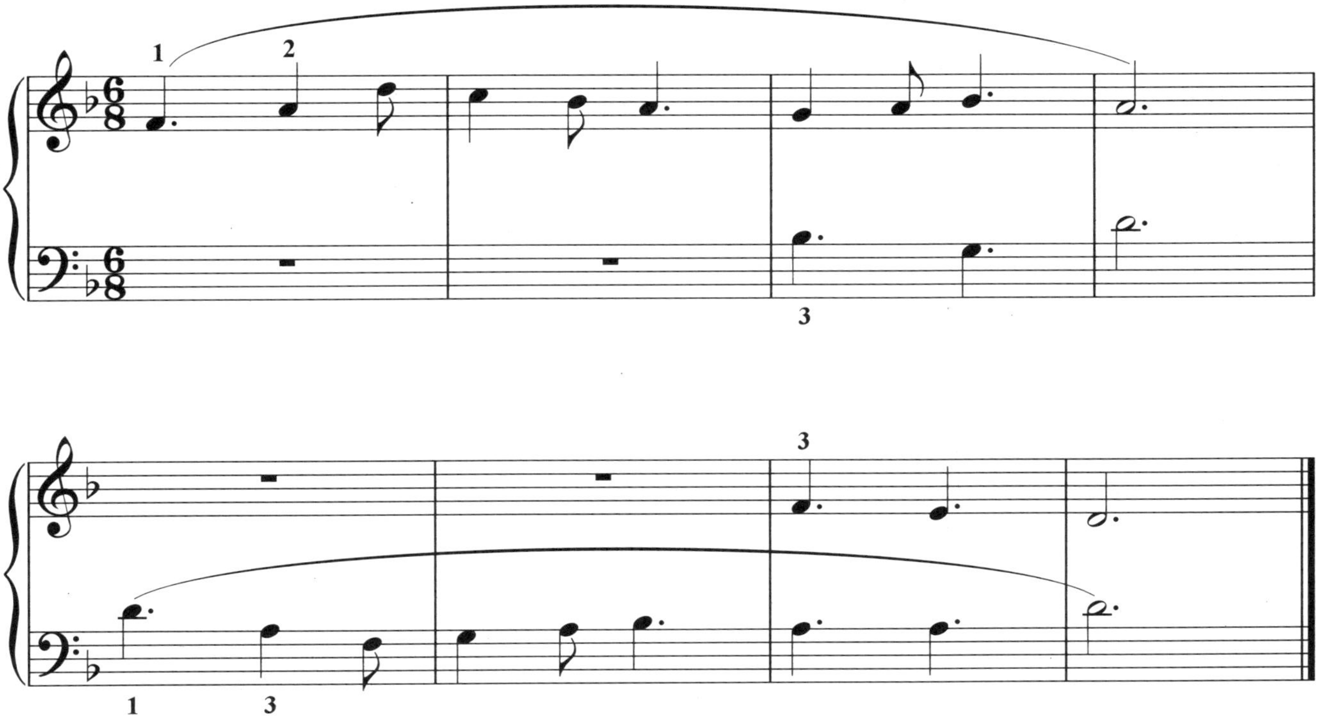

82

73

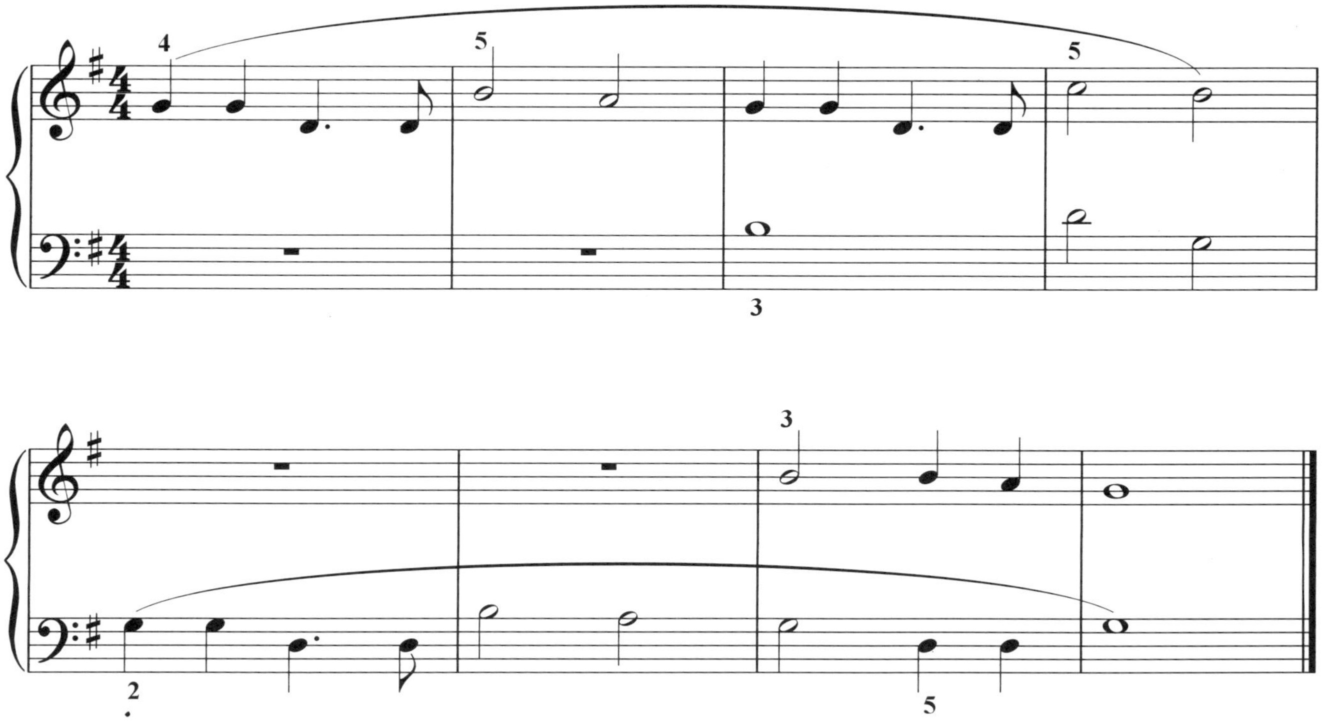

74

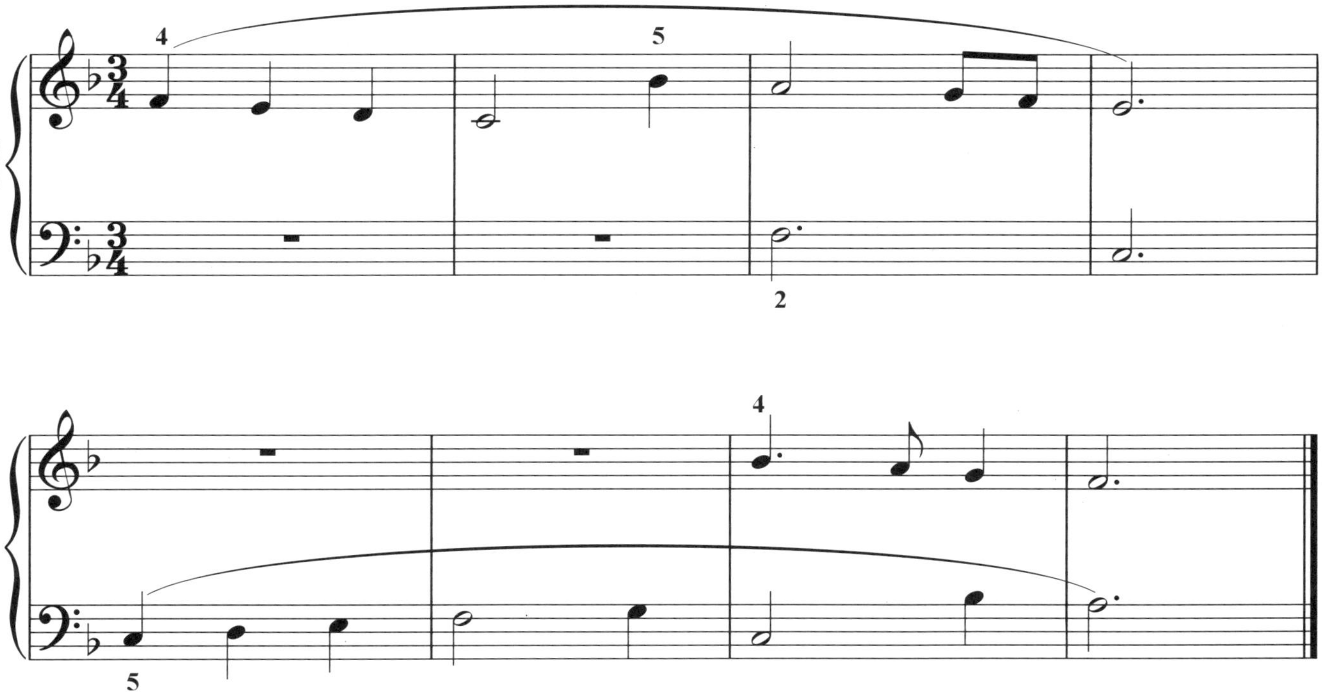

75

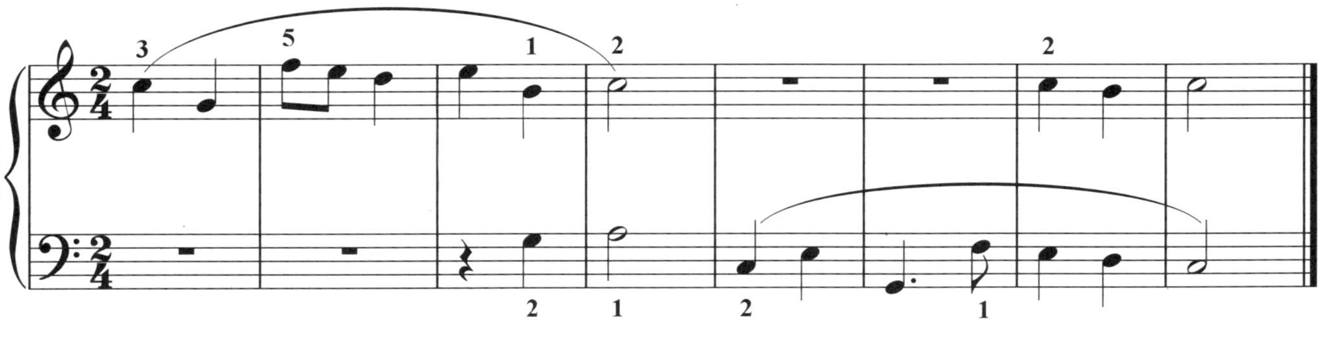

76

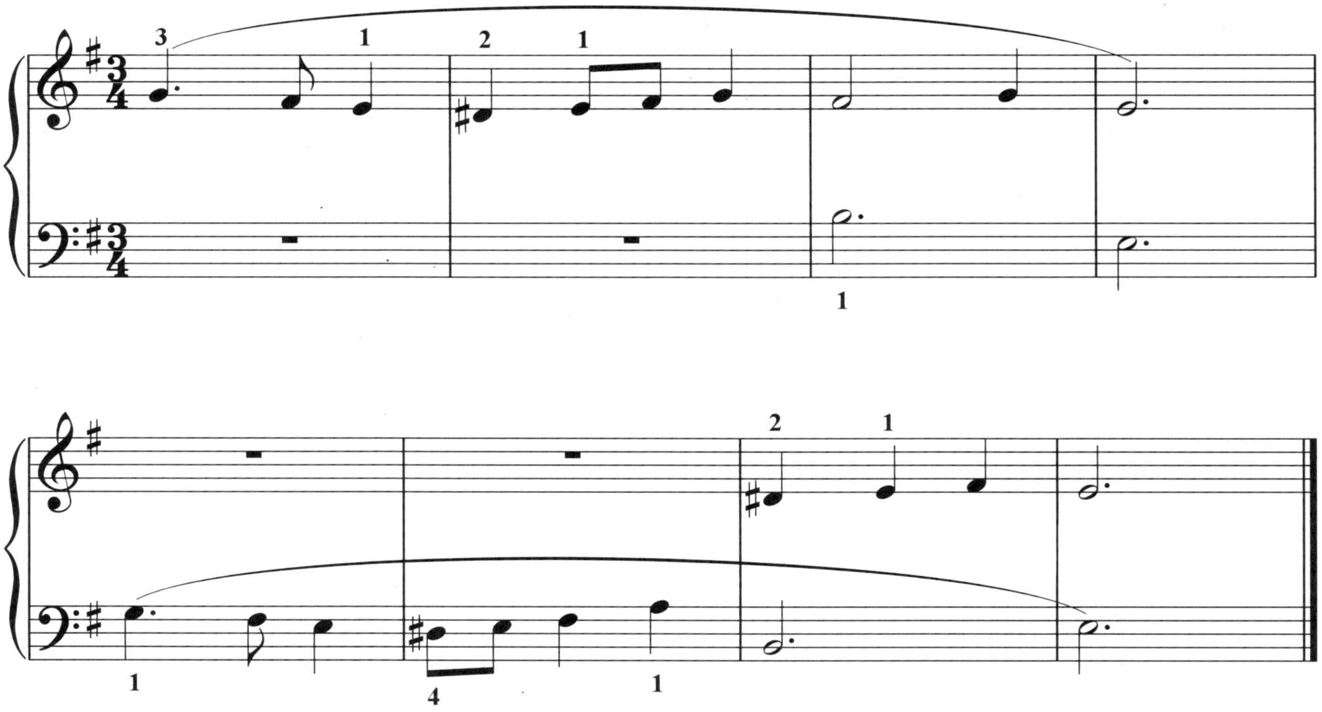

77

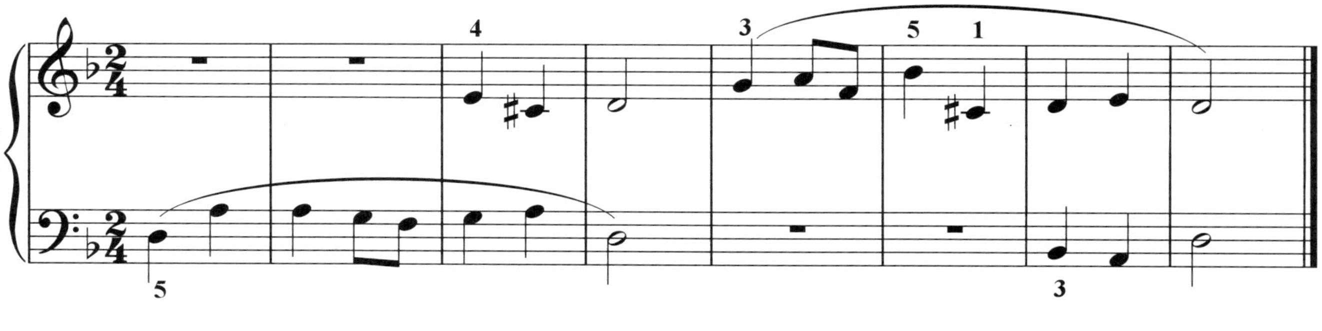

78

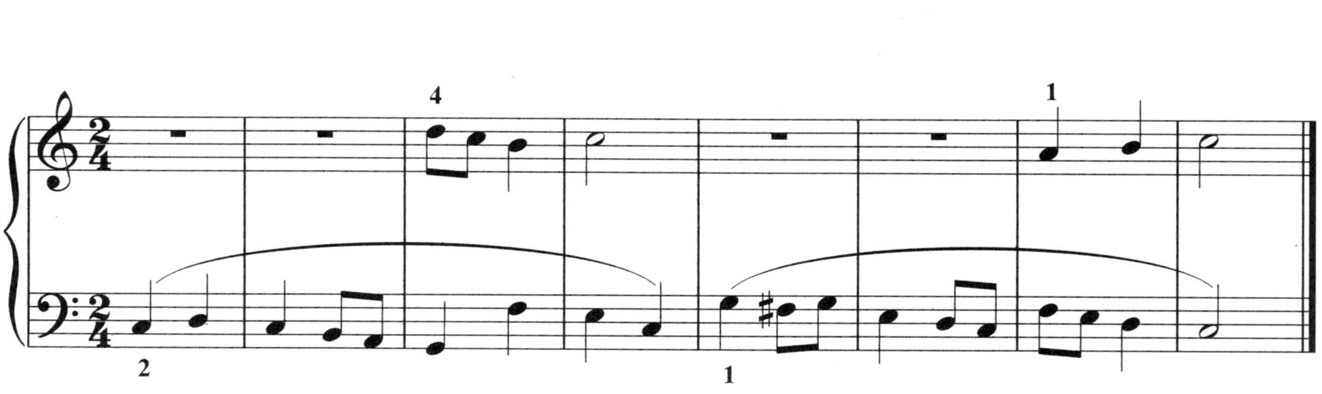

79

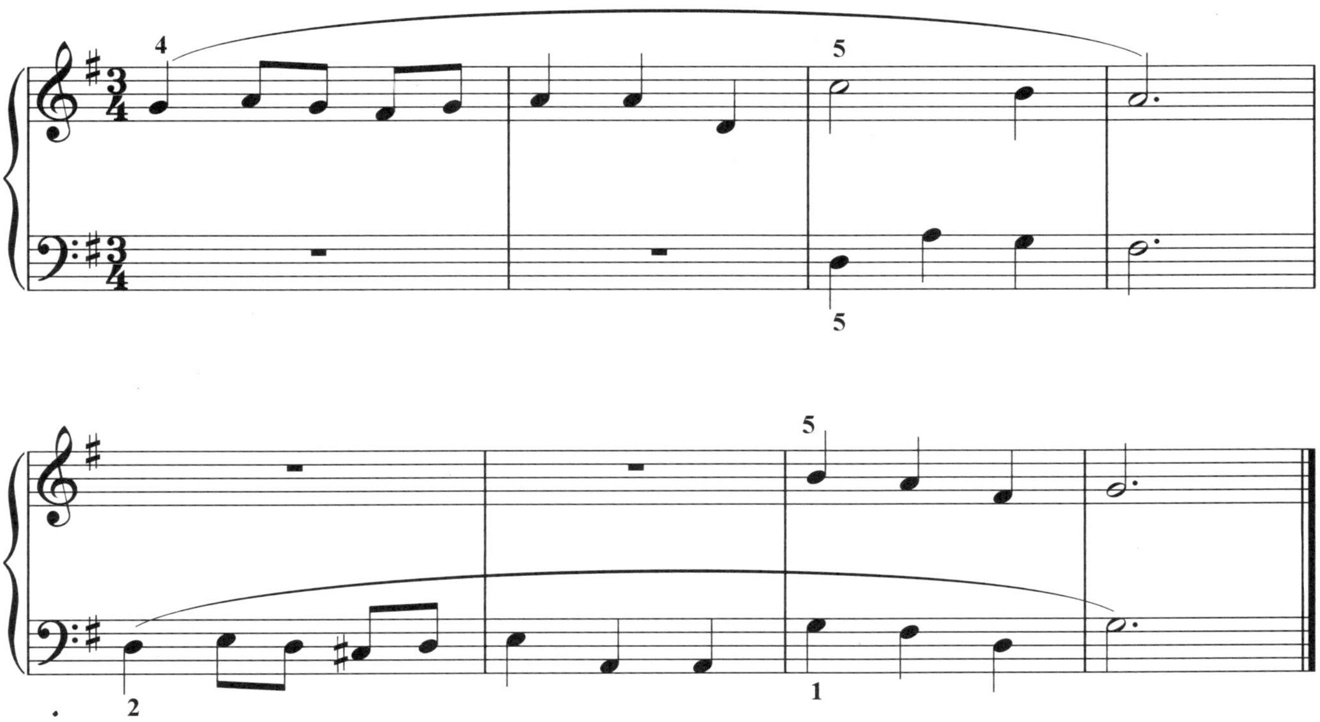

80

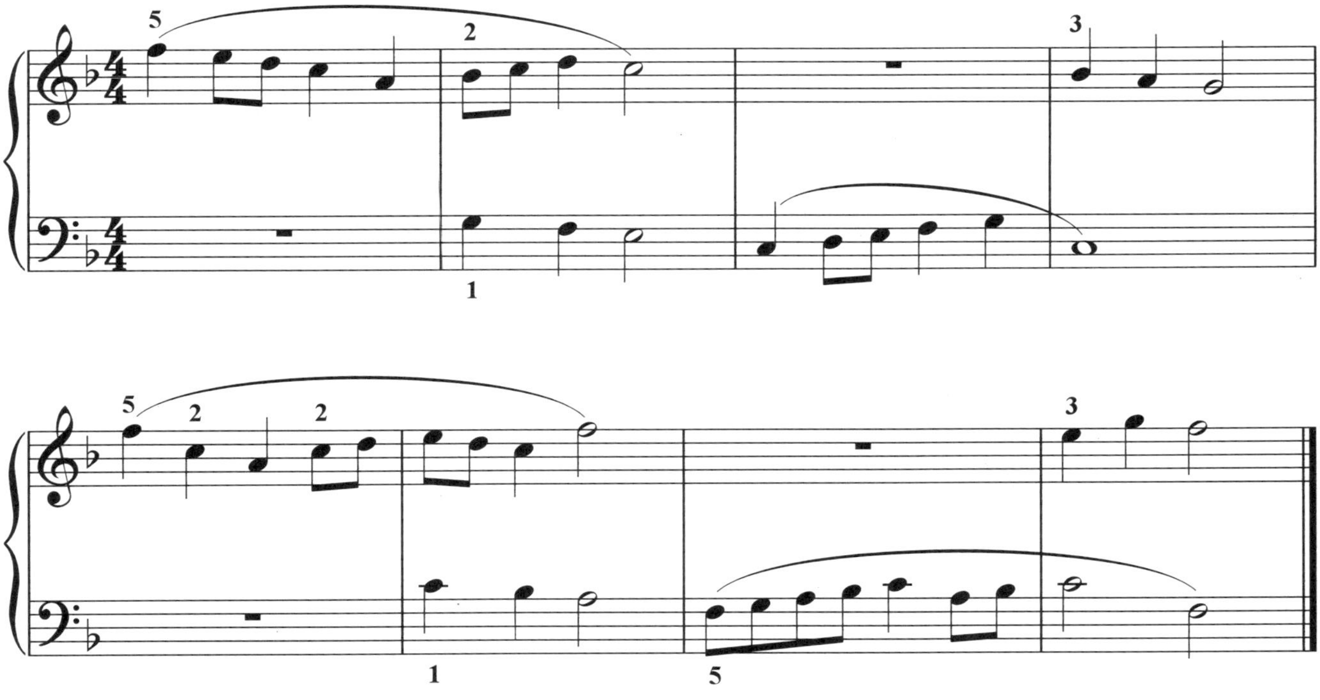

81

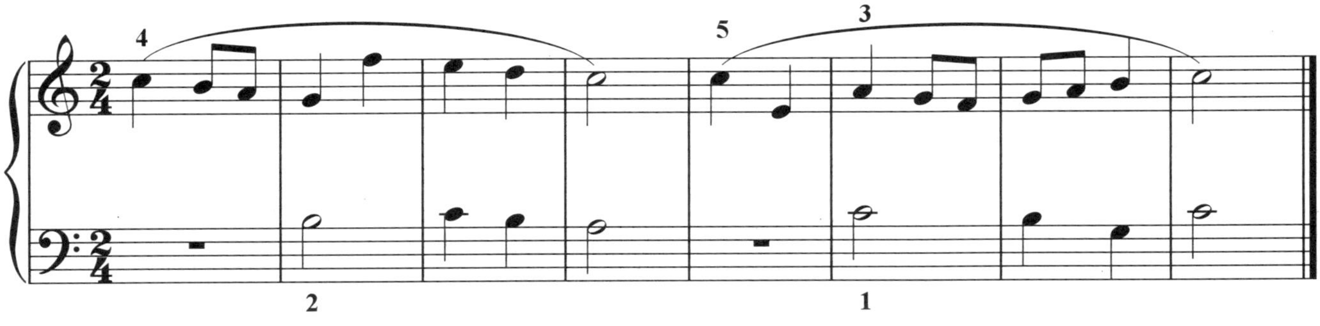

82

83

86

84

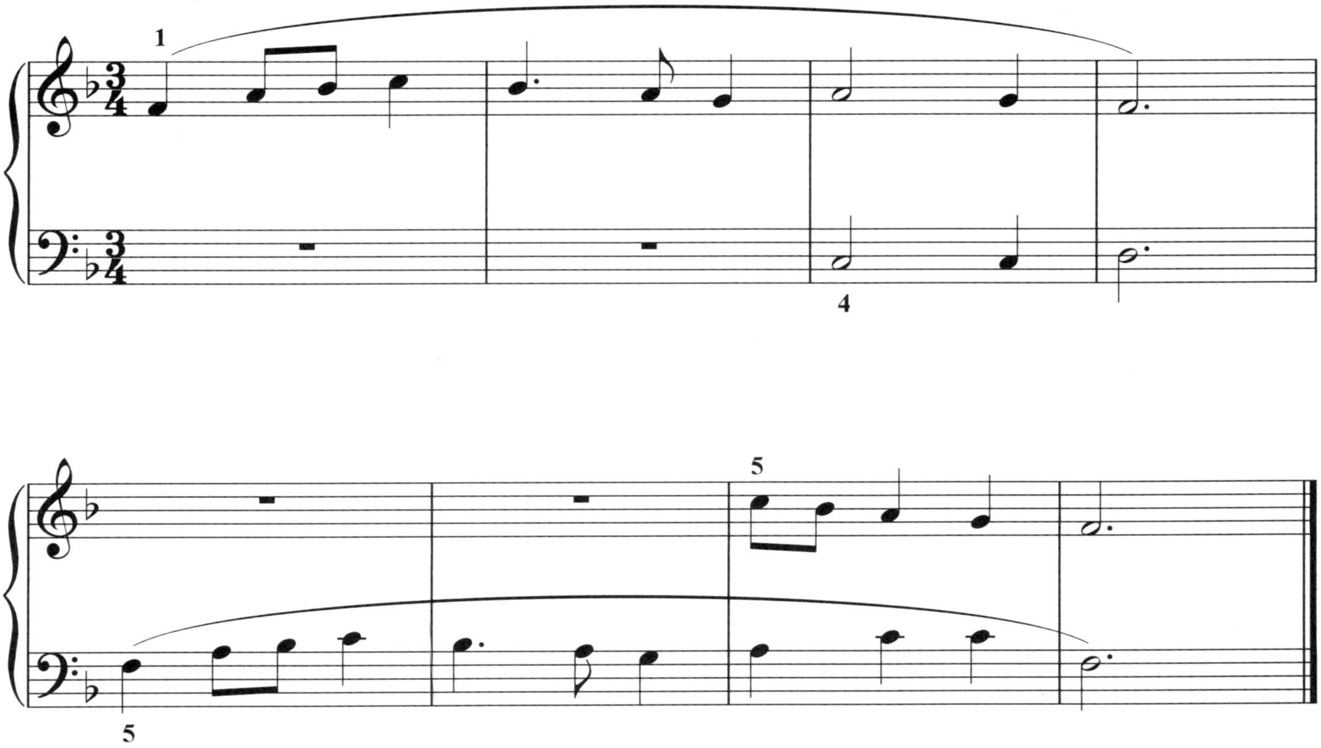

85

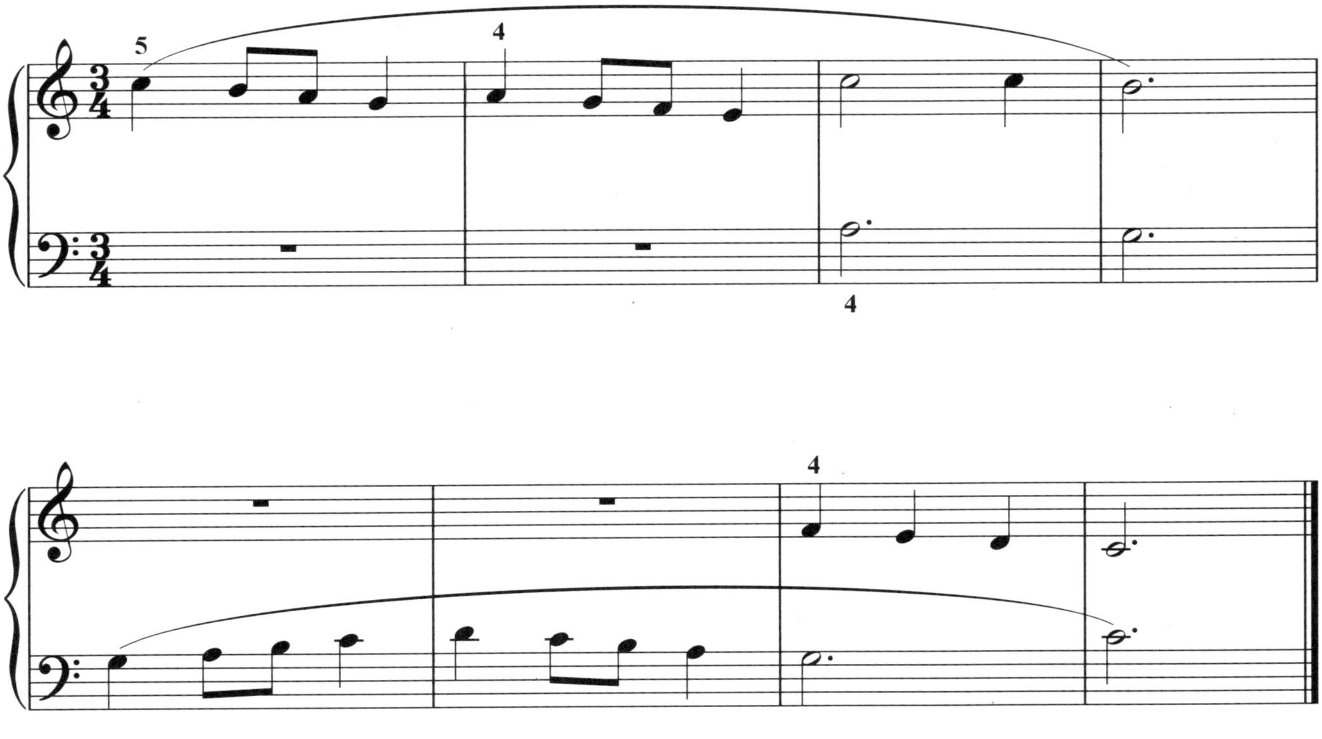

86

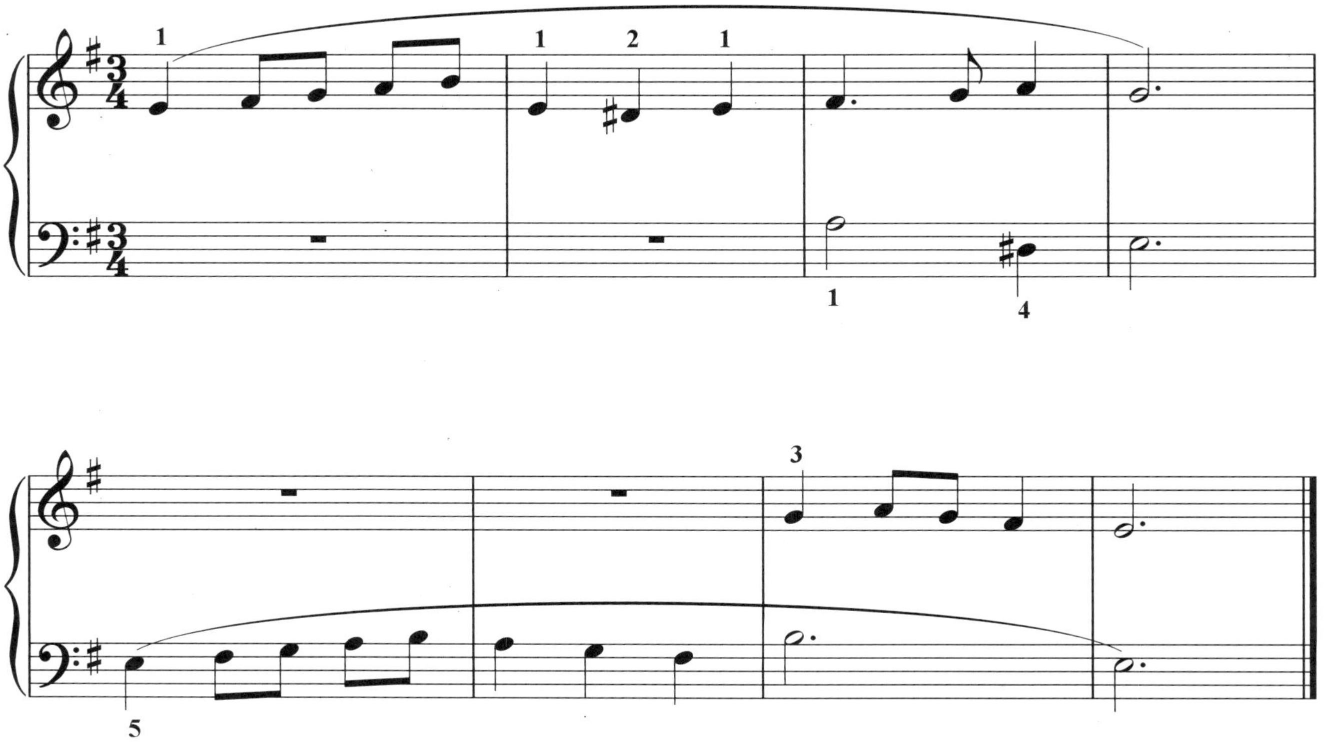

87

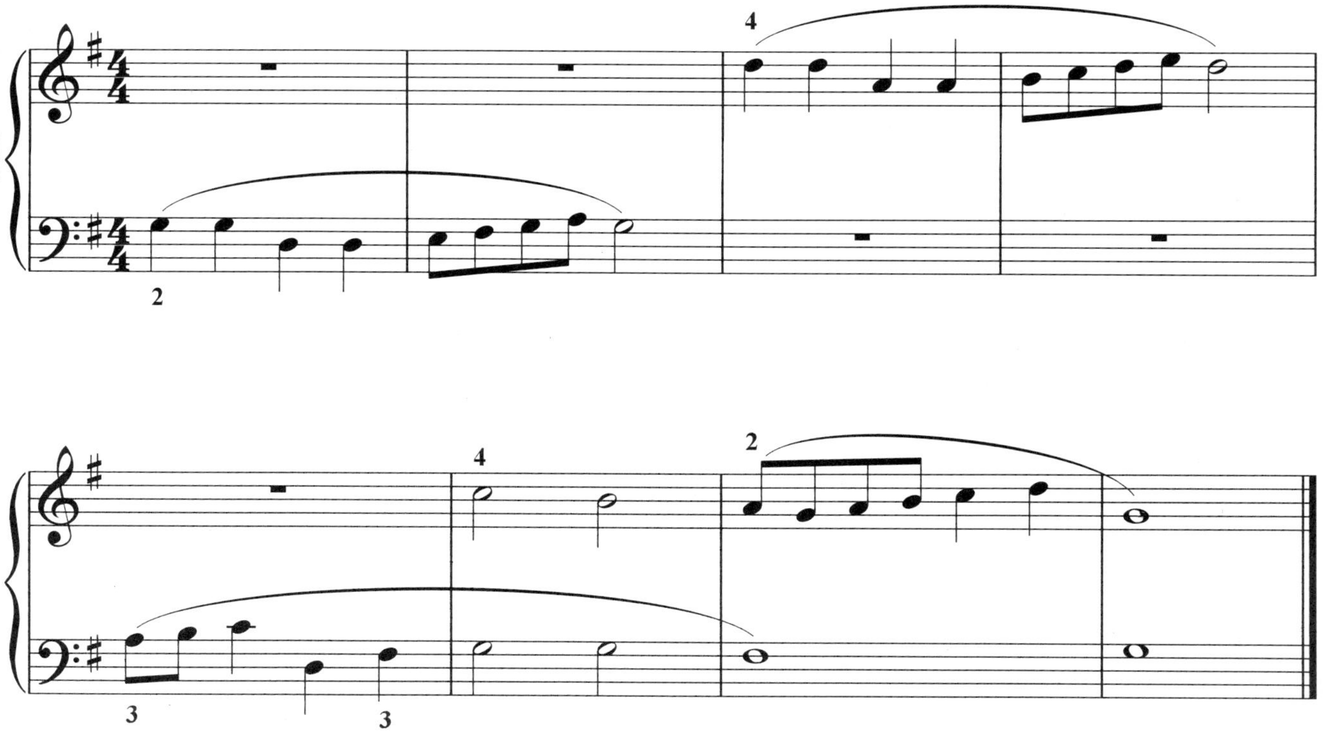

88

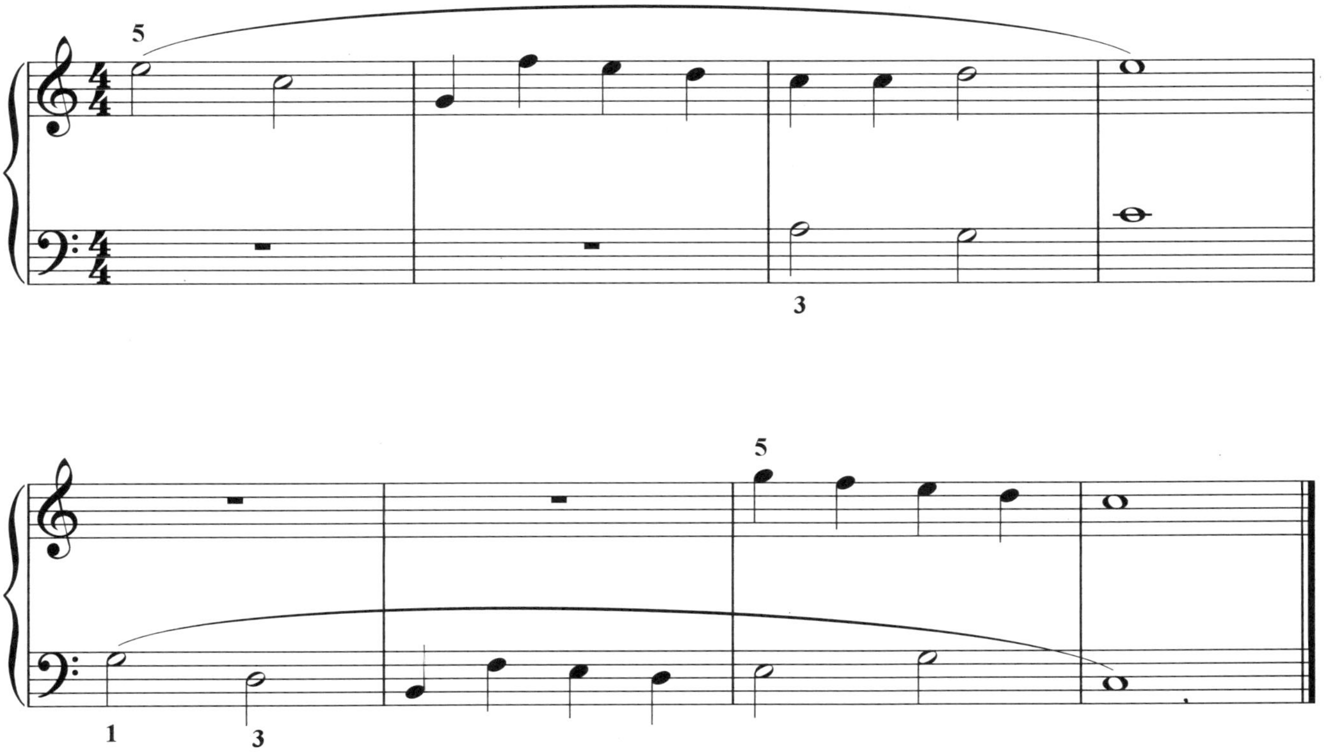

89

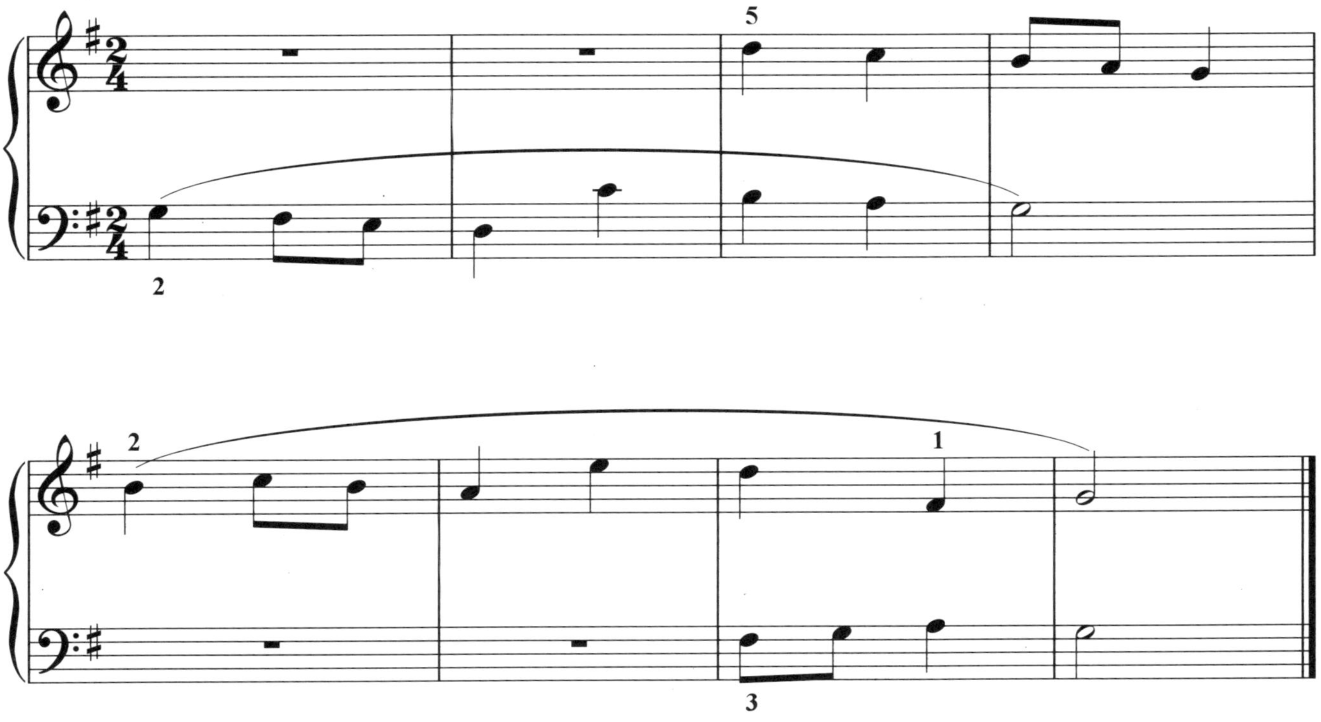